THE

GOOD

SHUFU

THE

GOOD

SHUFU

*Finding Love, Self,
and Home on the
Far Side of the World*

TRACY SLATER

G. P. PUTNAM'S SONS

New York

PUTNAM

G. P. PUTNAM'S SONS
Publishers Since 1838
Published by the Penguin Group
Penguin Group (USA) LLC
375 Hudson Street
New York, New York 10014

USA · Canada · UK · Ireland · Australia
New Zealand · India · South Africa · China

penguin.com
A Penguin Random House Company

Library of Congress Cataloging-in-Publication Data
Slater, Tracy.
The good shufu : finding love, self, and home on the far
side of the world / Tracy Slater.
p.   cm.
ISBN 978-0-399-16620-4
1. Slater, Tracy.   2. Sex role—Japan.   3. Man-woman
relationships—Japan.   4. Women—Social conditions—Japan.
5. Marriage—Japan.   6. Housewives—Japan—Biography.
7. Married people—Japan—Biography.   8. Japan—Social life
and customs.   I. Title.
HQ1075.5.J3S53   2015   2014039143
305.30952—dc23

Printed in the United States of America
1   3   5   7   9   10   8   6   4   2

Book design by Marysarah Quinn

FOR TORU,
OF COURSE,
AND IN
LOVING MEMORY
OF
MAMORU HOSHINO

INTRODUCTORY NOTE

The following is a work of nonfiction, and in calling it so, I feel a grave responsibility to honor that definition, but I acknowledge that it rests on the limits of my memory. I've recalled each aspect of the story as best and accurately as I can, and as literally, with the following creative exceptions: 1) I've re-created the dialogue from memory, not notes taken at the time, except on very few occasions (such as times I wrote down verbatim things my husband said because they struck me as so unique). Therefore, the conversations recorded here are a combination of my best approximations of what took place and my attempts, when possible, to consult the other people involved. 2) To protect the privacy of certain characters in the book, I have changed some names. 3) In a very few instances, for the sake of narrative consistency or brevity, I have combined multiple minor scenes that happened over time into a single minor scene.

Any other inaccuracies or errors in the text are both unintentional and mine alone.

D
E
P
A
R
T
U
R
E

Most if not all descriptions of culture shock indicate a progression of attitudes regarding one's self and others from a lower to a higher level of development . . . [in] the form of a three-to-five stage U-curve. . . . [But] the actual progression of culture shock is seldom as neat and orderly as a U-curve suggests. Only rarely will a person achieve as high a level of functioning in the host culture as in the previous home culture, suggesting a backward J-curve as perhaps more authentic.

• Paul Pedersen, *The Five Stages*
of Culture Shock

Whatever you do, *don't* fall in love over there.

• My mother

ONE

I MET HIM IN KOBE, JAPAN, in May 2004. Three weeks later, he told me he loved me. At least I thought that's what he said.

We were hidden away far past midnight in my dorm room at a corporate training center. He was balanced above me on his arms while I stared up from below. I was a new faculty member in an East Asia executive MBA program. All twenty of my students were men. He was one of them. I'd already fallen in love with him, too.

I was supposed to be teaching these men business communication: how to lead teams and run meetings in a language and culture not their own. I knew almost nothing about English as a second language—or ESL—and had been hired under the flawed assumption that since I taught writing to American MBA students in Boston I could coach this group of Asian businessmen to talk like native English speakers.

I began to realize what I was up against on my first day of class, when I learned that most of my students had never worked with a woman who didn't serve them tea. Anyway, by now, a few weeks into the job, I was already failing miserably in the classroom, never mind my extracurricular late-night transgressions with a student who could barely speak English but had already begun to make my heart spin.

BACK IN BOSTON a month and a half earlier, on the day I'd been recruited for the job, I'd been warned I might confront challenges as a young American woman teaching senior Asian businessmen. It was early April, and the Korean faculty director of the program had tried, indirectly, to prepare me. I had yet to learn that in East Asia the most important communication is almost always indirect, where meaning is often a destination arrived at through multiple circuitous waystops.

The director was sitting behind the broad desk in his office, books piled high against the wall, when he introduced his pitch to me. The window behind him boasted a panoramic view of the Charles River, Cambridge stretched out beyond. One of MIT's domes stood proud and gray in the distance, as if nodding sagely at its lesser colleagues across the water.

"The executive students all work for global Japanese and Korean corporations," he said. "You'll be traveling with them to Kobe, Beijing, and Seoul for each of the program's monthlong summer modules, where they'll see firsthand the manufacturing sectors across a range of markets. Then they all come here for nine months." He drew his hands wide in an expansive sweep, as if displaying the whole group in miniature right there. "They'll finish their degrees in Boston before returning next spring to their homes and companies in Asia." He smiled broadly, then sat back and folded his hands.

"You won't be giving them grades. Just sit with them at meals, get them talking, go to their marketing and strategy classes with them. Help them on their case studies and assignments. Some may be demanding, but you can handle this, yes?" He leaned forward toward me, both hands on his desk. "You have a Ph.D., so you're a professional, no?" Sitting back, he laughed then, at what I wasn't sure, but I laughed along with him. I wanted to suggest that—for the business-class tickets and a summer semester of highly compensated travel as a kind of "conversation coach"—this was work I could easily manage.

In truth, not only had I never been to East Asia or taught ESL, my Ph.D. was in English and American literature, not linguistics or organizational behavior. Moreover, I barely had an interest in cultures other than my own, although within my liberal academic circle, my provincialism wasn't something I'd easily admit.

That April morning, just hours before the director offered me the job, I'd woken in my street-level studio apartment in Boston's South End, the city where I'd always lived and planned to settle for good. As the sun streamed through my old floor-to-ceiling windows, I lay in my high-thread-count sheets and savored both the stillness and predictability of my life as a left-leaning, thirty-six-year-old confirmed Bostonian: over-educated, fiercely protective of my independence, and deeply committed to the cultural values of the liberal northeastern U.S.

Around me in the silence, the light swept across my bookshelves, full of volumes leaning left and right. Somewhere in the middle of all the Shakespeare and Milton, the Hemingway, Mailer, and Morrison, and the barely skimmed pages of literary theory, stood my own thinly bound doctoral dissertation on gender and violence in the modern American novel. On the floor lay a half-read copy of *Vogue*. My laptop was perched on a makeshift desk in front of kitchenette shelves stuffed not with dishes or pans but with papers and syllabi from ten years of teaching at local universities, which were crammed next to shopping bags and old tax returns. In the storage loft above the mini-kitchen were all the shoes I couldn't fit in the studio's small closet, rows of heels and boots and little ballet-slipper flats stacked on wooden racks.

As I did most days, I lingered awhile before leaving for my meeting on campus, luxuriating in the quiet, grateful for both the life I'd built around me and what it lacked: no complicated marriage or crying child to colonize my time. Then I climbed out of bed, showered, dressed, added a swipe of makeup, and stopped at my usual café for a soy chai before heading to the Boston-area university where I now taught. On my way out for the day, I ignored the mezuzah my mother had insisted I hang on the door frame, its tiny Old Testament scroll hidden in silver casing.

The only time my regular morning ritual differed, before my trip to East Asia changed everything, was the one day a week I'd go to Norfolk Correctional Center, a men's medium-security prison. Then I'd wake at dawn, skip the makeup, wear an old pair of flats, and drive the barren highway west. I'd reach the barbed-wired complex early, then pass through a series of electric gates before arriving at the classroom where I'd spend three hours teaching literature and gender studies in a college-behind-bars program to male convicts. This was the work I truly valued, one in a string of progressive education jobs I'd had: running writing classes for homeless adults, preparing inner-city teens for college, teaching first-generation undergraduates at a public university. The writing seminars for American MBAs funded my work in these other programs.

Either way, whether I was headed to prison or the ivory tower, I always began my morning firmly rooted on the exact path I had scripted for myself, what one ex-boyfriend termed "your life as a nonpracticing communist." I had a large circle of like-minded friends; a combination of academic jobs that satisfied me politically, socially, and intellectually; plus cash to buy great shoes. I'd planned each aspect of my world meticulously until together they created a kind of bulwark against the handful of mistakes I swore I'd never make: to take blind leaps of faith, give up my home in Boston, become dependent on a man, build a traditional nuclear family like my parents had, or, most important, cook dinner on a regular basis.

When he sought me out, the Korean director knew me only from my reputation around the business school. The year before, the deans had hired me to create a new writing curriculum for their on-campus graduate management program, and though I told him I'd never even been to East Asia, let alone taught there, the director had convinced himself that I was the woman to turn his foreign execs-in-training into English conversationalists—and to start in just a few weeks' time. Once he floated the idea by me, I assured him (remembering my Spanish- and Vietnamese-speaking students in lockup), "Well, I *have* had nonnative speakers in my literature classes before, lots of times."

"Excellent." He nodded, confirming my perfection for the job.

I played along. After all, I reasoned, the money they were

offering for three months of work was more than *five times* what I'd make in a whole year teaching in prison, and I liked to travel. Besides, what could these East Asian executives possibly throw at me that I hadn't already seen either behind bars or in an MBA classroom?

IN THE WEEKS before I left for the Far East, I made only modest preparations. I bought sightseeing books about the three countries I would visit. In their brief introductions to each culture, I read that all were more conservative about gender than the West. *But surely, this won't extend much into corporate life in multinational corporations,* I assumed. Not until many months later would I learn that, in Japan particularly, even the majority of professional women become what's known as *shufu*[1]: housewives who after marriage give up their careers.[2]

My travel guides also introduced me to the phenomenon of culture shock, the five or so stages visitors can pass through in foreign places. The names of these stages sounded both mysterious and like pop psychology: *Honeymoon, Disintegration, Reinte-*

---

1 That the term *shufu* remains singular even when referring to a group reflects one more lesson I'd come to acquire: Japanese contains very few plural forms, as if no meaningful distinction exists between the individual and the communal.

2 Even today, this relative lack of women in Japan's workforce persists. See for instance a recent *Japan Times* article on women after marriage, which reports that "74 percent of college-educated women [in Japan] quit their jobs voluntarily—more than double the rate in the United States (31 percent) and Germany (35 percent)" (http://www.japan times.co.jp/opinion/2013/04/21/commentary/saving-japan-promoting-womens-role -in-the-workforce-would-help/).

gration, Autonomy, Acceptance. The books promised a kind of euphoria followed by a crash and then—if one spent enough time abroad—a whole other, more integrated self could emerge, combining one's native and new multicultural identities. I dismissed these notions, too. *I won't be in any of these countries for long enough.* So I turned my attention to matters I considered more relevant: buying outfits for my new short-term global gig.

When I arrived in Kobe in mid-May, the faculty director from Boston was already there. He'd come early, affording him a few days of golf with the Japanese head of the training center where we would be staying. My trip from the East Coast had taken almost twenty-four hours, and I was exhausted. But as a formal welcome, we went to dinner at a traditional restaurant downtown. Its entranceway was a mini-garden, tiny bonsai trees dotting the white stone steps from the outside door to the dining room threshold. A gentle glow from paper floor lanterns lit our way. Removing our shoes, we stored them in little wooden cubbies, then glided in slippers over polished floors to our table. Even through the blur of jet lag, the effect was serene, magical.

At our seats, the faculty director poured sake for me, his golf buddy, and another woman who had joined us, Ji-na. She was the young Korean program coordinator who would travel with me and the executive students throughout the entire summer. She had recently moved to Boston with her Jewish-American business-professor husband, then took this job for the chance to travel back to Seoul once a year to visit family.

Ji-na explained proper drinking protocol in Asia, her small face and thin frame leaning in toward me, her hair swaying like a shiny black curtain. One person poured, and then, when everyone's glass had been drained—or better yet, when they were almost but not quite empty—we would take turns giving refills. She picked up the little round ceramic sake pitcher, holding it between delicate fingers, and did the honors.

For the first course, a kimonoed waitress brought sashimi. The entire fish was propped on a series of sticks over a plate of shaved ice, head at one end, tail at the other. Tucked inside its carved-out torso were slices of white flesh arranged in a neat row. I stared at our meal's profile, its mouth slightly open as if caught by surprise, one black pupil facing me like a laminated disk. I'd never been able to bear raw fish, nor a meal that made eye contact, but I gamely picked up my chopsticks, dangling them a few inches from the platter while I tried to build an air of nonchalance. That's when I noticed the tail waving, a slow arc through the air like a metronome.

"Um, it's moving?" I observed. "Is it. Is it . . ." I could feel my eyes grow wide, my expression between confusion and horror.

"Yes! It's still alive! So we know it's delicious and fresh!" the faculty director enthused. I knew the polite response would be to tuck in with feigned relish or at the very least try a tiny nibble. But I couldn't bring myself to do either. I put down my chopsticks, my face hot, my smile weak, and drained my sake cup completely.

THE NEXT MORNING, after jet lag propelled me through a deep but uneven sleep, I had time to explore the training center where we would be working, eating, and sleeping for the next month. Its air felt arid, disorienting. Every inch was tidy, basic, uniform: identical seminar rooms with long, tiered, curving desks; orange upholstered swivel chairs; plain gray carpeting; wall-length whiteboards with black markers spaced evenly across their trays. The faculty bedrooms occupied their own wing, separated by a hallway from the students' rooms, but they, too, were basic and bare, with a narrow single bed, a nightstand, three sets of drawers for clothes, and a small white bathroom.

Classes officially began the next morning. It didn't take me long to realize that the university had made an awful mistake. I was terrible at the job, not knowing anything about the field of ESL, how our brains acquire words, or how to help foreign speakers exercise the muscles in their mouths to shape new sounds. My students realized the same thing.

I learned immediately that although the Japanese and Korean participants were unable to differentiate between *v* and *b* or *r* and *l* (so "evaluate" became *ebaluate;* "product" morphed into *ploduct*), they were expert at discerning when a young woman who supposedly occupies a position of authority is, in fact, woefully bereft of experience. "When you meet a Western colleague, you shake his, *or her,* hand, look directly into his, *or her,* eyes," I enunciated loudly as I stood in front of the classroom on the second day, my chin raised high. The hot sun baked the ground beyond the window, but inside our classroom and the hermetically sealed walls of the training center, the air conditioner was blasting. The room was bright, sterile, cold.

Twenty pairs of dark eyes stared at me. A few heads nodded politely in slight acknowledgment. The two youngest students in the room—Toru and Makoto, both Japanese, both in their early thirties, and both the only ones my age or younger—smiled kindly, but the other faces before me remained impassive.

I began to sweat, my cheeks feeling bright. I opened my mouth to begin again, but instead of speaking, I gaped silently. *I'm alienating them*, I thought, *and I'm not even sure why*. Turning to glance at the clock, I swallowed, my throat like sand. *Ten minutes past. Twenty more to go. And still no clue how to engage them.*

What I did know: my Ph.D. meant nothing now. The confidence I had been trained to project as a professor in the U.S. came off as an insult here, an uncouth display of ignorance about my real status, determined by my age, my gender, and, most of all, my lack of knowledge about their countries. *Why didn't the faculty director warn me what an offense it is to show ignorance of their cultures, when he knew I'd never taught abroad before?* I felt a flash of anger. But underneath, I knew the fault was mine. It was a foolish miscalculation to devote my few weeks posthire to reading travel guides and crafting business scenarios for reenactment instead of really learning about the homes and histories of my future students.

"The right, um, the American way to greet colleagues." I plowed on, and the entire class stiffened. "I mean, in the West, in Canada or, or in North America." I fumbled. "The usual way to greet people you work with . . ." I tried to backpedal, realizing my sloppy word choice suggested a terrible insult: that the American way is best, all others lacking. I was tongue-tied and sweating harder by the second.

Later, Ji-na, the program coordinator, pulled me aside. She explained that the students had designated one Korean and one Japanese participant to be their leaders and spokesmen. In both cases, they chose the eldest, men in their late fifties, since their companies' Confucian hierarchies equated age with authority.

"The students are . . . commenting," she said, after a pause. She looked down for a moment, then raised her eyes toward mine, resting them somewhere around the middle of my nose. "They like how . . . clear your voice is," she added encouragingly. "But . . ." She stopped, looked down again. "Could you . . . talk more . . . quietly? Perhaps?" Then she giggled, her small, thin fingers coming up to cover her mouth. "Show less confidence? You know," she said, waving her tiny hand in front of me. "Be more shy. Like women here are supposed to. Like the students are used to." Later, in the dining hall, neither of the group leaders would acknowledge my presence, their eyes sweeping past me, their shoulders high and proud.

FOR THE REST of the week, we mostly stayed inside the training center, sallow under its wash of fluorescent lighting. The students began referring to it as "Kobe Jail," its interior so sparse and ordered, so utterly removed from the outside world. Despite my experience teaching in a real prison in the U.S., I felt even more confined here. At least in Boston I could leave lockup after my three hours a week of teaching were up.

The few times I did venture out, to a nearby supermarket, I handed my ID to the guard at the security gate, then blinked into a sun made improbably bright after the dull glare of the training center's lights. Outside, in a residential area on the outskirts of Kobe proper, I could communicate with no one. Children on the road stared shyly at me or hid behind their mothers, my long, wavy, blond-streaked hair looking very foreign to them, I supposed. Most of the brightly colored goods at the store remained mysterious to me, with vivid packaging and unintelligible black calligraphy dancing across their tops or down their sides, a kaleidoscope of the indecipherable.

When I found a bag showing peanuts on its front, with crescent-shaped rice crackers glowing like little orange moons, the women at the checkout counter smiled and bowed and laughed kindly as I struggled to count out correct change. Between the outside environment and the world inside the training center, I felt at once like a child in wonderland and like that fish on the platter my first night in Japan: flailing, stuck, utterly exposed.

After my talk with Ji-na, I spent the next week both ashamed and uncomfortable in the classroom. I spoke more softly. I looked down often, buttoned my shirts an extra notch around my neck. Except for the encouraging smiles of Toru and Makoto, I felt nervous meeting the eyes of the men around me. In the contest between the ideals that defined my life in Boston and the gender expectations of the East Asian classroom, I caved.

I did find some moments of reprieve, though. Especially outside of class, I was touched by most of the students' polite manners, even as I could sense they wanted someone more experienced teaching them business conversation. "Oh, you like white rice!" a few would exclaim when they saw me in the dining room with an overflowing bowl. They'd incline their heads in welcome as I pulled out a chair at their table and set my tray down. They found it hilarious when I dumped soy sauce and wasabi over my serving, since in Japan and Korea, white rice is usually eaten plain. "This, this is *natto*," a student named Sato told me when I eyed his dish of beans bathed in yellow gravy, sticky strands of sauce hanging from the end of his chopsticks. "Americans don't like! Can you eat?" he asked. "Strong smell! But good taste! Good taste!" I shook my head and widened my eyes as I peered into the bowl, then pulled back abruptly as its scent hit me, and the whole table laughed good-naturedly.

While most of the students remained distant in the class-room, Makoto would repeat everything I said under his breath, practicing the movements with his mouth. *Vertical marketing*, he'd mouth silently. "V-V-V," he'd practice, trying to push his teeth into his bottom lip to pronounce the *v* that Japanese replaces with a *b*. "Bertical, *v*ertical, *v*ertical marketing," he'd repeat under his breath.

Then there was Toru. At thirty-one, he was at least a decade younger than most of his classmates. Not until I'd spent a few days watching him did I realize I was drawn to him. He'd tilt his head calmly in thought, search through his portable electronic dictionary for translations to English words, and smile slowly. Sometimes he'd stare off into space, then nod and bend his head over his compact laptop, spiked black hair and fine-edged cheeks suspended over the keyboard, muscled forearms peeking from his shirt. Next he'd raise his dark eyes, cock his head, and think some more, all angular features and unhurried gestures. When he laughed, his quiet expression would break into a grin.

"Can you help?" he'd ask me sometimes after class, handing me a case study with the vocabulary he didn't understand cir-cled in blue ballpoint. He'd nod slowly and seriously as I ex-plained each word, watching my emphatic hand movements with interest. "Market *launch*," I'd explain, mimicking a rocket in flight, my fingers slanting upward. "*Ahhh*, yah, yah, *yah*," he'd say. "Okay, thanks you very much," he'd add as we finished. "I'm appreciate you."

Between my failures in the classroom and my disorientation in Japan, Toru's shy sincerity washed through me with bright relief.

ONE NIGHT, a few days after she first broke the obvious news that the students were unhappy with my teaching, Ji-na and I were slumped together in one of the training center's barren lounges. Her job was proving no easier than mine: since she was a young woman, and a Korean one at that, the elder Korean students treated her more like a secretary than the coordinator of an international executive program who had already earned her MBA. Mainly, they expected her to xerox their assignments and fetch them tea and snacks while listening to their litany of complaints. The air-conditioning was too high in some classrooms, too low in others, they insisted. The software for their marketing simulation was unsophisticated and slow.

Ji-na and I gossiped and giggled over beer and a Japanese approximation of Doritos. She told me which students she liked best, the few she thought were handsome and kind, and then I confided my small crush. In the twilight zone of the Japanese corporate training center—where we were the only women besides the uniformed cleaning or cafeteria workers who bowed silently to us each morning, where everything was more tidy, ordered, and sterile than our actual lives a world away—neither one of us dwelled on practical concerns such as professional boundaries or academic ethics. Instead, Ji-na pointed out how happy she was with her Jewish-American professor husband in Boston ("Just like you and Toru, sort of!"), how much calmer Toru seemed than the more senior, restive students in the program. How much she disapproved of my latest ex-boyfriend back home, the award-winning scientist with multiple diplomas and persistent fidelity issues.

That night when I slept, I dreamed about Toru, a hazy landscape of confusion and turmoil brought still by the shelter of his body. In the dream, I felt more comfort and warmth in his presence than I had ever known with another person—real or imagined. I woke feeling not so much excited as calm and safe. Then, although Toru and I could barely communicate, we came from entirely different worlds, and he was a student in a program where I was failing miserably as teacher, my feelings gave way to an even more surprising thought: *this might not end disastrously.*

THREE DAYS LATER, at an *izakaya*, a Japanese pub in Kobe's center, the entire program had an official celebration of our first weekend. We drank and toasted and drank some more, a common practice in East Asian corporate culture, where getting drunk together builds the trust necessary to do business. In general, getting drunk and doing business seemed pretty strange to me. But getting drunk and making a pass at a student suddenly struck me as a great idea.

I thought I had noticed Toru staring at me that first week in the classroom. He had begun to hang back and wait for me when the group walked down the hall after class to the cafeteria or shuttled to the program's factory tours. I imagined I felt heat rising off his skin as he sat near me, but then I'd think, *I'm being crazy; he's a student.* Even though we were all adults and, divested of the power to give grades, I held no meaningful authority anyway, I was still supposed to consider him off-limits. *Not to mention the disaster I've already made of this job without adding inappropriate sexual conduct to the mix.*

None of this actually stopped me from checking my contract to see how the university defined fireable offenses. After all, I'd spent years dating lawyers in Boston. *Interesting,* I thought, as I read through the document. Relationships between teachers and students-of-age were not, per se, forbidden, as long as harassment played no part.

That morning, before our celebration at the Kobe *izakaya*, Toru and I had sat together on the train when the whole group headed to Himeji Castle for sightseeing. The others paired near us, Ji-na sitting with one of the younger Korean students, the two talking a blue streak in their native language. Toru made me laugh by imitating the white-gloved conductor bowing again and again to no one in particular. Then he checked repeatedly to ensure the open window wasn't whipping too much wind into my face, brushing his arm against mine for a fraction of a second as he pushed himself up to close it in one quick, liquid movement. I was ecstatic, then chagrined. Then ecstatic again.

Now, at dinner, he was sitting next to me. Getting drunk like I was.

Afterward, we filed out of the restaurant as a group, crowding tipsily into the elevator. "We're going karaoke!" someone announced. On the street, everyone turned toward the karaoke bar.

I touched Toru's arm. Then I ducked behind a pillar, out of sight from the rest. Toru grinned and joined me, our backs pressed against the concrete slab, Kobe's neon signs blinking through the night air around us. We watched silently as the others departed. When they were halfway down the block, we turned to look at each other. His eyes were dark but very still. I pivoted the other way, and he followed. We were finally alone, together.

TWO WEEKS LATER, he told me he loved me.

The night of missed karaoke, we'd stayed late at a bar in Kobe, kissing furtively in a corner between bottles of beer, then snuck back to the training center, holding hands the whole way until we parted at the guard gate. For the next couple of weeks or so, he'd sneak into my room after midnight, the other students tucked into their single beds or studying under the pale light of single-bulb lamps in their bare rooms. He'd leave around three a.m. Each Japanese student had been paired with a Korean one, and soon his Korean roommate, a shy man approaching middle age, was impressed, exclaiming to the group how studious young Toru was, how he'd stay late into each night in the computer lab working diligently on his solitary assignments.

Now, as Toru declared his love for me, I feared at first I'd misheard him through his accent. The curtains were drawn against the midnight moon, Toru's spiky black hair jutting out in urgent tufts. He looked straight at me when he said, "I lub you."

In keeping with my dismal performance as an ESL coach, I didn't nod with brisk encouragement or prod him patiently to enunciate his syllables. Instead, I blurted out, "You *what?*"

If he was saying what I was hoping, it would be one of the best things I'd ever heard, since he'd already turned my own heart upside down. But still, I'd only known him for three weeks, this man who'd spent his life half a planet from my home, who bowed when I shook hands, ate miso soup for breakfast while I ate cornflakes. I didn't want to think he'd said, "I love you" when, in fact, he'd said, "I live far from you."

But he repeated it again, and a third time, and when I finally answered, "You do?" he said simply but unmistakably, "Yes, I'm love with you." And somehow, right then, I knew I'd found a lifetime perk to the worst teaching job I'd ever had.

THROUGHOUT THE SUMMER Toru and I were together, though we spent very little time alone. We kept our relationship a secret, and during the week, in classes or sharing communal meals, we would go about as executive MBA student and faculty member. But on weekends, when the group would scatter for sightseeing or side trips, we would get away for overnights in Kyoto or downtown Kobe, and when the program moved to China and then South Korea, we'd escape to Beijing and Seoul. Away, we'd lie entwined for hours.

The initial heat of infatuation that had infected me like a fever didn't so much dissipate as mellow, and alongside my yearning for Toru, I began to grow fond of him in a quieter, more balanced way. After a fifteen-year string of Ivy League academics, lawyers, doctors, and entrepreneurs who had impressed me with ambition and inspired me with wit but still left me empty in my chest, I'd finally fallen in love with a man I actually *liked*.

One weekend in Kobe, we stayed in a small hotel near the harbor. Like most spaces in Japan, our room was tiny but as sleek and modern as I'd ever seen: the clean, precise lines of the furniture edging its dark mahogany burnish; evenly placed pillows lined perfectly against impeccably white sheets pulled so taut that the sheer absence of wrinkles belied their buttery softness. One whole wall was a window opening to Kobe's skyline, its pointed tower winking in the distance, headlights glowing in the street below, tall buildings with square windows stacked up like newly minted Chiclets. Off to one side, the sparkle of the city laced the dark expanse of water.

That night, lying face-to-face, I asked Toru about his family and his growing up. He told me of his middle-class, stable childhood in a small Osaka apartment and his parents, who loved and protected him and his younger sister with a mix of warmth and reserve that he found wholly unremarkable in Japan, but that I found intriguing compared to family dynamics in the West. "They could love me well enough, so I always knew I was safe," he said simply.

"Did you feel lonely?" I asked, as he told me of the day he first went to school at five, when his parents said he should stop calling them Mama and Papa and use the more formal *Okāsan, Otōsan*: Respected Mother, Respected Father.

"Lonely?" he repeated. "No, not lonely. Maybe a little . . . a *little* sad. But proud. Now I was real *boy*, not baby, so I felt good. More good than sad."

"Did your parents hug you?" I asked, getting ready to psychoanalyze. After six years in a Ph.D. program perfecting theories about the hidden meanings of literature's greatest works, there was nothing I liked better than dissecting a real-life story—especially when it involved a romance of my own.

"Yes, of course, lots!" Toru answered. "Until I was older, in school. Until about five. Then, we didn't touch so much. We Japanese, we don't touch so much." He nodded as if this were the only sensible choice.

"But still, you always felt . . . you always felt *held*, anyway?" I asked, crossing my arms over my chest and rocking my shoulders to pantomime a child's sense of protection.

"Yes! Always *held*, yes. Even though not a lot of hugging."

His parents never once went out to dinner without him and his sister, he told me, nor went away without them—child-free vacations being a concept so novel to Toru that it took me a few tries even to explain. In fact, they hardly ever went out to dinner at all. "No need," Toru said, in response to my surprise. "We were happy at home."

Memories of my own parents, grim-faced but impeccably dressed, flitted through my mind: leaving instructions for the housekeeper on the way out the door, my mother's French perfume scenting the air around me as she'd lean down for a quick kiss, her voice then permeating the large, dark house by intercom—"Kids, we're leaving now. Corita will have dinner ready later." Or, best of all, when they let us four children dress up and come out with them. I'd order shrimp cocktail at Josephine's on Newbury Street and explain to my father, as he'd stare off into space, how the mirrored foyer made this restaurant my favorite. I'd feel safe then, as if anyone could see that nothing bad would happen among the gilded walls, the clinking crystal, the bathrooms with little lettered towels, all the pretty people in the rooms around us.

Back in the Kobe hotel room, though, all I said to Toru was "Huh, interesting."

THE NEXT MORNING, we both woke a little giddy. We'd have to head back to the training center soon, and the anonymity of the hotel threw into stark contrast the confinement of the MBA program. Toru threw open the curtain and the sunlight glinting off of Kobe's skyline tumbled into the room.

I began to recite the opening lines of Nabokov's *Lolita*, a little pretentious academic humor that I knew he wouldn't get anyway, so he wouldn't be able to call me on my intellectual posturing or challenge me to recall anything beyond the book's first few lines (a literary fluency I lacked). "Light of my life, fire of my loins," I called to him from my cross-legged seat on the bed, my arm flung out dramatically, my long hair a tangled mess.

Toru turned from the window to throw me a silent smile, seemingly unconcerned that he couldn't get my meaning. Then he swiveled back to the view. I felt equally unconcerned, and then surprised, as I suddenly thought how many relationships would benefit from a lack of shared linguistics, from the absence of expectation that our partners would, or even could, understand us most of the time.

A few minutes later, Toru turned toward me once more, his grin huge as he tried to remember and return the quote. "Love of my life, tenderloin of my heart!" he offered proudly.

I threw myself back on the bed in giggles, pounded my hands and feet up and down. "Tenderloin of my heart! That is *so* great!"

Toru smiled at me, head tipped to one side, looking quizzical. Then he couldn't help breaking into a full laugh himself as I rolled around in the sheets, hiccupping. "What's funny?" he asked, diving into the mayhem on the bed.

"Tenderloin is a *steak*!"

"Oh, terrible. Terrible mistake." Toru shook his head with mock gravity and plopped himself onto the pillow beside me.

Still, I couldn't help but notice that his was a proclamation more visceral, touching, and eloquently twisted than any I'd ever read in the entire Western canon.

ONE NIGHT A few weeks later, we were hidden away again, this time at the Chinese government's Ministry of Commerce training center in Beijing, where the entire program had moved for the middle leg of our Asia tour. Toru would have to leave in a few hours to creep silently along the dark hallways and make it back to his own room before dawn. We had become less careful in China, since the facility there sprawled with multiple wings, affording privacy to the faculty suites. We still hid our relationship during the day but had lapsed into more frequent late-night sneaking around.

The night was dark and heavy beyond the window, the air-conditioning churning out a constant, guttural hum. I flitted in and out of fitful dreams while Toru lay quietly beside me, his breathing soft and even. I had grown to love the peacefulness of his slumber, so different from my own turbid sleep. He eased softly into the gentlest part of night while I was always wrestling to grab hold of a meager rest, like fistfuls of shadow I had to yank from an unwilling darkness.

I'd always been prone to angst-filled dreams. Sometimes they would hold scraps of films I had seen as the child of first- and second-generation American Jews with a Holocaust fixation. Despite having lost no direct relatives in the camps, my parents enthusiastically promoted our duty to "never forget"— and then extended that to "always be remembering." In homage to this vigilance, my mother had even initiated her own version of America's favorite prime-time activity: family Holocaust movie night.

When I was four or five and our temple showed live footage from the genocide in the adult service, my parents yanked us out of the children's sing-along so we could fulfill our duty to bear witness. Half a decade later, when the network miniseries *Holocaust* aired, we brought notes to our Protestant private schools explaining that we should be excused from homework while we observed this latest chapter in our history of ethnic calamity, reenacted for network TV. I clutched the thick, lemony yellow notepaper my mother had given me, monogrammed along the top in rich red lettering, FROM THE DESK OF CHARLOTTE SLATER, and proudly handed it to my teacher before recess.

In addition to the mourning and anguish for those who perished in the camps, however, my parents hinted at another theme roiling just below the surface of these images. Or maybe in my confused efforts to grasp the ungraspable I just imagined a deeper message: the fatal naïveté of the victims. For these were the Jews who didn't get out in time, who somehow failed to recognize or admit the gathering storm. So what I took most clearly from my Holocaust education was not my responsibility as an American Jew to blindly support Israel (my mother's intended message, reinforced with a collection of window decals proclaiming I AM A ZIONIST! for each of our bedroom windows). Instead, I learned the importance of never being foolishly optimistic, never under-estimating the potential for disaster, and never, *ever* assuming you could leave life up to fate.

Now, in the black of a Beijing night, lying next to a Japanese executive-in-training I had met just six weeks earlier and with whom I could barely converse, I was immersing myself deeper and deeper into a relationship that would eventually require some sort of optimistic stretch—or most likely a wild leap of faith—to sustain itself across two hemispheres. *Am I just fooling myself here,* I wondered, *just inviting some messy, bicontinental breakup?*

Then suddenly, Toru began to stir. I turned toward him, ready for him to cry out while I guessed about his own night-mares. The outlines of shapes—a wooden dresser, an aging TV, a book on the nightstand—ghosted softly in the dark. As Toru tossed beside me, then began to murmur quietly, I paused, weighing whether to wake him from his dreams or let them pass.

But then he laughed, a chortle bubbling up through slum-ber, like a child with a joke. I looked at his face, and the stress I expected there was absent; in its place, a small smile curved his lips, his cheeks peaking above a satisfied grin, almond eyes squeezed shut and crinkling at their corners.

Next he turned over, sighed, and fell back into peaceful rest.

Holy shit, I thought. In the inky black of night, Toru didn't dream of horror and tragedy, didn't dwell in fragmented scenes of Nuremberg, Nagasaki, or Nanking. Instead, he chuckled.

Hearing Toru laugh, I was struck with a new thought. *Perhaps utter vulnerability and pure peace really* could *coexist, surrender sometimes culminate in quiet joy, not destruction.* And right there, in the People's Republic of China's Ministry of Commerce training center, in bed with a Japanese businessman I had met less than two months before, I fell further in love than I'd ever thought possible, my heart crashing through a floor I didn't know existed, revealing a deeper comfort than I ever guessed another human's presence could embody.

TWO

ONE NIGHT TOWARD THE MID-
dle of our stay in China, almost eight weeks into the MBA program, Toru and I were curled together again. I lay on my side
facing him, my head propped on one elbow, my other forearm
extended on the sheets between us. He smiled at me, then looked
down and passed one finger lightly over my forearm, near the
top crease of my wrist bone. He traced two small, faint scars
nestled there, little pale parentheses cradling a minor vein. He
looked up at me, knit his brows.

"I made them once," I admitted. "It wasn't such a big deal. It
wasn't dangerous or anything." Toru nodded wordlessly, con-
ceding that they were nowhere near the underside of my wrist,
where tender skin separated artery from air.

These were marks made during a particularly confused period of adolescence when I had wanted not so much to destroy
myself as render tangible an invisible grief so it might begin
somehow to dislodge and recede. "I felt pretty bad then . . . in
my late teens and early twenties," I tried to explain. "I just
wanted . . . some way to feel better, and I know it sounds weird,
but this was the only way I could really think of."

I told him my family had been wealthy but "kind of screwed up," aping the irreverence of Northeast academics discussing shrinks and psychopharmacology, personal pathology, and other upper-middle-class woes. "Like, not totally okay, you know, between people," I said, wagging my finger from my chest outward and back again, miming personal connection.

"A-*ha*," Toru said, as if starting to see a picture. Then I tried to tell him of my family's demise, our inability to hold it together even after we had been handed so much. The morning I was eight or nine when we kids woke to a wall of kicked-in kitchen cabinets, their smooth cherry doors splintered and gaping, one in the shape of a mouth caught mid-surprise. The wreckage of a mismatched marriage, how we would hear my parents shut into the wood-paneled library of our house, my mother's voice rising among the antique leather volumes until it reached a high-pitched scream; my father's murmurs soft and strained; we four kids ducked low at the top of the staircase or huddled in a silvery guest bathroom while the sound of our parents' voices would come to us in waves of hisses and low pleads. The one child—my middle sister, Lauren—with whom my mother never seemed to bond and who for years slid deeper into a depression that wouldn't quit; the other child—me, the baby—crowned my mother's favorite, the difference so obvious that even my father proclaimed I was her chosen one.

In truth, although I never could quite figure out how I'd gotten pinned a parent's favorite or why Lauren bore the brunt of such opposing luck, I assumed my status depended on playing the perfect little girl—and while my heart broke for my sister, I grasped on to my own role. It made me feel safe, or maybe it really just held at bay some sense of terror and helplessness I couldn't understand. Either way, I grew to believe that the more perfectly I behaved, the more fixed my safety and place in the world would be, and the more firmly my family's cohesiveness would hold.

Of course, I was wrong.

One day when I was ten, Ms. Wing, the headmistress at Lauren's all-girls school, called to say they had found pills in my sister's locker. Upon admitting her urge to take the whole bottle, Lauren had been dispatched to Mount Auburn Hospital's psychiatric ward. My father was somewhere in Texas that night. My mother claims he declined to take her call.

But I remember a friend of my parents', Mrs. Birnbaum, coming home from the hospital with my mother. Her hair was light brown streaked with ashy blond, piled high in a seventies sweep, and she bent over my bedside in the dark while my mother did something in the kitchen (Cried? Flipped through her Rolodex to find a lawyer? Checked the fax machine for the latest on the Middle East conflict?). Then she tried to explain that Lauren had gone away. Two weeks later, my father moved out.

My parents broke the news of their separation while Lauren was still in Mount Auburn, calling the rest of us into the library. We sat among the plush leather upholstery and burnished bookcases, the glass-shelved bar and Baccarat tumblers, and they said my father was leaving for a while. Then we went to the country club for an afternoon swim and Sunday barbecue, and I, in particular, tried to smile on cue for the other families.

After a few weeks in the hospital, Lauren moved in with her English teacher, an arrangement my parents funded privately: the upper-middle-class version of foster care without the stigma of state involvement. Years later, Lauren would tell me that her new family had been gentle and kind, although she still spent more than a decade going in and out of psychiatric wards. As if her insides had been crushed beyond repair.

Within a few months of Lauren's first stay in Mount Auburn, my brother, twelve, went to boarding school and my eldest sister moved in with my father, who had now left for good and for a new, Texan wife. Meanwhile, as if frozen into the separate spheres where our family's roles had flung us, Lauren and I lost touch for years until she went to college and I left home myself for boarding school at fourteen, and then we began to grow close. That was the year our mother remarried, too. Over time, I grew to value greatly the stability both my stepparents brought to their marriages, helping certain jagged family holes to begin to soften, to hold some hope of evening out. But still, sometimes while I was in college, Lauren would call me to her bedside when her hands itched for another bottle of pills, and I'd sit with her in a darkened room and wonder how you stopped someone from wanting to die.

Eventually, despite her crippling depression and the indelible effects of her childhood pain, as an adult Lauren graduated from psychiatric patient to gifted author and psychologist. She earned her doctorate and became renowned for writing lyrical, some-times controversial essays about mental illness, science, and med-ication. She married, built her own family, and published books about her raw struggles, her extensive involvement with phar-macopeia, and even her experience seeing patients in the same psych ward where she once lived.

As for myself, I flirted as an adolescent with my own share of suburban angst, though much more modest in nature. I passed with total unoriginality through the requisite self-starvation and attendant crises of my ilk: boarding-school girls from chaotic families who turned their anger and shame inward. In college, I dwelled with indecent relish on existentialism and death, the maudlin English major's porn: Camus, Kafka, Levi, Arendt. But then I stopped and made myself a promise that at the time seemed wise. I'd never again become dependent on any family unit. Or anyone at all, for that matter. I bought one of those T-shirts that proclaimed A WOMAN WITHOUT A MAN IS LIKE A FISH WITHOUT A BICYCLE. I swore I'd never become marooned in another messy, unpredictable world—especially one that required me to sacrifice all I'd squelched in my childhood efforts to play perfect, or where I was helpless to hold disaster at bay.

I knew I was lucky to be able to make such a promise to myself. I had the money to pay for years of therapy, the insurance to keep my Prozac prescription filled, and the good fortune to find the combination of counseling and psychopharmacology remarkably effective. I eventually took my tribe's early turmoil and, like in many a bourgeois tragedy, turned it into a career: my doctoral dissertation on violence and power, my jobs teaching gender studies and literature at universities and in men's lockup, and the business writing work that guaranteed me total financial independence from my family.

Now in Beijing, as I narrated the broad outlines of this story for Toru, he caught enough to understand, at least, what "kind of screwed up" meant. He held my gaze with unblinking eyes. He didn't ask me how I felt about any of it. He didn't say a word. He just took my hand and smiled sadly.

Unexpectedly, Toru's silence comforted me more than any commentary could. I didn't need to try to explain perfectly (nor would there be a perfect explanation anyway) the vague but persistent mix of embarrassment, guilt, and fear I'd always felt, mocking me through the fabric of my family's privilege. Toru simply let me know that he sensed both my grief and my numbness, and that his heart hurt for me, and actually that was enough—in fact, it was the only thing that mattered.

Of course, I didn't know how to tell him that night in Beijing, as he reached out to take both my hands in his so we could lie nose to nose and palm to palm and not say anything, how much his silent embrace meant to me. But even so, as he fell asleep that night, he never let me go.

BY THE TIME the Beijing module was winding down, Toru and I had begun to talk about what we would do when the MBA program ended, after the entire Asia tour was over and the following nine months in Boston were, too. He was expected to return to his country and company, and climb the corporate ladder, since his firm had funded graduate school. We didn't make any concrete plans, but I suspected he might consider moving to Boston, at least eventually. He had enough money saved, he told me one day in passing, to pay his company back for his degree. He'd also lived in Malaysia for three years before starting the MBA program, working as head financial officer for one of his firm's factories there, and now he was doing graduate work through an American university. *He* must *be open to settling outside of Japan,* I reasoned.

My moving outside of Boston, however, was inconceivable. I'd lived my whole life in the city's vicinity, and it represented the only sense of rootedness I'd ever really trusted. For me, safety felt cartographical: the familiar, stable contours of a place I knew by heart.

One night during our last week in Beijing, on a couch in my faculty suite, I tried to explain my attachment to Boston, my dread of leaving it, and my fear about what this might mean for us as lovers from opposing corners of the earth. I told him of how, when I was finishing my Ph.D. program seven years earlier, I had turned down the possibility of a few full-time academic jobs outside of New England after realizing I wasn't willing to move from the Northeast, even for a tenure-track literature position.

Because Toru was less dramatic and more optimistic about everything, he didn't understand why I felt so sure I could not live far from Boston—but neither was he especially concerned. "It's okay," he said, with a small smile. "We don't need to worry on this now."

On one hand, I knew logically it was much too early to analyze our long-term future. On the other, rooting out possible disaster was my *thing*, my unique forte. Moreover, Toru's lack of angst about sustaining our relationship frustrated me. *Does it mean he's fallen less in love?* Perhaps most surprising, he proved strangely unanxious about *my* anxiety: very different from the other men I had dated, for whom any display of emotion trumping cool rationality hinted at the unseemly and any question over "where this relationship might be going" blinked like an urgent exit sign.

Now in China with Toru, I stared across the faux-opulent faculty apartment, its heavy green curtains framing each window, the sheer white liners underneath hiding the Beijing grime.

Then I did something I had never done before. I considered giving Toru and whatever was happening between us the benefit of the doubt. Maybe his lack of concern over our future—and my own related anxiety—meant he didn't care as much as I. Or maybe he was just optimistic that we could work out our relationship when the time came to do so, and my tendency to believe the opposite didn't faze him. At first, this idea of seeing the glass half full careened into my mind as merely a novel thought. I prodded it mentally for a moment, as if jutting my tongue into the fresh gap of a lost tooth.

Then, somehow, my mind took the leap itself, and suddenly I'd made the decision to go with the better possibility. The moment I did, it felt strangely right and solid. Perhaps, I thought, instead of uncaring, Toru was simply sure and strong. Perhaps, I thought next, Toru really would move to Boston, and into my meticulously cultivated life there I could add the one thing that had always eluded me: a deep and steady love.

A FEW DAYS LATER, we had our first fight. It was early July, and the Beijing afternoon was brutally hot and humid, the air wet-cotton heavy. As dusk neared, Toru and I went to a running track near the training center. I tried to go every few days, as did a few of the executive students, who would run with their bright white tube socks pulled halfway up their shins. The track was dusty, the grass in its center brown and old. We jogged slowly because of the heat. Toru's socks, I noted approvingly, were pushed down around his ankles.

I had a vacation coming up when we got to Korea, a week off when I planned to go to a spa alone on Jeju Island, lie on the beach, have massages, and forget the sound of businessmen trying to speak English. Now I suggested Toru join me in Seoul the Friday my vacation ended so we could spend a night or two at a hotel in the city before heading back to the Korean training center, where the whole group would be staying for the program's last month.

When I proposed the plan, breathing hard from the jog and the heat while Toru's inhales and exhales stayed smooth, he only answered, "Maybe."

"*Maybe?* What do you mean, maybe?" I exhaled harder.

"Maybe I can come. Depends on weekend's assignments. What's happening with program schedule."

"Uh, okay," I said flatly, straining to keep my frustration inside. "When can you let me know?"

"Maybe at Seoul. When I know schedule better."

Suddenly, he didn't seem very eager to spend a weekend together. *Has something happened?* My mind ticked back through the last few days. I couldn't locate any rift, but now Toru seemed a few degrees cooler in his pragmatism.

"I need to go shower and change," I said, as we wound down our slow loops around the dirty trail. A few other people were at the track, too: no one from our program, but I didn't want to have an obvious disagreement in public. Even more, I didn't know exactly what to say, but his nonchalance stung. Confounded, I gathered my water bottle, turned toward our dorms.

Toru waved as I left, bending down to begin his stretches.

We spent the next twenty-four hours avoiding each other. I

got to dinner late that night, slowed by a sudden heaviness in my limbs. I sat with Ji-na at a different table than Toru, avoiding his gaze in the cafeteria, where the buffet always made me shudder. The Beijing training center kitchen specialized in fried chicken feet and a dish of sautéed rooster crowns, the scrawny claws and flimsy, yellowing cartilage pooling in oil at the bottom of their metal pans. I had been eating a lot of fried rice.

The next day in the classroom, Toru and I continued to keep our distance. Everything around me suddenly felt grayer, the fascination of East Asia fading to a dirty scrim of strange accents and nauseating foods. That night, we still had not acknowledged each other except for quick, sad nods in the dining room. Then the whole class went to one of the training center's karaoke halls, where we were joined by members of the Chinese Ministry of Commerce for some sort of celebration—the cause of which I never fully understood but assumed had to do with the ubiquitous combination of business, drinking, and letting down your guard.

The music was booming, and three older Chinese ministry men grabbed me and Ji-na to join them onstage for a song. I had always hated karaoke, but I knew I had to play along. We chose a Beatles number and, blushing wildly, I muttered along while the men threw their arms around my and Ji-na's shoulders, swaying back and forth, and belting out "Hey Jude" in their accented English. I noticed Toru slip out during our performance.

Ji-na giggled madly, but she was used to karaoke, and she stayed behind for one more tune while I bolted off the stage as our song ended.

They chose "Let It Be" next, and I sat on one of the tawdry

lounge's faux-leather couches, watching them sing under the too-bright lights from the little stage, and I smiled a frozen grin while the other students laughed and high-fived me. "Good job, good singing!" they enthused kindly. "You shouldn't so embarrass! Berry good!" another added, until tears welled in my eyes. I was suddenly, poundingly, miserably homesick. The adventure of the last two months felt small and diminished, and the thought of making it through my last month of the program without Toru as my secret salvation seemed intolerable.

"Headache," I said, pointing to my forehead, and I made another mad dash, this one for the door.

I walked around outside for a while, the training center and other campus buildings gloomy in the twilight, dark shapes hovering in humid air. I was rounding the corner of one building, heading back to our dorms, when I saw Toru on the path in front of me, a figure emerging out of the dusk.

"Oh. Hi," I said.

"Hi," he answered, looking down, kicking an absent stone with his shoe.

"I had to leave, I . . . you know I hate karaoke," I stumbled.

"I feel sad," Toru said simply, looking up at me, meeting my eyes. "Don't know what's happened, why we don't talking, but I feel low. Too low." The lamps from the path haloed the space around him, his dark eyes reflecting a slice of their light.

I felt a swish of relief, as if the gray inside me were being swept by cool wind.

"Me, too," I said. "I don't want to fight, don't want to not talk."

"So what's happened?" he asked. "Why did you change so sudden?"

"Why didn't you want to come to Seoul with me for the weekend?"

"I didn't say didn't want. I said maybe." Toru looked at me carefully, narrowing his eyes.

"Well, why only maybe?" Now I looked down and kicked my own imaginary stone, my little ballet flats growing dusty at the toe.

"*Maybe*, maybe I can come, I tried to explain," he said. "I don't know what program schedule will be, don't know if I can take time away that weekend. Of course I *want*, but don't know if I can. So maybe. I said maybe because it's true."

"Okay." I was relieved but still frustrated. "But I need you to make clear that you *want* to come away with me, that if you don't come, it's only because you can't. I didn't understand that. I needed you to explain that."

"So just misunderstanding?" he said, his expression loosening into softer planes. Then he shook his head. "Don't like to say something that's not true." A pique of annoyance crept back into his tone. He glanced down again, then back up at me. The pathway light left half his face in shadow. "So I said maybe."

Then he sighed and reached out to grab my hand. He told me he'd been too low without me next to him, that everything since the night before had felt too bad. "Doesn't really matter, I guess," he said, "why misunderstanding was. Just let's be together again."

I squeezed his hand and brought it quickly to my chest. Then, looking around to make sure no one could see us, I dropped it reluctantly. I still didn't understand why he needed to be so literal all the time. *Why did he have to focus on the "maybe" part, the pragmatic part, instead of on the part that matters, instead of explaining he wanted to be together?* But I was too tired, suddenly, to work it through; I didn't even know how to explain the term "pragmatic," and mostly, I just wanted to surrender to the relief inside me.

We turned to walk back together in the direction of the dorms. "Yes," I said gratefully. "Let's just be together again."

BY THE END OF JULY, we were staying just outside Seoul, our last stop in Asia before the students headed to Boston to finish their degrees. I'd gone to Jeju Island for my vacation, and on my way back, Toru met me for an overnight at a hotel in the city. I felt a spike of joy at having a whole day and night alone with him when I could hold his hand in public, when he didn't have to rise before dawn to sneak back to his room.

We explored the city's downtown, then rested at a café among the cobbled streets and antique houses of the Insa-dong area. We drank sweet *yuzu* tea, hot and thick and lemony. Then we went to get haircuts in the neon-lined Gangnam neighborhood at a salon whose windows advertised American hair products, suggesting they might speak some English.

Sitting in the high salon chair, I turned my head while the Korean hairdresser cut and combed, and I watched Toru through the mirror on the room's other side. I flushed warm at the ease and fluidity of his movements reflected back at me, the carefree shake he gave to his own clipped hair. He ran his fingers over his strong round skull, the baby whiteness beneath. He was turning toward me with a smile when the phone call came.

Hearing it ring, I turned my eyes back to my hairdresser, listened to the snipping shears slicing through my hair, watched the severed lanks in their slow deadfall to my feet. It wasn't until a few minutes later that Toru reentered my line of vision.

At first, I didn't notice the difference in his expression, didn't see the disbelief fixed across his features. But then I heard him say, through the soft chops of scissors, "There's been an accident."

He stared blankly at me for a moment. Then, "I must to go back to Japan."

My hair half cut, I turned fully toward him. "What?"

"I must go back, go home. I need to take cab to the airport and go back. Now."

Confused, my hair still lopsided and unfinished, I paid the bill quickly, throwing money onto the counter, then followed Toru into the street. As if in a dream or slow-motion movie, we hailed a taxi. His mother was lying in a coma in a hospital in Japan, he told me as the cab veered toward the highway for the airport. A devout Catholic who went to church each morning, she had been run down by a drunk driver while walking just past dawn to pray. The car had dragged her some distance before the driver sped off. That had been Friday. Now it was Sunday, and Toru's father and sister in Japan, who had been searching all weekend, had finally located his mother in an Osaka emergency room. They waited until they were sure to call Toru.

Suddenly, he shivered, and then, for the first time, I saw him break. Tears, then a shaking through his limbs.

By the time we reached the airport, the last flight out to Japan had already left. Toru would have to wait until morning.

I stayed with him at the airport hotel while he became too numb to cry. We slept on and off, tears seeping down my own face as he lay rigid and still.

He left at dawn, and I went back to the training center, now numb myself. The Korean faculty director's face was dark with anger as my cab pulled up. I had phoned the night before to tell him I would be staying with Toru at the airport. Now, as I stepped out of the idling taxi, he eyed me sideways, then sighed as if he had always known what was coming: this awful breach of decorum by his young American female faculty member. But I no longer cared. The secret of our relationship was out. *Let them fire me*, I thought, then turned silently on my heel, my hair still lopsided, and walked away.

When Toru flew back to Korea a few days later to finish the program, I went again to meet him at the airport. "My mother will never wake," he told me. "The doctors say there is no chance she will live. But she will stay in coma for about a month."

"Why did you come back?" I asked, unable to hide my shock. "Why not just stay there, forget about finishing the program?"

"It's my duty to finish," he said softly. "I'll see her again in two weeks, when I go back to Japan before starting Boston module. She won't wake anyway before then, they're sure." He paused. "And what can I do there, just waiting," he finally said, not a question, not a finished sentence, not venturing to name what would come at the wait's end.

I nodded, hoping mostly just to support him even though I didn't really understand why he'd returned. *Maybe the program's scheduled normalcy will help him cope*, I thought. Maybe he'd find some relief for a few more weeks before going back to say his final good-bye, to watch his mother slip from unconscious sleep to death. It was a reprieve I was praying would soothe him somewhat, until we got another call that night. A few hours after Toru had boarded his fight from Japan to Korea that afternoon, his mother died.

MY HEART BROKE for Toru. But I knew immediately what would happen next, and what it would mean for us.

I had learned enough about Toru's culture and family, his place as *chonan,* or eldest son, to know that eventually he would return, indefinitely, to Osaka to care for his now-widowed father. In Toru's worldview, one never, ever shirked one's duty. So in nine months' time, after finishing his graduate work in Boston, with the late May sun shining gloriously through the soft New England air, he would undoubtedly go home.

And if we were to be together, at least for the foreseeable future, I, too, would have to go back to Asia. I'd have to leave the only place I'd ever truly believed I could live with some sense of stability and security. And I would have to find some way to begin making Toru's world my own.

I had two thoughts when I realized these were bound to be my options: *there is no way I will be able to do this,* and *there is no way I cannot try.*

THREE

TORU RETURNED TO SEOUL
almost immediately after his mother's funeral in Osaka, finishing the last week in Korea with the rest of his class. He was
quieter than before, but he had always been reserved, especially
in public.

For our last week in Asia, we still aimed for discretion, even
though our overnights at the airport had clearly outed our relationship. In our few private moments together, I held Toru close,
but I never saw him cry again, at least not until he was back at
the airport nine months later, this time in Boston, leaving me.

When he first arrived in the U.S. on a warm August day
soon after the Seoul module's end, our life together in my hometown felt as close to perfect as I'd ever known. Toru's company
rented furnished apartments near campus for him and each of his
Japanese colleagues. Only Toru and Makoto, the two youngest
students, were unmarried, but none of the other Japanese men
brought their spouses or children with them to the U.S., even
though they would be gone for almost a year. This was not
unusual: Japanese businessmen are frequently expected to have

greater loyalty to their companies than to their wives. Most *shufu*, or housewives, I would come to learn later, accept this as fact. In a common arrangement known as *tanshin-funin*, many married couples live apart because of the husband's job. Even Toru's parents had done so for a few years, his father shuttling back from Tokyo to Osaka on weekends when the children were young.

I had quit teaching in the Asia executive program almost immediately after arriving home, but we decided I would never spend the night at Toru's apartment, since the other Japanese students lived in his building, too, and we thought it would be weird to run into them as a couple. In addition to my one class that fall at the prison, I was also still teaching writing on the regular campus at the business school—four sections for first-year standard MBAs—so we rarely spent any time together there, either.

But on weekends, Toru would come to my little studio in the South End, and it felt like my world was pretty much complete. I was home, in a place I could navigate almost with my eyes closed. Unlike in Asia, when I walked down the sidewalk in Boston, not only could I read every street sign or store name, recognize all the food on market shelves, I could read the *people*, too. When someone smiled, laughed, shook his or her head, I knew exactly what was meant. The subtle but constant disorientation of the Far East lifted like a fog burning off in bright, sudden sun.

Weekday mornings, I would wake in my apartment and luxuriate in the feeling of *home*. On the weekends, I took Toru to my favorite café in Central Square. I'd read the Sunday paper over a steaming soy chai latte and strawberry scone while he flipped through his business textbooks, eating plain buttered toast and drinking black tea with milk, exactly as he did every morning in Japan.

We went running along the Charles River from Boston to Cambridge, and I loved turning the corner together by the BU boathouse on the loop back, the huff of our breaths in sync, the city skyline rising along the water. Thin white boats unzipped the river's surface as their rowers pulled their arms in unison. The air was crisp, gliding over my skin, a weightless force holding me perfectly in place. Beyond, sailboats bobbed in the distance like little Brahmin toys, while Beacon Hill rose up, the golden crown of its statehouse winking in the sun.

In public, our roles had reversed, especially from our dynamic in Japan; I was now the one who knew the language and culture. Of course, Toru could read English quite well; almost all his fellow citizens can. But most learn it in school from native Japanese instructors who teach grammar and vocabulary, not speaking. Despite his enrollment in an American graduate program, he still struggled verbally. When we went to restaurants, Toru would try to order with broken syntax—"Ahh, I'll gonna have a steak?" he'd say, pointing to the menu—and the servers would always turn to me, even if Toru had been basically understandable, as if the very idea of communicating with an accented speaker made them nervous. I'd feel protective of him then and annoyed at the person waiting on us. But I couldn't be sure that, in all my years of waitressing during graduate school in my twenties, I hadn't done the same thing.

By now, our own communication challenges had woven a familiar rhythm into our relationship, fodder more often for humor than prolonged frustration. Toru had become used to my sayings and intonations, and I with his. Of course, there were still times when our conversations got tangled. One night at a Thai restaurant, he tried telling me about a giant crab he'd seen in Thailand, and I thought he was talking about a *club*, some kind of disco. He mimed jerky arms and legs, and I thought, *Oh, he must be trying to explain a dance club. Weird-style dancing though.*

Then he mentioned a huge "hand."

"Wait . . . wait," I stopped him, "are we talking about a *club*?"

"Ya, ya, *crub*," Toru insisted, and it went back and forth until he mimed pincers and I realized we were discussing a crustacean.

But we had our usual gestures and jokes we knew by heart, and these became a fluency we shared. "*Saitei!*" was my fallback, which technically means "worst" in Japanese, although I co-opted it as an all-purpose protest, as in "That's the worst!" Toru, for his part, liked to say "That's *so* suck" after hearing me complain, "Well, *that* sucks." In homage to our verbal games of Twister and to Ji-na from the summer before, who had once mistakenly called him "Tofu," I gave him the nickname "Tof."

When we had disagreements or moments of confusion that really mattered, we tried to keep clarifying, repeating back what we thought the other meant, to avoid a more profound mis-understanding like we'd had in Beijing. This sometimes made conversation slower, but it also helped keep things simple and encouraged us to be careful, ensuring we'd think through what we needed to say before blurting it out.

Of all the everyday interactions we had, my favorite was also one of the most mundane. In Boston, as he'd always done in Asia, when we stepped off a sidewalk, even along a barely trafficked road, Toru would ensure he was on the outside, shuttling me away from potential cars, blocking my body from the street with his compact but solid presence.

Despite my passion for self-reliance, when Toru shielded me, even from my own world, I felt safe and at home in a way I'd never imagined. I felt, quite simply, cocooned.

I decided it was time he met my mother.

THAT FALL, I introduced Toru twice to my mother and stepfather. The first time was soon after he got to Boston, before they went to spend the fall and winter in Palm Beach. We both felt nervous about the meeting, but we loved each other, and I couldn't imagine him *not* knowing my family, despite the potential culture clash between my quiet but strong-willed Japanese boyfriend and my loud and strong-willed Jewish-American parents. Toru bought a new jacket, and we went to dinner at Aquitaine, a French bistro in the South End.

My mother, then in her late sixties, swooped in with her Ferragamo handbag and heels, her honeybee pink lipstick and matching manicure, and her twice-a-week salon-styled hair sprayed to such perfection that it seemed not even a Boston nor'easter could disturb a strand. She shook Toru's hand, kissed my cheek, and then settled down with her martini—Smirnoff, twist, stemmed glass *only*—to interrogate Toru as to why "your countrymen are so hard on the empress for failing to produce a male heir."

For his part, Toru nodded earnestly, then agreed, "Hmm, yes, makes no sense, doesn't it?"

My mother repeated this same question immediately upon meeting Toru the second time, when my parents came back to Boston for Thanksgiving. Toru again agreed graciously, this time adding "poor empress" for emphasis.

My stepfather, a retired banker in his early seventies with an expansive laugh and Gucci loafers, smiled frequently despite responding "What was that?" to almost everything Toru said. Then he patted Toru warmly on the back and generously picked up the bill, waving his hand when Toru reached for his wallet.

My parents had taken us to dinner at their country club this time, and my stepfather even called over David Shwartz, who had fought in the South Pacific and then started a successful postwar business with offices in Tokyo. "We bought up half of Japan!" Shwartz fondly recalled. Toru paused for a beat, tilted his head a few degrees above his jacket and tie. Then he smiled politely and said, "Oh, great!" They grinned expectantly at each other for a moment longer, and finally, all conversation apparently exhausted, Shwartz gave Toru's hand a robust pump, then turned to my stepfather to discuss the markets.

Through it all, Toru was unflappable. He sat a little stiffly, propped upright by the tension of English conversation in an entirely new environment. But he was unfailingly courteous and persistently unruffled, interested in the scene but also removed from it, like a director on someone else's set. I held his hand under the table, and he told me both times before my parents arrived that as long as I stayed next to him, he'd be fine. And he was.

"Good practice for English!" he told me after we left my parents at the restaurant and then again at the country club. His strongest impression was that both my mother and the club were "kind of too gorgeous," an adjective I later learned the Japanese use to mean "fancy."

I didn't have the heart to tell him of her calling me in my office at the university a few days after Thanksgiving, when she realized that Toru and I were not breaking up anytime soon, and trying to fix me up with the son of one of her Palm Beach friends. "He's a *fine* person. An investment banker in New York," she told me. "He's getting divorced, but his parents are fine, fine people. Very close friends." She left the "Jewish" part unspoken, although eminently clear, but she couldn't help adding, as if I hadn't picked up on the Palm-Beach-investment-banker part of the equation, "*Very* wealthy." Pointing out that I wouldn't be teaching in a prison if I cared about money—and conveniently ignoring my cash-driven work at the business school—I told her I wasn't interested. I loved Toru and knew that he loved me. I had to believe we would find a way to make our relationship last when he went back to Japan.

ALTHOUGH I FELT a unique sense of completeness with Toru in Boston, he didn't necessarily take to American culture. While some might assume the lack of shared fluency would present the greatest challenge in a relationship such as ours, I found the difference in our customs a harder gulf to cross. Where once I'd hoped that Toru, like some people I'd met from abroad, would find America and its casualness a relief—as if they could finally exhale a breath they hadn't realized they'd been holding—now I saw Toru was not likely to embrace my world as some sort of long-lost beacon of his soul.

Out for lunch one day, we went to a bakery in Cambridge.

Toru raised his eyebrows in anticipation as we waited to order, watching plates pass by, sliced meats and cheeses bursting from thick slabs of homemade bread. But the line moved slowly, sometimes in no particular fashion, and when we got to the front, the cashier was chatting away, first with another customer who was well past ordering, then with a coworker. Her nose ring glinted in the light from the windows, and then she turned suddenly and disappeared into the kitchen.

Behind us, a man complained loudly to no one in particu- lar, while a teenager popped her gum. A woman interrogated someone over her cell phone about their desired sandwich choice. When the cashier returned, Toru and I stepped up. He opened his mouth to order. She turned to chat some more with a young woman who had abruptly poked her head through an opening from the kitchen. Then she laughed, her back to us. "You know it, *girl!*" she called to the white-coated pastry chef. Toru's face turned darker.

After we finally ordered, we went to get seats at the bakery's communal center table. Toru was removing his coat when a woman in pressed jeans and leather driving shoes burst through the door, a scarf knotted neatly at her neck, a trio of fresh- scrubbed children trailing behind. She took an imperious look around, stepped through the crowd, and made a beeline toward our seats. Drawing near, she clucked her tongue at Toru, shooing him to the end of the bench to make room for her oxford-shirted offspring.

A protest arose in my chest, but I stifled it as it reached my tongue. *She's shooing him like she would a puppy,* I thought in dis- gust. *Would she be so dismissive if he were some big white guy?* I glared at her, but confounded as to a proper response, I said nothing. I felt chagrin at myself rise alongside the mute objection in my throat.

"I don't like," Toru said, irritation cutting through each syllable, his eyes slanting toward the woman. He shook his head in one fierce motion, then turned away from her, and he seemed to shrink into his own skin, hunching his shoulders, pressing his lips together in a closed line as if insulating himself from the rude disorder around him. The clucking woman stuffed her children into seats, oblivious.

An image of the white-gloved train attendant we had seen in Kobe flashed through my mind. The stiff formality, the insistence on bowing at each end of the car—despite whether anyone was looking. It was the conductor's role to be polite. It was unthinkable not to do so. But in Boston, no one even noticed when decorum failed or order unraveled. I tried to stifle the disconcerting thought that, if Toru were to build a life here with me, this cultural chasm would alienate him on every level, both personally and professionally—even more than the actual language barrier.

Toru's inner distance from my world emerged in other ways, too. The most surprising was his lack of interest in being with my friends. In Japan, Toru told me, couples rarely socialize together. Husbands and wives go to dinner in lone pairs but rarely in a group of couples. Double dates and even mixed-gender outings are uncommon, especially for adults.

Toru couldn't understand why, just because he was my boyfriend, he would necessarily spend time with my friends. He wasn't opposed to them—he appreciated their kindness, their humor, and especially their warmth for me—but he didn't get the concept of being friends merely because you loved someone in common. He was also quite shy. Where I was boisterous and social, Toru, even at home, preferred being alone when he wasn't at work.

One night in Boston, we went with five of my friends to Pho Republique, a funky French-Vietnamese place on Washington Street in the South End. Sitting at our long, rough-hewn table, swilling a lychee martini, I sprinted from one topic to the next: giving Robert a cultural analysis of the gender politics in men's prisons, where the weak are labeled women; complaining to Jenna about the tragedy of having to teach writing to MBA students for income. The other end of the table was laughing about Rod's miserable first date, while Louise anguished over her upcoming tenure application, everyone popping fried wonton strips into their mouths and leaning forward to gossip more closely, elbows splayed.

Toru sat quietly beside me at the end of a bench sipping his Sam Adams beer, politely trying to listen, throwing back his head to laugh when the conversation deemed it appropriate, but clearly not in the spirit of the moment. From time to time, I squeezed his hand and smiled at him. Occasionally, I tried to draw him into the conversation.

"Tof, tell them how Makoto kept mistaking police cars for taxis. How he spent his first week in Boston hailing cops at every corner," I urged.

"They couldn't understand, *why* this skinny Japanese guy waving at them all the time?" Toru told the table, and we all laughed. But once the hilarity faded, Toru leaned back, looking more relieved for a chance to escape the spotlight than eager to continue the conversation.

Still, my friends all liked Toru, admired his quiet humility, his down-to-earth aura, his bravery at pursuing an MBA in English when he clearly wasn't fluent—and at pursuing a relationship with me when I couldn't speak his language at all. Most of all, my friends liked how grounded and happy I was with Toru. It felt as if for years I'd had a motor spinning in too high a gear somewhere deep inside, its calibration skewed, and now with Toru next to me, the revving slowed to a smooth and even hum. My friends noticed. After all, they were the people who'd supported me through years of boyfriends with high ambitions, top degrees, and prestigious jobs, all of which had still left these men ill equipped for simple intimacy—or for my own not-so-simple neuroses.

Toru's distance from my social circle made me feel a little lonely in a different way, like I had two halves of my life that I couldn't bring together. But as consolation, I considered there might be wisdom in the Japanese tradition of *not* combining a romantic partner with friends. *After all, one person can't be everything at all times.* I turned the idea around in my mind for a while. *Maybe it's healthy to find some fundamental social sustenance outside your relationship.* As long as I was home, ensconced in the place I knew so well—and the people who knew me—I felt rooted and content enough, especially with Toru by my side, his love adding heft to the gravity holding my world in place.

What unnerved me even more than questions about my compatibility with a man so different from me socially, was Toru's inevitable return to Japan in May. Lately, I'd been silently mulling over moving to Osaka. Then I would think, *How did I become* this *person? This woman, the one who would consider forfeiting her way of life, her home, her world for a man's? And for a country like Japan, where women hold so little power?*

I tried to justify my deep reluctance to leave the U.S. as a form of political resistance. Like my suspicion of marriage as an institution created long ago to codify female servitude—both historically accurate and handily consoling every time a previous romance failed—my refusal to change my life for a man felt central to my identity as an independent, modern woman. But, in truth, my reluctance went deeper than the intellectual or political, dipping down into a place of plain, bald terror.

The world I had created for myself in Boston, so perfectly planned and shaped, was built upon that promise I had made myself in early adulthood when I swore never to sacrifice too much for someone or something else. I'd seen where dependence led and I was loath to lose myself in another situation I couldn't control or navigate on my own. Now I wondered if building a life with Toru in Osaka could possibly guarantee anything other than the very loss of self and home I'd sworn never again to relinquish.

2.

T
H
E

H
O
N
E
Y
M
O
O
N

S
T
A
G
E

The typical description of [culture shock's] progression . . . starts at a higher stage of fascination, adventure, optimism, or excitement called the honeymoon stage. [But] this is followed by feelings of inadequacy, disappointment, disillusion, alienation, and self-blame.

• Paul Pedersen, *The Five Stages of Culture Shock*

Please enjoy your time in the pocket park in a city.

• Advertisement for my morning café in Osaka

FOUR

THE DAWN was bright through
Logan Airport's tall windows. It was late spring 2005, about a
month after Toru had returned to Japan, and I arrived at five-
fifteen a.m. to check in for my early flight to Chicago and then
on to Osaka's Kansai Airport. My bags were overstuffed, my
hair in a loose ponytail still damp from the shower. A line had
already formed despite the inhumane hour, and in it stood a
clutch of women with Japanese passports bound for my same
itinerary. Most stood stick-straight and impeccably coiffed, their
makeup subtle but flawless, their bags compact and neatly arranged, gliding forward on perfect, tiny wheels.

They waited patiently to check in while I tapped my foot
nervously, trying to straighten my unruly ponytail, lugging my
bags awkwardly as the line inched forward, my suitcase scraping the floor in a minor cacophony. Still waiting, I called Toru
to tell him I had made it to Logan on time. At just past six
p.m. in Japan—hours before traditional salarymen like him leave
work—he couldn't talk for long, but he urged me to call from
my layover in Chicago, telling me he loved me, reminding me

he would be waiting on the other side of customs at Kansai Airport. "Thank you for coming to here," he said.

In the weeks before he had left Boston, we had decided I would visit him in Japan from mid-June through mid-July. This would take the edge off his May departure from the U.S. without interrupting my fall teaching schedule, still leaving me plenty of time to prepare my September syllabi. Toru had convinced me that even though I couldn't imagine actually *living* so far from Boston, I might as well explore Osaka a bit before I insisted on the impossibility of making a life there. "Why not just come, see what it's like?"

"Well, maybe I could," I had tentatively agreed. I let the idea take form in my head, solidifying slowly like liquid hardening into shape. Given the intensity of Japanese corporate life, Toru wouldn't be able to take more than a day or two off from work, but there was a national holiday (Marine Day, which he termed "respect for the sea" day) in mid-July that provided one long weekend. Plus, it would be the rainy season and airfares would be cheap.

As I approached Logan's ticket counter, I felt a sudden pressure behind my eyes and in my throat. *This is going to be our life from now on*, I thought. *This is how we'll live, with me returning a few times a year to this early-morning line, calling him thirteen time zones and half a world away, then boarding a plane for a twenty-four-hour trip across the planet.* Unless I agreed to move to Japan or we decided to break up.

When Toru had arrived home in May, he had confirmed my fears about his sure place in Osaka. His father was spending whole days in front of the TV, his weight dropping as he declined food during daylight either because of mourning or apathy. Tremors had begun to shake his hand.

Grasping the phone in my studio in Boston, listening to Toru's report of life back home, I hadn't mentioned the possibility of his being transferred to America. Instead, I stared off into space and clutched the handset hard as, silently, we both agreed he needed to be in Japan, at least for the foreseeable future.

Now, standing at Logan Airport, I was swallowing back tears. Then a uniformed woman at the counter called, "Next!" and I shuffled forward. The rush of activity pushed back the burning in my eyes and throat: handing over my passport, removing my shoes and unloading my laptop at security, buying water and a paper near the gate, boarding the plane to my tiny economy seat.

Twenty hours and one layover later, I woke to the plane's descent, its hulk banking through the clouds until Japan emerged below. I saw dark blue ocean and pancake-flat earth, urban sprawl jutting against gray mountains in the distance. Bays and basins dotting the land were topped with cargo ships, slivers of blue and white atop the shifting water. I had seen this landscape once before, of course, just over a year earlier when I had arrived in Japan to teach. But this time felt different. This time, I was landing, potentially, in a whole new life. I forced this thought from my mind. *All that matters now is that soon I'll be through immigration and customs, and then I'll be with Toru again.*

Touching down, I could see air-traffic attendants on the runway dressed in dark blue jumpsuits and light gray hardhats, red and white batons in hand. They stood still and straight as the plane slowed to a roll, their arms crossed at their thighs. Then they bowed simultaneously, lifted their batons aloft, and signaled us toward the gate. Watching them, I felt a little thrill, their polite choreography all the more delightful for the mundane labor of their task.

Thirty minutes later, the doors from customs swung open and I saw an ocean of Japanese people, some holding signs written in sloping English, others standing immobile in the late-afternoon light. Then there he was.

He started toward me with a hesitant smile. His black hair and dark eyes blended with the others', but the familiarity of his face and gait stood out unmistakably to me. In a flash, I was pressed against his chest.

WHEN I WOKE early that first morning in Osaka, the sky peeking through the curtains was slate, promising a day with no sun. I glanced at Toru in the tiny bed beside me, taking in the room I had been too tired to notice the night before. He'd rented us what the Japanese call a "weekly mansion," little box-apartments available for short-term lease. *The "mansion" part must be an attempt at humor,* I thought. I would come to learn that nonsensical phrases like this are everywhere in Japan, a culture that gleefully and unironically co-opts foreign terms without regard for spelling, grammar, or even meaning.

Toru's father, named Tetsunobu, had invited me stay at the apartment where he and Toru lived together. I'd already met him briefly when he and Toru's sister, Kei, had come to Boston the previous Christmas for a quick visit. He was kind, unassuming, and dapper in his five-foot-two frame, and when we'd met in December, he'd grabbed my hand and given it a friendly shake. "Nice to meeting you!" he'd said in English with a grin, and when I'd bowed awkwardly, he inclined his head as we both laughed at our attempts to assume the other's culture.

Tetsunobu-*san*, as I called him (the "*san*" denoted respect), had made an unusual offer when he'd asked me to stay at his apartment in Osaka. Toru had told me that in Japan, families rarely meet partners until an engagement becomes official. Neither Toru nor Kei had ever introduced a girlfriend or boyfriend to their parents, or even mentioned having one before me. But Toru wasn't surprised or overly impressed by his father's hospitality. "We're not so conservative family," he explained.

I knew enough already about his history to know this was true: Toru came from a long line of liberal academics, his grandmother even attending college and becoming a teacher in prewar Japan, when most women ended their education at grammar school. One aunt had been a scientist, another taught at university, and his uncle, whom we called the "Communist Professor," had studied Marxist economics and been a student leader in the Tokyo University protests of the 1970s. Even his mother's Catholicism in secular Japan had been a mark of quiet independence.

When he learned I'd be coming to Osaka for an extended visit, Tetsunobu-*san* not only invited me to stay with him and his son, he told Toru he wanted to prepare me a toast breakfast every morning. He worried that I wouldn't be able to order food at a restaurant or go to the market on my own. But by U.S. standards, their apartment was tiny, with one small bathroom and a sliver-sized extra bedroom, although it was the same place where Toru had grown up in a family of four. Touched by Tetsunobu-*san*'s kindness, I had asked Toru to decline for me. Toru, more

annoyed at his father's impracticality than moved by his generosity, had immediately agreed that we needed privacy.

The studio he rented us was slightly more than two hundred
square feet, too cramped even for a full-sized bed, leaving us
both squeezed into a twin, under which Toru had pushed my
suitcase. The place boasted a hot plate and a mini-refrigerator,
a rice cooker, a pint-sized toilet/shower/bath room, and a tiny
washer-dryer tucked into a small closet. It also had another little
closet for clothes, one Lilliputian set of drawers, and a televi-
sion broadcasting three local channels. Toru and Tetsunobu-*san*'s
apartment was just blocks away, so at least we didn't have to
make room for two sets of clothes.

Now, the studio's curtains glowing faintly with a hint of
daybreak, Toru lay straight and silent on his back beside me, his
breathing steady and gentle, his expression tranquil. I resisted
the urge to wake him with a kiss. *This is what I love most about
him,* I lay thinking, *this serenity in the face of life's twists and turns.*
Soon his black eyes popped open, and he gazed at me, blurry for
a moment. Then he focused his pupils and said, "Hi, my love.
Ohayōgozaimas! [Good morning!] You're at Japan!" And just like
that, he was awake and happy.

His bright confidence burned off whatever haze of unease
I had about being in Osaka. And then we were up and dressed,
and I was ready to meet his life in this new land.

JAPAN IS STEREOTYPED for be-
ing vastly different from the West, a country of intense confor-
mity rippled with astounding strains of weirdness. In the days
that followed, these stereotypes struck me as utterly true. Being

sequestered in the training center almost 24/7 the summer before, I hadn't had a chance to experience the country except in the most cursory way. This month would be different.

I learned that Kansai is Japan's second most populated metropolitan area, and Osaka, Kansai's capital, holds almost ten million people. Its streets combine modern high-rises and mid-rise seventies-style buildings slotted next to each other like mismatched teeth, a maze all the more striking for its utter tidiness. The sidewalks are bare of trash. The entranceways brook no disorder. Wedged between buildings sits the occasional traditional Japanese house (a few survived the city's near total destruction in World War II), their gray scalloped roofs undulating in little swells.

Yet unlike most other huge cities such as Tokyo, Osaka's population is surprisingly uncosmopolitan. Even in a country notorious for its homogeneity, Osaka has comparatively few foreigners: a much more modest ratio of *gaijin*—literally "outside people"—than even the smaller cities of Nagoya, Kyoto, or Kobe.

Toru took the first Monday off from work after my arrival and, holding my pale hand in his smooth palm, he led me through the Umeda subway station in the city center, then along its vast underground mall, between cascading waves of dark-suited salarymen and schoolgirls in blue kilts. *I've never seen so many people moving at one time*, I thought as hundreds of bobbing black heads waded through the subterranean halls, a sardine-can crowd that somehow kept pulsing smoothly forward.

In my guidebook, I'd read of the Japanese saying "The nail sticking up will get hammered down." In Osaka, the fierce sameness of people's manners was on full display, as was how much I, in turn, stood out, a woman simultaneously conspicuous and utterly irrelevant. On the sidewalk near our weekly mansion or in the subway neatly dissecting the city's vast underground, mine was almost always the only (bottle) blond head visible. Except in Osaka's commercial center, three stops from our studio apartment, where the Hilton, Ritz-Carlton, and U.S. Consulate had taken up residence, I could go for whole days without seeing another Westerner. Most passersby either stared at me quickly or pretended I didn't exist, their eyes boring into the empty space in front of them or around me but never drifting to the contours of my body. Even the people who did stare looked away immediately when I caught their eye. Toru told me this was an act of politeness; in such a crowded country, making eye contact can be an invasion of privacy.

But the opposite would frequently happen when young mothers rode by on their *mama-chari,* ubiquitous one-speed bikes whose names were a riff on "mama chariots." Their toddlers, tucked into little baskets in front, would often crane their necks to stare, tiny round heads and wide eyes following me as they swooshed past. Being so seen yet also so erased felt strange but not entirely disagreeable. I had unwittingly inherited a curious power: to be both a bright mystery and a blank space all at once.

On the subway, men in business suits read porn, flipping pages with an ease bordering on ennui. Next to them, schoolgirls in kneesocks and kilts texted madly on sequin-covered Hello Kitty cell phones, equally unfazed by the bondage scenes splayed across the newsprint of their neighbors. On the street, women in summer kimonos, called *yukata,* walked side by side with modestly dressed housewives and adolescent girls in short shorts, fishnet stockings, and stilettos. Sometimes a group of Goth-doll teenagers would walk by, feet plugged into black-and-white shoes atop preposterously high rubber soles, their short frocks decked with bolts of white lace jutting outward at the hem, thigh-high striped socks covering skinny knees. They would clasp their hands over their mouths as they giggled, radiating a mix of defiance and self-consciousness, a desire to stand out and shock but only in the context of a uniform group.

I felt my eyes widen and my stomach contract at these scenes. On one hand, it all looked so *regressive*, and a slew of academic arguments began to coalesce in my brain about how these trends must disempower the girls and women who adopted them. *The schoolgirls with their sequined cartoon characters next to porno-reading men? The stiletto heels on teenagers in shorts? The middle-aged women's bland invisibility?* On the other hand, I had to admit I was riveted.

DURING THE WEEKDAYS, with Toru at work, I spent most of my time reading or walking Osaka's streets under a humid drizzle. Tucked into random spots throughout the city were tiny Shinto shrines, wooden or stone structures usually no bigger than a large cardboard box, festooned with colored strings or hanging chains, bells sometimes hooked among their links.

My guidebook explained that Shinto was Japan's original spiritual tradition. When Buddhism arrived via China in the sixth century, it gained equal prominence, although it did not usurp Shinto. Unlike in the West, most Japanese saw no contradiction in worshipping within two belief systems simultaneously. A form of animism, Shinto considers the earth one vast pantheon, with gods embodied in random rocks, trees, patches of grass, or even, apparently, concrete roofing. From the window of my tiny weekly mansion, I could see a mini-shrine erected on the top of an adjacent building, although I never saw anyone visit it, despite keeping watch for a rooftop supplication.

Near the city center at the intersection of two busy streets stood my favorite trace of Shinto. The road circled awkwardly around the base of an enormous tree, its trunk bulging like a well-fed belly swelling to embrace an orange hut a few feet high. The tree, Toru informed me, was supposedly a god, and the public works department had respectfully rerouted the pavement to accommodate the leaf-bound deity. Like so much of Osaka, the shrines were tiny treasures in an advent-calendar world, every corner revealing a minor wonder.

I was equally surprised by the city's children and my reaction to them. Although I had never been drawn to kids before, I now loved seeing the little students with their yellow hats, dark uniforms, and identical boxy, red-leather backpacks. One afternoon, I watched a pair of teachers leading a long line of children who looked no older than six. They filed onto the subway platform, the boys in shorts, the girls in pleated skirts, hat straps snug under chins. When the train pulled in, one cluster broke off from the line and stepped onto the subway. Then they turned and bowed to the row of teachers and students still waiting for the next car, who bowed back in mirrorlike precision, two parallel lines of yellow caps dipping and rising in unison, mini-hands shooting up and waving to Japanese-accented cries of "Bye-bye!"

For a split second, a jolt of longing pierced me. I wondered what it would be like to hold one of those tiny children close. *If Toru and I had a baby, would it stand here one day, too, a little bright-*

capped being in a freshly pressed uniform, all chubby fists and polite bows? But when I tried to focus further, the image blurred. *Wouldn't having a child bind me to Japan, in one way or another, for good?* I turned my back then to watch a train on the opposite track arrive.

Between walking and taking the subway, I could navigate much of the city alone, ever more bewitched by its crazy constellation of opposites. Most of the main stations had English transliterations on their signs, so I could find my way around with a phonetically rendered list of central stops—Umeda, Shinsaibashi, and the one near our weekly mansion, Tanimachi-Rokuchōme. Toru bought me a cheap cell phone with a prepaid plan so I could call him if I got lost. He also made a copy of our studio's address spelled in Japanese characters, printing out a map and marking a big X over the black-and-white grid where our apartment lay among a maze of streets. I could give the paper to a cabdriver if I couldn't reach Toru, since even pronouncing our address, let alone giving directions in Japanese, was impossible.

Although most people in Japan know how to read English, I was surprised to find that few in Osaka actually spoke it, and fewer still were willing to talk with a foreigner. Sometimes on the subway, people would move if I sat down next to them, and frequently the vacant seat to my side would be the last taken. Then I'd be left in the crowded car, the only white face among a swell of passengers, the empty orange seat next to me like neon blinking news of my otherness.

When I asked Toru why people were so reluctant to be near me, he explained they were probably afraid I was going to ask for directions or speak English to them, and then they'd be embarrassed by their lack of fluency. "Face is very important here," he said. "People don't want to do things they'll feel shame for." If they could not converse perfectly, they were loath to converse at all.

One day, Toru took me to a bookstore with a section for English books, although the sign marking it was in Japanese, so I couldn't have found it again myself. I wanted to buy some expat magazines, learn more about the English-speaking community in Japan. Most were published in Tokyo, but two came from Kansai, covering Osaka, Kyoto, and Kobe. They were printed on matte paper and staple-bound, not like my glossy magazines at home. Their thin, folded spines told me what a flimsy slice of life foreigners occupy in Japan.

EVERY MORNING while Toru was at work, I'd go to one of the many nearby cafés where, whenever a customer entered, the identically clad staff would proclaim in unison, *"Irasshaimase!"* "Welcome!" My two favorite places had pictures on their menus, so I could point to a photo of coffee or buttered toast, and the cashier would bow his or her head in little dips of respect, then smile, count out my change, and set my order on the counter.

The air would become heavy with smoke as the seats filled up. The "smoking sections" seemed a mere formality, placed smack against the "nonsmoking" areas—or sometimes even sur-rounding them. One morning, waving a puff of tobacco from my eyes, I gazed out the window, watching lazily as business-men in suits rode by on three-speed bikes and cars idled quietly in traffic. Something about the urban scene's tranquility struck me as odd, but it took a moment for me to identify what. Then I realized I had yet to hear anyone do something as obtrusive as honking.

At the intersection, I watched pedestrians at the curb. The walk sign was red, a white silhouette of a man in a suit against a glowing crimson square. No car approached, but still the people waited, obeying the mechanized order not to cross. They stood without moving until the sign changed, the white cutout figure now angling forward, arms swinging across a green background, calling its human followers to motion.

Then an immaculately washed, tiny purple garbage truck ambled past, bright pink flowers painted on its side. Two uniformed garbagemen sat in front, their expressions earnest despite the melody warbling like a nursery rhyme from a speaker on the roof. Written in white English letters across the top was their slogan: CLEAN OSAKA!

As morning extended into noon, I watched the café fill with office workers. Men in plain dark suits sat together, smoking and drinking coffee. Nearby, women in matching skirts and white blouses chatted at tables of their own. Toru told me these women were called OLs, a bizarre, shortened version of the English term "office ladies" (although, since the Japanese lexicon lacks a hard *l,* the second letter was pronounced as an approximate *r,* becoming even more bizarrely, *O-er-uus*). At most traditional companies like Toru's, women wore uniforms while men—with the exception of factory workers—did not. If a female staff member reached management level, she could trade her OL uniform for business attire. In Toru's office, that had never happened. He knew of few places where it had.

At the café, the OLs spoke quietly, nodding their heads rapidly, clutching frilly handkerchiefs in their laps, knees pressed together, sensible black shoes tucked under their chairs. When they laughed, some covered their mouths modestly like I had seen Ji-na do the previous summer. The businessmen at their own tables bantered more freely, their legs and arms spread out like branches.

Once again, I was surprised by the gender divisions around me, but even more surprised that they failed to rile me much. I wondered if that was racist of me: if I cared less about the status of women who looked different from me, whose skin was darker and syllables more staccato than my own. But I felt so *removed* from the world around me in Japan—as if I were walking around inside a giant bubble, rolling through a landscape fascinating yet untouchable. *This is not your country*, I saw written across the polite but closed faces, the unreadable street signs, even the kind but paternalistic surprise people showered on me at restaurants when I picked up chopsticks or when they asked Toru if I could eat soy sauce. When people's eyes looked through me on the street or hawkers quietly pulled their advertisements back as I passed, I felt gently but firmly reminded of my outside status.

At times this left me alienated and lonely, and I wondered how I would cope if I actually moved to Japan. But tucked within the folds of this concern, I found unexpected freedom and relief. *This is not my country. These are not my problems to solve.*

ONE DAY, we headed to Kyoto, about forty minutes away by train, to visit the Kinkaku-ji, the famous golden pavilion. Covered in gold leaf and rising out of a pond, the site was once a shogun's villa and then a Zen temple. I'd never seen it but had read about it. "Very famous. Very beautiful," Toru told me. "Kind of big, golden temple," he said, and for a second I flashed back to the Chinese restaurant my mother and stepfather loved in Brookline, the Golden Temple. I pictured plump fried chicken fingers and glossy, ruby-colored spareribs, but I didn't mention this to Toru.

Waiting on the platform for our train to Kyoto, we were flanked on one side by a white-gloved station attendant tasked with ensuring no one strayed too close to the edge. On our other side stood a young man dressed in khaki trousers and a plain white button-down, the sleeves pushed up to reveal thin arms. He stretched one limb aloft, straining to lift some sort of device above his head, angling the apparatus toward the tunnel's mouth.

"What's *he* doing?" I asked Toru.

"He's *densha-otaku*," Toru said, his voice suggesting a minimum of interest. "Train nerd. Obsessed with trains." Toru explained that Japan bred *otaku* of every stripe, fanatics passionate about one phenomenon or another: *manga, anime*, even *cosplay*, where adults dress up and walk around as characters from video games, movies, and comic books.

Densha-otaku study schedules and ride trains, sometimes all day. Then at home, they replay the sound of trains rushing in and out of stations. I imagined the man next to us sitting in his house alone, listening to his recordings while a frisson of locomotive-inspired delight surged through him.

"It's *so* dumb," Toru said, his laugh dismissive. But I was fascinated, a little thrill of my own shivering through me at the weirdness and surprise this country constantly offered up.

"Tof," I said, "I know the U.S. is odd and crazy in its own way, but this country is just totally *bizarre*." Toru emitted a small *huh,* somewhere between begrudging amusement and utter disinterest, and then we turned to watch as the train approached. The *densha-otaku* held his device even higher while the uniformed station attendant stood still and stick-straight until the cars slid into the station.

Then the attendant bowed to the similarly white-gloved conductor, who in turn bowed back, his head leaning out the window as he slowed the train until it reached a thin white line on the platform marking the exact spot at which the front end should stop. The conductor pointed to the line with a quick two-fingered flourish, nodded his head again, and proclaimed *"Hai!"* ("Yes!"). On the wall, the clock confirmed the cars' presence at the precise time printed on the hanging timetable. Our train had arrived.

In Kyoto, Toru and I walked the grounds of the golden pavilion, staring up at its gilded walls, a soft gloaming in the pale afternoon. Like so much in Japan, the temple stood tranquil, stately, and in stunning contrast to the bizarre hypermodernity of the *densha-otaku* we'd seen earlier.

Another weekend toward the end of my stay, Toru took me to Kyoto again so I could see a Japanese tea ceremony. We rode through the flatlands of Kansai, houses of white, beige, and gray with dark-shingled roofs swooping by our window while mountains rimmed the distance with dusty blue. In Kyoto, we followed the Philosopher's Path, a grass-bordered walkway along a small stream. The ground was damp, the famed cherry-blossom trees lining the path now well past bloom, rising in a green canopy under a wet sky. Little stores and restaurants flanked the path. Fat gray and orange carp broke the stream's surface, gaping their mouths in awkward yawns before slipping back under the waterline.

At a small house advertising an abbreviated form of tea ceremony, we removed our shoes and stepped onto a platform of straw tatami mats. Instead of whisking the green *matcha* tea in one communal bowl and then passing it for each person to sip— as in a traditional ceremony—this teahouse offered individual bowls, served on a porch overlooking a Japanese garden. A white couple was already there, and from the brown sandals they had left at the entryway and the socks pulled up along their shins, I guessed they were European, maybe German. While we waited for our tea, the woman whispered something to the man, her accent guttural, while I asked Toru quiet questions about the tea ceremonies he had told me his grandmother had taught, all of us hushed for no clear reason.

I felt a sudden wave of conceit go through me. I grabbed Toru's fingers, pride surging that I was there with a Japanese man who held my hand, unlike the obvious tourists sitting next to us, those poor souls lacking any real access to this mysterious world. I glanced pityingly at their tube socks and fanny packs, my compassion feeling generous. Then my knees began to ache from kneeling. I shifted uncomfortably, letting go of Toru's hand. Apparently, my short skirt did not lend itself to a demure, cross-legged position on the tatami.

From across the hallway came a woman in a kimono. She held a tray with four small bowls and plates bearing tiny domed sweets. Removing her thonged slippers, she padded silently across the mats in white *tabi* socks, sewed with a separate compartment for her big toe. She held the tray perfectly immobile, balanced so it never betrayed a hint of movement. When she reached us, she bent fluidly to her knees, tray still in hand, and set the dishes down in utter silence.

"*Irasshaimase*," she said softly. She placed a bowl in front of each of us, turning them forty-five degrees until they were positioned exactly as protocol demanded, then setting the small plates with sweets alongside our tea. She moved unhurriedly yet with complete economy, as if any extra motion would be an affront to tradition, an inexcusable sloppiness. The loose sleeves of her kimono dipped and rose as she served, and I caught my breath as they waved close to the tea, but they hovered perfectly, never grazing anything but air.

We sipped the frothy drink, its rich, dark green sediment washing across the bottom of the bowl. Toru cut a piece of bean-paste sweet for me, wielding the tiny wooden knife balanced along the lip of my plate. I rolled the confection around on my tongue, grainy and too sweet but a right balance to the bitterness of the tea.

"Tof, I'm kind of fascinated by this country," I admitted. We stared together through the wall-length open window, the garden lush and still. "I even think I could consider spending more time here." Inside, with all the newness and mystery crowding me, I was starting to feel like a new person myself, as if the bizarre but mesmerizing world around me had started to seep through my pores and reorganize the molecules of my body, opening me up to places and experiences I had never before known how to imagine.

"I'm happy," Toru said, still staring out at the garden. And then, because he wasn't like me and didn't need to analyze every possibility at the moment of its conception or prod every happiness for signs of future demise, he looked at me with a contented smile, grabbed my hand, and left it at that.

BEFORE I LEFT TORU ten days later at the airport, we went one night to an Italian restaurant. The room was flushed with candlelight, the jacketed waiters hovering just past earshot. Toru read the menu, Japanese with Italian subtitles, while I flipped vaguely through it, looking for words that resembled English ones, wondering in half interest if the waiters might mistake me for European, if my gauzy tank top and strappy sandals might project Continental chic. Before Toru began translating from the parchment page, I put aside my menu, clasped my hands along the table's edge, and leaned in. "Tof," I said.

Then we hunkered down to address in detail what options remained for our bicontinental bond.

Toru had a week off in October, and he suggested coming to Boston for a four-day visit—what would be left of his vacation after the two and a half days of travel the trip would devour. We agreed. I took a breath.

"What if I came back in December for a month or so, and then again next spring for longer? Like, three or four months?" I said. I could take the spring off from teaching or come toward the end of the semester and stay through the summer. In the meantime, I could try to pick up some freelance writing work to do from overseas.

Toru smiled wide, then nodded more than once. "Of course, I'm happy if you can do that."

We discussed the plan over the multicourse meal. If the pattern worked, I might even continue going back and forth, spending part of the year in Boston, the rest in Japan. "If you feel too hard, moving to Osaka for full-time," Toru suggested, "maybe we can build life together this way, and you can go home whenever you need. And if we want to, we can marry." He nodded his head again, this time a graver gesture.

"Do you want to get married?" I asked, one fingertip running nervous arcs along the bottom of my wineglass.

"I want to stay together. Married or not married is not so big deal to me. But stay together, yes." He looked straight at me. Then, looking down, he added, "If we can."

I exhaled a little wisp of relief. But my mouth still felt dry and tight. I picked up my wine and sipped. I looked at Toru.

Despite my fears about marriage and becoming dependent on someone, I'd grown to long for an enduring, hope-to-last-forever bond with Toru. I still didn't necessarily need a piece of paper as much as I needed to trust that he wanted to stay together, grow old in each other's presence. Knowing that he did, I felt stung with joy. *But how to fit, long-term, both Osaka and Boston into the equation?* The question terrified me.

"So, do you think, if we got married, we could move to Boston . . . or at least the U.S., in the next couple of years? Would your company ever transfer us?"

"Maybe, sometime in next few years," Toru said. "Maybe to the U.S. To California, San Diego. Or else, could be Kansas City." He held my gaze. "But to Boston, or even East Coast, probably not," he said, shaking his head, his eyes still locked on mine. "To Boston, no."

"Kansas City?" I gasped. Then, more quietly, as if I needed to get used to the words themselves, I repeated, "Kansas City."

I had never been there. But I had my ideas. It was far from the Northeast. It was not Chicago or San Francisco, or even Seattle. It contained the word "Kansas" in its name.

"We have an office there. There and San Diego."

I knew that in Japan, and especially in traditional jobs like Toru's, most men stayed with one company for life. Switching jobs signified a failure of loyalty, and loyalty was one of the culture's most fundamental values. Looking for a position at another Japanese corporation—one with offices in New York or Boston—could hurt Toru's career. I also recognized the slim likelihood of his succeeding as a nonnative English-speaking manager in an American company. Or of my supporting us both in Boston, even if I quit teaching in prisons and taught business writing full-time.

I'd already done the math. If I lived in Japan and worked as a freelance writer, I could go back to Boston when I wanted, as long as I could continue to afford the flights, and, I supposed, we remained childless. If Toru lived in the U.S. with a corporate job, he'd have a few weeks a year, at most, to go home.

And, of course, Toru was his family's eldest son. He—and eventually his wife—would be expected to stay in Osaka and care for his father now that his mother was gone. Unless his father agreed to move with us, too.

I both loved and hated Toru's honesty about our dismal prospects for life together in my hometown. It made me trust him more to know he'd never offer hollow promises. But at the same time, a piece of me longed for him to hold out some tiny sliver of hope, or at least soften the blow. To admit a little less forthrightly that if we built a home together the closest we'd probably ever get to Boston, until he retired in thirty years, was Missouri.

Ultimately, though, I knew as I set my teacup down on its bone-china saucer, there was only one thought whose relief matched the intensity of my worry: *when I leave Toru again at the airport, at least it won't be for good.*

WHEN SHE CAUGHT wind of the plan a few days later by phone, my mother reacted with considerably less relief. She baldly assured me that I was getting deeper and deeper into an "unsustainable arrangement." I didn't tell her we had discussed marriage, but I admitted I was planning to return to Osaka in December, and then again in the spring to give living in Japan an earnest try. "Oh, for God's sakes," she chided me, the long-distance line sounding tinny, "are you really going to prolong this situation even further? Unless you really are considering *moving* to that country." She paused. "Where you'll be a foreigner for the rest of your life," she helpfully elaborated.

But surprisingly the idea of being a foreigner, at least part-time, was no longer so awful. After all, Toru had made me feel so protected in the past month. Never before as an adult had I been so unable to do things for myself; the flip side revealed the sheer comfort of having someone take care of everything for me. Instead of feeling helpless, most of the time I felt safe. I was ashamed to admit it, but in Japan, I found a delicious release in the unexpected taste of utter dependence.

I thought about my Boston-bound hunger for social challenges: writing my dissertation on violence and gender, teaching in prisons, hoping the classes might encourage my students to think about masculinity and power in new ways, that their degrees might help them get jobs when they got out of lockup so they could return to their own children and break the cycle of recidivism. But now I began to question whether passion or some confused mix of guilt and ego fueled my motivations. What if I lived in a world where I *couldn't* confront these challenges? Sure, I'd be more limited, less useful. I'd also be playing into some gender stereotypes of my own: a woman dependent on a man to take care of her. But wouldn't I also be absolved of the responsibilities accompanying both the privilege and potential of my American life? That absolution, that freedom, felt terribly seductive.

FIVE

I DIDN'T FEEL THE SHIFT, THE particular Americanness, of the space around me until halfway through my layover in Chicago. At first, the specifics of my surroundings blurred together. I was so obliterated by exhaustion after the fourteen-hour flight from Osaka, with another two-and-a-half-hour leg to Boston in front of me, that I still have only a vague memory of passing through passport control and customs. I hazily recollect lugging bags from a metal carousel, crossing broad hallways and wide wings to domestic departures, and shuffling once more through security.

What eventually brought me to sharp attention, cut clean through the fog of my fatigue, was the woman on the cell phone. Her voice. Her volume. And most of all, her apparent—and complete—lack of impact on almost everyone around us.

She waited in front of me at the gate for Boston, her scuffed, overstuffed backpack slung loosely over one shoulder, long hair in a dark brown mutiny, blue jeans barely containing her backside. "The plane is delayed!" she shouted into the phone. "This fucking flight isn't going to take off for *at least* another hour!"

Then silence, followed by "I *know*! The airlines *suck*," before she slapped the handset closed.

Now it hit me: I was home.

For the first few seconds, the shift jarred me physically, as if my body were still inhabiting a world where politeness and self-possession were premium, rather than one prizing self-expression above all. *Doesn't she know she's screaming into the phone and annoying everyone around her?* I felt embarrassed by her lack of restraint.

But everyone else appeared to take her yelling in stride. The man behind me rolled his eyes, but otherwise, no one even noticed. Then, as the space around her absorbed her emphatic style with a minimum of concern, my own annoyance began to dissolve. I felt myself slipping from stern disapproval into grudging tolerance, buoyed by a low expectation of politeness that I realized had always permeated the American air I breathed: a barometric pressure utterly foreign to Japan.

I was too bleary-eyed to muse for long over my first stage of reimmersion, though. As I reached the counter, I confirmed that my seat was, in fact, on the aisle and that the flight was, in fact, delayed, then slumped into the thin cushioning of a blue vinyl seat in the waiting area. As I sat with my eyes closed, my brain felt grainy, barely able to grasp that I still had hours more to go before reaching Boston and my soft bed in my South End studio.

I was asleep somewhere over Ohio when a flight attendant announced that we had to turn back to O'Hare. One of the toilets in the back was clogged, it was close to overflowing, and with most of the flight still ahead, the captain didn't like the risks. "We'll have you on the ground and transferred to another plane as soon as possible," her monotone assured, an implicit injunction not to react with any sort of gumption.

No luck. Groans of protest rose across the plane. "We don't want to turn back!" a man yelled. "Let's just keep going and not use that bathroom!" He seemed incredulous that such an obvious solution hadn't already been arrived at by the uniformed people in charge. A few others roused themselves to action, jamming plastic trays into position, stuffing bagged nuts into seatback pockets, propelling upward to their feet, their brusque determination belying the undignified state of their wrinkled laps as they prepared to advance upon the galley.

Then the captain came on. "Ladies and gentlemen," he began, his voice like a stern uncle's. "Please return to your seats." He allowed a soft pause, adding, "I'm captain of this craft, and I've determined that turning her around is our safest option."

I began to wonder at the weirdness of calling the plane "she," until his next words stopped my thoughts and filled the canned cabin air once more. I imagined him sitting upright, grasping a microphone with steady hand, silver-winged pin flashing smartly on his lapel. "It's my call," he announced, his tone now dipping low, a leader who would brook no dissent, "and that's what I intend to do."

Brief silence followed. Then, seemingly satisfied that they'd lodged their best protest, their dismal expectations of the airlines once more safely confirmed, the offended passengers sat back down. I fell asleep again to quiet grumbling and soft murmurs, the passengers secure in the knowledge that their complaints were entirely justified and widely shared with their fellow commercial aviation victims, stuffed with mutual crabbiness into seats all around them.

. . .

"HELLO, this is speaking Toru!"
I heard on my voice mail two days later.

We'd mostly been playing phone tag and had only managed to talk briefly, quick snatches of *Yes, got home safely, finally! Miss you; love you.* I was surprised but also delighted that in the seventy-two hours we'd been apart and he'd been speaking only Japanese, Toru's English syntax had already started to slip back into its charmed contortions.

That night during an early dinner with a few girlfriends, I played his funny message back, pressing my cell phone to their ears so they could hear, watching happily as their expressions morphed from squint-eyed concentration to open-faced amusement. *So far, I seem to be able to balance this love in two worlds just fine,* I thought with satisfaction and then a rising thrill.

Since arriving home, I'd had the uncanny sense of everything as both familiar and new. Each site I'd seen so often before now revealed a fresh dimension, an edge of foreignness sharpening customary contours. Boston and Cambridge looked so different from the landscape of Osaka: at once smaller but more spacious than the sprawling, densely packed Japanese city. In my daily interactions walking down the sidewalk or waiting in line at my morning café, I had the once normal but now remarkable sense of myself as unexceptional, merely one of the crowd instead of a mismatched silhouette. Suddenly, I was again just part of the backdrop, not an outsider to notice, ignore, or both.

I was also still flattened from jet lag, and as I drove home from dinner with my girlfriends, I lumbered slowly in my aging VW. Creeping down my neighborhood's narrow streets, I peered through the windshield into the night, searching for the ever-elusive South End parking space. Turning a corner off Columbus Ave., I saw a car double-parked under a headlight, blocking the road. Still in Japanese public-decorum mode, I beeped softly, but the vehicle didn't budge. I beeped again. Nothing.

Maybe they've gone inside an apartment? It was too dark to see the driver. Annoyed, I hauled myself out of my VW, preparing a polite request. Before I reached the other car, its engine suddenly started. Then I heard a furious honking at my back.

A man in a beat-up, dark blue sedan had pulled up behind me, bumper dented, air freshener dangling from the rearview mirror. *He must be beeping at that double-parked car, too,* I thought, *honking in support of my patient protest.*

But then the driver behind me leaned out the window, jutting his head toward me in one angry thrust. "Jesus Christ!" he screamed. "Get back in the goddamn car, you *moron*. What are you *doing*? You're blocking the whole fucking *street!*" I began feebly to protest, to explain I was only attempting to clear the road. In response, he slammed his palm back onto the horn, emitting another series of long, irate, and humiliatingly loud rebukes.

In a rush, my exhaustion overwhelmed me. I didn't have the energy to absorb the full-throttled aggression of a Boston driver or the thick skin to deflect it—especially not after having floated in a bubble of extreme collective restraint for a month in Japan. I felt my cheeks flame in the night air, and then I burst helplessly into tears.

Suddenly, I longed for the more respectful, civilized manners of Toru's homeland. *What's* wrong *with the people in this country?* I thought as I hurried back to my car, slammed the door shut, and turned the ignition as fast as I could. *What purpose on earth does it serve to be so rude? Why are people here so . . . so* ill-behaved?

But as I drove away, the tears receded. An image of me startled and mortified under the streetlights flashed through my mind, and with it came a laugh, then a surge of release. *This is my crazy neighborhood.* I was finally back in a place allowing me and everyone around me to unleash whatever lurked inside; to display our internal states without a hint of shame; to announce ourselves and our minute-by-minute reactions to the world in a glorious rush of self-expression.

Sure, Japan's enforced harmony had been soothing at times. But it had also been suffocating, I realized now, a wall of decorum sealing shut with hermetic insistence any signs of discord. Sitting in my aging car's front seat, rumbling down my neighborhood's liberally potholed streets, I loosened my lungs in relief and even in strange gratitude for the infuriated driver who had been cursing me moments before.

I'm in America, I thought, almost giddy.

Perhaps we could sometimes be rude, self-absorbed, inconsiderate. But I suddenly thought of Americans' carefree expressiveness as our own curious form of mutual respect: an agreement to relinquish the façade of permanent politeness and bare our souls together. It's a skewed species of respect, I allowed, but when it works, without devolving into injury or violence, we forge a generous, communal trust: you be you and I'll be me, and somehow despite the annoyance and noise and clumsiness, we'll have faith that we'll all get by, ourselves, together.

.   .   .

MY NEW LOVE AFFAIR with the USA continued to bloom as I eased back into Boston life, although it emitted a patriotism that before had always seemed slightly tacky, wafting a subtle scent of the unintellectual or unexamined. Yet mine was a love affair made sweeter by the knowledge of distance, of difference. Everything continued to seem tinged with exoticism.

The streets are so wide! The cars so big! The supermarket aisles so enormous! Everything was suddenly not three- but four-dimensional. Even the SUVs, before always just annoying in their girth, had become interesting: unwieldy suburban gas-guzzlers transformed into culturally specific artifacts mirroring America's vast land, optimism, and consumption, like an ugly stepsister whose skirts suddenly gave way to a golden slipper.

This wasn't the first time I had traveled overseas and come home to see my world with fresh eyes. Besides having gone to East Asia the summer before, I'd been to Europe, the Middle East, Mexico, had even spent a college semester in France. But I'd always returned after playing tourist in lands clearly designated as not home. Now I realized how these places had always remained less real to me—partly because I had glimpsed many from resorts, but even more because I'd never imagined actually *living* there. I had certainly never considered adjusting to them as the new normal. In turn, they had never wielded the power to make me view my own world as potentially foreign.

Even more surprising yet harder to pin down was an abstract but unmistakable new sense of being *at home*. I quickly realized that just walking down the street in Boston or Cambridge felt different than it had in Osaka. My movements were the same. My gait, my breath, my heartbeat. But *I* felt different.

Was I unconsciously responding to the familiarity of the New England air, the particular calibration of its weight or humidity? Did hearing the flat sounds of American English or the consistent hum of some Northeastern traffic pattern send untraceable signals from my eardrums to my skull: that I was where I belonged, where I was most used to being? Was the force of gravity slightly different here, rooting my feet just so to the native concrete—and could my heart sense that, even though my brain couldn't define it?

Whatever the specific cause, my sense of being at home felt distinctly different, more powerful, from my age-old certainty that Boston was where I wanted to settle because of its safe familiarity. My attachment to the place and its pulse went deeper now. My home in Boston had become a part of me in an entirely new way: not only was it the city where I wanted to live, it was where I *belonged*, because I so clearly hadn't belonged in Japan.

I had inherited a rare experience for a white, middle-class, educated American: that of being a minority, and how escaping that identity feels like nothing else ever will. After spending years of academic reflection on inequality, power, and belonging, of being appropriately guilty over my own privilege, I'd touched outsider status in a new way. At the same time, I realized how fundamentally far from this status I would forever stay, since it was something I could easily shed with a plane ticket and twenty-four hours of airport snacks.

Regardless, I was utterly grateful for this indefinable aware-ness of *home*—even as I acknowledged that its potency was fu-eled by the prospect of a life in Osaka. Ultimately, it was Japan that had made home coalesce into a new, more magical force.

NOT SURPRISINGLY, my family, and my mother in particular, found my budding enthusiasm for bicontinental living less than exhilarating. When I tried to explain my new postmodern theory of home—how the foreign-ness of Osaka only made my attachment to Boston that much sweeter, but, in turn, my enhanced love of home now depended on my simultaneous life in Japan—my mother was impressively, or perhaps just realistically, unmoved. She had hoped my com-ing back to the U.S. would cure whatever illusions I held about finding happiness with an Asian salaryman eight thousand miles away. But more than that, I was still her baby. She longed to protect me from what she saw looming, plain as any two-state solution for Israel and Palestine along pre-1967 boundaries, like a disaster on my horizon.

When I announced I had still not abandoned my plan to go back to Osaka that winter, and then again in spring to try set-tling there at least part-time, my mother's eyes widened in alarm. "Give it a try, at your age?" she asked crossly. Then, "You'll be almost forty after you experiment like this for just one year, if you persist in dragging out this arrangement with Toro." She stared evenly at me, her eyes level with mine but still somehow seeming to glare down from a height of unappreciated wisdom.

"I know, Mom," I said. "And his name is Tor*u*, not Tor*o*."

Her face remained immobile, a perfect mask of blazing eyes and pink lacquered lips drawn tight.

"Toro, just so you know, means 'fatty tuna' in Japanese, like the sushi."

"And, in the best-case scenario," she went on, ignoring my lesson in pronunciation, "if this, this *situation*, were to work out, and you were to actually *marry*, how would you have children if you spend six months a year alone in Boston? You'll be a single parent half the year and an outsider the rest," she warned.

I nodded simply, acknowledging that success, in this case and in the traditional definition of relationships, would surely doom me to some such fate.

"And if it doesn't work," she continued, her voice rising, her face reddening at the hairline, "if it falls apart—and in my world, spouses do *not* plan to live half their lives apart; it's a sure recipe for disaster—what will you have then?"

The answer, I knew, was nothing. I looked silently back at my mother, her stare still fixing mine like an entomologist pinning a specimen to a sheet.

But as the days in Boston turned into weeks, as Toru's visit passed in a blur of excitement, jet lag, and close-clasped limbs, and my return to Osaka loomed ever closer, it was a nothing I became increasingly willing to risk.

ANOTHER AVENUE where I confronted doubts about my relationship was in therapy. My shrink never voiced these misgivings out loud. In fact, I can't be sure how many she herself even harbored, or the extent of them:

predictably, or just appropriately, when I tried to ask her about them, she turned the issue back to me with a gentle yet firm suggestion of "projection." As in, perhaps, I was projecting my own doubts onto a concern about hers?

What she did say was something like this: "Your fears about this relationship seem consistently focused on logistics. Where you and Toru will live. How you could possibly build a life with a man from Osaka. How to balance your image of yourself as an independent woman with the potential that you might give up your way of life for a man. But—and I don't mean to suggest these aren't important questions—they still all seem just a little . . . *abstract*." In the pauses between her words I could hear traffic from the road below: honking, a lone siren going by through Cambridge's Central Square.

Then she pushed a little further. She noted that I rarely mentioned any worries about whether Toru and I were interpersonally compatible. She wondered, did we ever fight? What did I do with my fears and feelings about him as a *person* and a potential partner, not just as a potential partner in a relationship with some pretty steep logistical challenges?

I shrugged. "I don't know how to explain it," I admitted. "It's not like we have a perfect relationship or anything. Neither one of us is a fighter, necessarily." I tried explaining how when we had misunderstandings or frustrations, we often just went silent for a day or two, like we had in Beijing, rather than exploding in argument. "But I just don't feel the worry, or at least not the terror, about us interpersonally, not nearly as much as I do about the geography and logistics. I guess I never really expected to be happy in a relationship, and for the most part I am now. Or at least so much more than I ever thought I could be."

I struggled to clarify to her, to both of us. I wasn't sure this was the answer, or the full one. But however incomplete, it was the best, even the most honest, one I could come up with.

Of course I was lonely sometimes, thinking about how compartmentalized our bond sometimes felt, with Toru on one side and my friends on another, or how, despite our great affection for each other, because of the language barrier we didn't share the kind of intellectual connection I always assumed I would have with a partner. But somehow the warmth and calm I felt with Toru outweighed everything else. Except for my fears about Japan.

I had to admit, sometimes it did seem like the country, or the whole "bicontinental issue," was an animate object instead of a challenge of place or culture, like a loitering former lover, a tangible threat that got more of my attention than any dynamic between me and Toru. I didn't know what to make of that realization, though. Neither did my shrink.

"Well," she sighed eventually, "let's keep an eye on this, keep talking about it." She wondered if my expectations were low because of my family's chaos, what she called "trauma," although I still struggled with that word, especially in a context as privileged as mine. She offered that perhaps any relationship tipping the scales toward harmony felt like a bounty to me. *Huh,* I thought. *Maybe I've been underestimating the benefits of childhood turmoil.*

IN THE MEANTIME, while cracking my risk-averse heart open more and more to a life least expected, I latched on to a new obsession: starting a reading series in Cambridge. Due to her notable literary success, my sister Lauren had participated in many author events around the country, and she lamented how staid most were. She agreed to be one of my first readers, as well as help me contact other literary figures in the area.

I decided each event would be free, themed, and feature four published writers reading in a kind of evening salon. My friend Louise suggested the name Four Stories. And, Lauren added, why not include some type of entertaining question-and-answer feature, emphasizing the comical rather than the intellectual? I could run the events when I was home and put the series on hold or find other writers who could host when I was in Japan. Most important, the evenings would combine the two things I felt every literary scene required: alcohol and appetizers.

Throughout graduate school in my twenties, I had waitressed at an MIT-area bar called the Miracle of Science, where I'd worked with a friend named Gary, who'd now opened a lounge in Central Square, the Enormous Room. It had soft lights; long, slouch-worthy couches; low Moroccan-style tables and cushions; a small stage backed by a great sound system; a whole menu of tapas and exotic fruit-spiked drinks with names like God in Small Pieces. It was perfect.

Another friend, Tim, who owned a popular local independent bookstore, helped me publicize. I planned to meet him for drinks one evening at a bar near his bookstore. "I always thought you and Tim would make a great couple," Lauren said. He was Southern. "Very smart, sexy accent," Lauren weighed in, "a real flirt, too." I wondered if her words were more an attempt to persuade than caution.

Tim ordered a Wild Turkey, neat. I was driving, so I stopped at my first glass of wine, then ordered a soda water with a twist. We talked about literature, the MBA in nonprofit management he'd earned before he opened the bookstore. We laughed about Lauren—So eccentric! But successful!—and the literary scene in Boston. He gave me ideas about how to make Four Stories work and names of press contacts. He leaned in when I spoke, stared at me for long moments with his smooth brown eyes. He stroked his beard absentmindedly, gentled the air with his slight Southern drawl. Lauren was right: he was sexy.

But my heart didn't pull toward him like it did with Toru. I was gut-deep relieved, but also confused, that a man with whom I had so much more in common, such a fluid intellectual connection, didn't tempt me in any profound way from Toru. I could be attracted to Tim. *Easily*, I thought. But somehow, Toru was like a key whose crags and slopes, curved edges and empty spaces, fit inside my chest. I was driving back to the South End after meeting Tim when Toru called, and I told him Tim had given me lots of great contacts, that I had decided on the themes for all the fall events and had lined up most of the authors. "I think this might work, Tof!" I said. "I think I might have found a way to stay connected with the literary community here even though I may not be living in Boston full-time for a while."

"Congratulation!" Toru said, his voice like a bright bell through the phone line. "You know," he said, "I feel proud you."

And just like that, I could feel his presence, his heat with me, although he was halfway across the world. The directness of his emotion came to me through his words and tone so plainly then, as if, without sophisticated vocabulary or complex commentary, I could feel his pride and support right next to me, unadorned, straightforward, pure. Nothing, I realized, would ever feel as warm to me as that. I didn't know why, but I knew it to be true.

WITH TIM'S HELP, the charm of the Enormous Room, my sister's and my own academic contacts, and my obsession with a seamless plan, Four Stories opened to a standing-room-only crowd. Before the event began, I slipped into a clingy top, swiped my lids with sparkly shadow, and downed a God in Small Pieces cocktail. Then I got up onstage, grabbed the microphone, mispronounced the names of a few literary figures, and introduced the night's readers. And people laughed! I drank another God in Small Pieces and admitted to choosing one of the authors because I thought he was cute. People laughed some more! Then I circulated Four-Stories-logoed question cards, encouraged people to ask each reader the funniest, most creative, or dirtiest question, and promised free drinks to the audience members whose queries I picked. I started in on my third cocktail and went with dirtiest. Soon the *Boston Globe* was quoting the director of the literary organization PEN New England, who claimed that Four Stories was "fast becoming the place to be."

Fired up by the sudden success of the reading series, I secured two additional career opportunities before I left for Japan that winter. The university had hired me to do some writing for their website, so I could work remotely and continue to earn income even when I wasn't teaching. I'd also managed to interest the food editor at one of Boston's major newspapers in an article about Osaka: a city famous for its unique but unpretentious food and its rough-and-tumble character, at least compared to the fierce refinement of Kyoto and Tokyo. Toru's hometown was known by the motto *kuidaore*, which I'd heard alternately translated as "eat yourself bankrupt" and "eat so much that you die and go to heaven happy."

Sitting in my office at school one fall day, I typed off a quick pitch to the editor mentioning my Japanese connections, my upcoming return to Osaka, and a previous publication (my first nonacademic piece) that had recently been accepted by a literary magazine. Though that article was about being a woman teaching in a men's prison, I must have made an adequate case for my track record writing about "other worlds"—prison, Japan, whatever—and she bit.

She e-mailed back the next day saying she'd be delighted to see my food article when it was finished. I was thrilled, ignoring that she'd failed to mention anything about meal budgets, contracts, or deadlines. But it felt like the beginning of a new self: bicontinental modern woman, half of a nationally and ethically blended couple, and now global food writer. *Could it really be this easy?* Exotic meals. Fashionable outfits at the latest restaurant openings in cities across the planet. Maître d's recognizing me with discreet glances. I was happy to fund a few meals on my own as an investment in my new career. In a whole new, more exciting *me*.

The idea sparked a little ember in my brain, even as my more practical mind tried to swat it away as foolish, a clichéd misconception. Staring off into space, looking at but not seeing the streaked computer screen in front of me, I would not have admitted these thoughts and feelings out loud, wanting to believe I was somehow above the silly trap of thinking that a new place could magically make you a different person.

But as I arranged my upcoming trip, the quiet glow of excitement burned on inside me. I mapped my first few weeks back in Japan, planning which restaurants to visit, what foods to profile. In the mornings, I fantasized, I'd bring my laptop to one of my neighborhood cafés and make lists or write up notes, and at night, Toru and I would eat. We'd taste, sip, discuss, and critique my way into a new international identity.

SIX

WHEN WE REUNITED at Osa-
ka's Kansai Airport, it took only a few moments to feel myself
melting back into shape beside Toru. His presence in my con-
sciousness had been so large over the previous months that, as he
came toward me in the crowded terminal, I felt momentarily
surprised to remember that he was my height, not taller. But
when I hugged him to me, bending my head slightly to bury it
in the corner between his neck and shoulder, his warmth was
expansive.

"Thank you for coming to here again," he said.

Scanning the schedule board for buses back to the city, a
white expanse crammed with black squiggles I couldn't even
begin to read, I felt myself surrender completely. The afternoon
light was waning, the air cold and damp, and as we stood on the
clean-swept sidewalk waiting to board our bus, around me flew
snippets of an indecipherable language. The sound reminded me
of a river running fast, only a modest gurgle rising up every now
and then in whose echo I could trace some semblance of meaning. When the white-gloved attendant approached to load my
luggage and inquire about our final stop, he looked only at Toru.

My American identity as an independent, competent adult with an advanced degree, two challenging jobs, and a high level of cultural fluency receded back into its little corner, leaving in its wake a curious mix of diminishment and relief; I was once again a foreigner in Japan.

I'd found a subletter to cover my rent in Boston, and Toru had booked us another "weekly mansion" in the same building as before. This time, since we were renting for more than a month, he managed to secure one with a "full-sized" bed, only slightly wider than a twin. These apartments were designed for single working people who might occasionally have an overnight visitor. Like my room the previous summer, the studio was spare and tiny, outfitted with bare whitish-gray walls, one window, and the same sliver of a bathroom—where two people could not stand with the door open—plus hot plate, closet, minifridge, and diminutive set of drawers perched on wheels.

Once again, Toru kept all his clothes at his and his father's house down the street, where every morning before work he would eat breakfast, shower, and dress. I kept half my clothes in the closet and drawers, and half in my suitcase under the bed, stuffing my heavy sweaters there and calculating how much shopping I could do before I would need to store things at Toru and Tetsunobu-*san*'s apartment, too.

As I had imagined, in the mornings, I would go to one of the neighborhood cafés I'd found the previous summer. The staff showed no signs of remembering me, although I couldn't tell whether their obliviousness derived from Japanese manners— since conversations between strangers were to be avoided—or simply my lack of having made any lasting impression.

In preparation for my new food-writing career, I spent morn-

THE GOOD SHUFU 101

ings flipping through the few entries in a Lonely Planet guide, a Frommer's, and a Fodor's and then searching the expat magazines for recommendations or even just advertisements. Since the Michelin guide to the area had yet to be published in Japanese or English, and the city's Zagat guide appeared only in Japanese, I compiled minor notes based on Toru's rough translation of the latter. "*Yakitori*," he explained one night, "like chicken on stick. You might not like, though, at least not some." Toru had kindly pretended not to notice the gaping flaw in my plan to play global food critic: my squeamish stomach. He referred only obliquely to it now.

"Some is like chicken . . . chicken *ass*," he said, his brow knit in an attempt to describe chicken tail. Then he mentioned octopus balls.

"*No way.*" I shook my head, my eyes bulging with horror.

"You know, little dough balls with *tako*, octopus piece, inside," he explained. "Like dumplings. Called *takoyaki*. Very famous in Osaka. Very Osaka food."

At night, as we walked to the restaurants I had chosen, Toru would hold my hand, switching sides to buffer me even when the street was empty. As always, he'd do so quietly, as naturally as breath. He never once forgot or neglected to protect me this way even if we were running late or immersed in conversation, as if he held some kind of homing device within his body, and home was wherever I might need shielding. Even more than my relief at being held by him again, than my skin's sense of rightness next to his, Toru's calm, instinctual protectiveness made me feel rooted in space alongside him, despite it being Osaka's skyline around us, not Boston's.

We went to a food stall at a neighborhood market and ate

those fried octopus balls: crisp *takoyaki*, crunchy on the outside but gooey within, the chewy tentacles and slimy, half-cooked dough sliding down my throat in a disconcerting slip. Next we tried *okonomiyaki*, Japanese savory pancakes, at a restaurant nearby. Its walls were plastered with cards signed by famous Osakan comedians and musicians. At the table next to us, a group of teenagers in low-slung jeans and grunge-chic skirts played quarters and smoked, laughing loudly.

The pancakes were made with mountain potato flour, cabbage, and egg, then layered with sliced pork and Worcestershire sauce, a drizzle of mayonnaise, and dried salted seaweed. I was happily surprised that I actually liked the seaweed topping, hoping my taste buds were maturing into a new global sophistication.

Toru proudly explained to the aproned waiter that I was a writer working on a piece for a Boston newspaper and would appreciate an interview with the owner. Moments later, an older man burst from the kitchen, blue apron smattered with food, round cheeks scrunched above his grin. I sensed from Toru's polite but hesitant tone and his gestures that he was making another introduction, and then the owner-chef emitted a volley of Japanese, Toru throwing back his head occasionally to laugh in a way I could tell was, at times, more manners than mirth.

Toru tried to translate for me as the man forged ahead with more zealous commentary. Although I couldn't follow his words, I laughed along with them, captivated by the chef-owner's effusiveness, his expansive hand gestures. Later, Toru defined him as a quintessential Osakan, outgoing, boisterous, and much less reserved than other Japanese people tended to be.

"He's saying *okonomiyaki* means 'as you like,'" Toru said, turning to explain, while I grabbed my pencil. The gist, I learned, was something about applying this "as you like" ethos to free experimentation with ingredients, which the chef then funneled into a "global culinary vision" using creative flavors from around the world. "So," Toru relayed, "this is why all world's citizens enjoy and . . . and feel at *home* with his food."

Another mini-monologue followed, and Toru nodded.

"He say he has many dreams." Toru paused, struggling for English. "He say something like 'But my final dream is to journey into black hole, into new universe, and make *okonomiyaki* in another world.'"

I looked up at the chef standing over our table. He laughed once more, mouth drawn wide, eyes wrinkling shut. Then he bowed a single salutation and returned abruptly to the kitchen, his culinary intentions explained, his ontological vision revealed.

Another night, we went to eat at the Hankyu department store in the central Umeda neighborhood. We passed an information desk manned by a line of young women in identical pillbox hats, then rode the escalator through levels of clothing boutiques, each one attended by more uniformed salesladies, their skirts pressed taut. At the top, we reached the Dining Stage, or *"dainingu-suteiji,"* as Toru explained it would be pronounced in the store's Japanese approximation of English.

The place was lined with tidy stalls from some of Osaka's most well-known restaurants. Customers could order at various counters, then wait at tables for aproned servers to bring their food. We ate crisp tempura, colorful slices of vegetables, and whole jumbo shrimp battered and dipped in the coarsely ground salt the waiter delivered in a little blue dish. Next we ordered sushi, an endeavor Toru approached with consternation after we'd first eaten it together the summer before. I had been bitterly disappointed then to discover that only in the West do rolls come with avocado and spicy sauce, or with tempura pieces tucked inside. Toru had frowned darkly when I'd asked where the California rolls and spicy salmon *maki* were. "Not real!" he'd said, shaking his head emphatically. "Not even sushi. Just fake food."

But here in the Hankyu Dining Stage, I was attempting to nurture my new persona as sophisticated international food critic, so I let Toru do the choosing. I bit into a shiny slice of fish draped naked atop an oblong of white rice. I didn't bother to ask what it was. My plan was to eat first without really thinking, just to get past the initial raw bite, and then take notes from the safe side of an empty plate.

All I could feel was slime. Before I'd even mustered my jaw to movement, my instinct to swallow—to get the slick flesh off my tongue—kicked in. I gulped, a small convulsion emitting an undignified little gasp from my throat. Then I snatched the beer in front of me.

Toru shook his head while I pushed the rest of my sushi toward him. Neither one of us mentioned the absurdity of my writing a food article on Japan.

SOME NIGHTS WE ATE dinner at Toru and his father's apartment. The summer we first met, I'd told Toru that I never expected to cook, not even if I got married, and that I never—"and I mean *never*"—cooked at home in Boston. "There's always takeout if you want to stay in, right?"

Toru had disagreed with a vigor I'd found slightly worrying. "Eating at home is most relaxing," he'd corrected me. "I don't want to go out every night. Too tiring." He'd told me that he didn't think it was realistic to have a family and never eat at home, even if you never had kids, that part of having a home was eating together in it. He hadn't bought my argument that not cooking, never cooking, was a viable political statement about women's independence, either. "Just not normal, never to eat at home, never once," he'd grumbled.

I could tell he'd thought I was a little spoiled or at best lazy when it came to domestic matters. Now I considered the possibility that he could be right. Maybe alongside my political argument—or rather buried secretly beneath it—was a classist irresponsibility I'd inherited in the large suburban house where I'd grown up. As kids, we'd cleared the table and had been instructed to put away our toys, but mostly we'd been spared chores by the housekeepers. Then I lived in dorms in boarding school and college until, on my own, I'd built up both a tolerance for messiness and a love of restaurants.

In our conversations about cooking dinner, I found Toru's sternness slightly rankling, felt somewhat disappointed by his failure to be charmed by my quirky undomesticity, but I also grudgingly admired how diligent he was about keeping our little weekly mansion neat. The apartment he shared with his father, where he'd grown up in a household of four, further highlighted both the differences in our backgrounds and his family's apparent contentment with modest, mundane domestic life.

At about seven hundred square feet, Toru's family home had two tiny bedrooms big enough only for single beds, one larger bedroom wide enough to hold a full, a kitchen that could seat no more than four people with legs near touching around a small

table, and a living room. The latter had one two-cushion couch
and an aging massage chair; trinkets from Toru's mother's visits
to Catholic churches around the world; a large rack for hanging
laundry; a TV atop aging wooden shelves; and two framed pictures of Toru's mother with a plain cross hanging between them.
The apartment also had one toilet room, just wide enough to
hold the toilet and a tiny cold-water sink, and a shower room
with a larger sink, a washing machine, and a small but deep
yellow-sided bathtub. On the wall near the washing machine
was the hot-water heater, which remained off until shower or
dishwashing time, when Toru's father would flick the switch
and wait for the heating mechanism to kick in.

In the kitchen stood a seventies-style stove, microwave, rice
cooker, and mini-dishwasher on the counter next to the sink,
designed for only a handful of items. The sink, built for Toru's
mother, who hadn't grazed five feet, was so low I had to hunch
over to wash anything in it. Luckily, Toru's father, at just about
five-foot-two, agreed to wash dishes on the nights I cooked.

The first time I saw Toru's apartment, I flashed back to my
childhood house in the Boston suburbs: the marble-floored,
window-lined plant room complete with burbling fountain; the
sundial patio overlooking the tennis court; the winding front
staircase we kids never used, since it bore an imported carpet we
weren't allowed to walk on; the dark-paneled library where my
mother and father had delivered the news of their separation.

My parents had been known for giving big parties, especially
as their marriage began to crumble, impressive affairs filled with
polite conversation that morphed into tipsy laughter as uniformed valets darted through the dark, and tuxedoed bartenders
served drinks in the library's low glow. I wondered if we'd al-

ways clung to our imposing house, its expensive decor, its enviable landscaping, as proof of some deeper worth, even—or especially—as our family imploded. As a child, I had felt soothed by the shelves of delicate china and cut-crystal glasses, the European upholstery, as if they could hold at bay the diminishment of the humans they surrounded.

Now I wondered whether Toru had felt slightly depressed or uninspired living in such a modest apartment, no material magic to distract the mind from its own torments. But both he and his father seemed completely at ease there, unconcerned by the physicality of their home beyond their commitment to keep it immaculately clean, safe, warm, and well functioning. Almost as if the house itself, as a material object, was irrelevant. There was, I recognized, a kind of integrity in this: unexpected, utterly foreign to me, but very wise.

Still, I wasn't entirely comfortable with the idea that if Toru and I built a life together, frequent cooking would be involved. But as my hopes of becoming a celebrated global restaurant critic waned, I acquiesced to making dinner a few times a week. "So if we did get married, could we at least agree to eat out, just somewhere casual," I bargained, "let's say three or four nights a week?"

"Yah, maybe three times a week, maybe sometime even four, but you know, not at expensive places. Not that often," he insisted.

"What does 'not expensive' mean?" I asked, wincing at the thought of those octopus balls at plain food stalls becoming our thrice-a-week night out.

"Like, not too gorgeous," Toru said, using his term for "fancy." "Like, not Ritz!" He held out a carrot he knew would appease me. "Like new Indian place, or somethings like that," referring to a dive we'd just found down the street that we both already loved.

Deal, I thought.

So I began trying to cook at the apartment Toru shared with his father. A few afternoons a week, while Toru worked long hours at his job, I'd go over and download recipes from the Internet, and Tetsunobu-*san* and I would sit together and list the ingredients on a little pad of white paper. I'd say each item aloud in English, and he'd write them down either in his tight English script or Japanese characters. Sometimes I would have to repeat the words a few times before Tetsunobu-*san* could understand what they were, and occasionally we had to look up translations.

"Pecorino cheese," I tried to explain one afternoon, "like, do you know what Parmesan cheese is?" I made a triangle with my hands. "It's kind of like that."

"Paa-meshan cheez-u," he repeated, thinking. "Maybe had better to be looking it up." Then we bent together over the computer in the tiny room that used to be Toru's mother's. Usually, we'd find that the market didn't have either kind of cheese anyway, and we'd settle for the little squares of cheddar they sold.

Tetsunobu-*san* would help me identify the food on the market shelves, since many items came wrapped in Japanese-covered packages. Yogurt and milk bore similarly shaped cartons, which I discovered only after trying to make oatmeal one morning on the hot plate in our studio: I'd ended up with a hot fermented mess. Even soy sauce was hard to identify, shelved alongside a slew of other brown sauces: *dashi* (bonito fish broth), *mentsuyu* (a noodle-dipping sauce), *gyōsho* (a southeast Asian condiment), and dark vinegar.

The first time I cooked at Toru and Tetsunobu-*san*'s apartment, I planned chicken parmigiana with a cheddar substitute. Quick, easy, simple, I reasoned. After Tetsunobu-*san* had taken me to the market and we worked out that *panko*, or Japanese breadcrumbs, contained the same basic ingredients as Italian ones minus a few seasonings, I carefully followed the recipe. Standing in their tiny kitchen, I added a dash of oregano I found in a cupboard, then layered each item on a large plate while Tetsunobu-*san* watched TV in the living room.

"Okay, Tetsunobu-*san*!" I shouted out to him when I was ready to put the whole thing in the oven. "Where's the oven?" I called out, thinking it strange I had never noticed it before.

"*O-ben* . . ." he mumbled as he gathered himself off the couch and made his way into the kitchen, substituting a *b* for the *v* the Japanese language lacks. "Hmmm," he said, when he saw me, plated bird held aloft.

"You know," I said, miming a door being opened, a rack being pulled out. "An oven. Where I can cook this. With a grill-like thing on the bottom."

"*O-ben* is, actually, it is here." He pulled out a tiny fish grill from a slot under the stove, no more than six by nine inches across, four inches top to bottom.

"No, I mean a big thing. Big black oven. Like that," I gestured toward the fish grill, "but bigger. For cooking," I added uselessly.

"Japanese house don't have *oben*!" Tetsunobu-*san* admitted, and then he tipped his crown back and laughed. He pointed at the microwave.

"How do you microwave chicken parmigiana?" I asked.

Tetsunobu-*san* went to the microwave, examined it for a moment, checking the dials, the row of Japanese *kanji* running up its side. "I don't know!" he finally said, laughing again. He had never eaten chicken parmigiana before.

Later that night after Toru arrived from work, he explained that you could set the microwave to a convection oven setting, but I had already sliced up the chicken and cooked it in pieces on the fish grill, smashing down the cheese topping so it would fit, splattering tomato sauce everywhere. The men were totally unperturbed by the strangely flattened bird. At least until they learned there would be no white rice accompanying it, a development they found utterly bewildering.

ONE EVENING, about halfway through my stay, Toru's aunt and uncle held a dinner for me, a special honor to welcome me to their city, their home, their nephew's heart. I knew this was a rare privilege in Japan, a country with houses so small and boundaries so cherished that usually only relatives are invited to enter. Toru's aunt was his mother's only sibling, and although I'd already begun to delight in Tetsunobu-*san*'s easy warmth, I sensed the other side of the family might be slightly more traditional.

Toru told me to refer to them as Michiko-*san* (his aunt's first name, plus the suffix denoting respect) and Hamatani-*san* (his uncle's surname, meaning Mr. Hamatani or Hamatani sir). They lived in a house on the outskirts of Osaka, larger than Toru's family's apartment but similarly modest in style. Michiko-*san* spoke barely any English; Hamatani-*san* was dean of the English department at a nearby private high school and spoke formally but clearly. I already knew from my own disastrous teaching two summers before that English in Japanese schools is taught for grammar and reading, not conversation, and students rarely learn from native English speakers, so I wasn't surprised by Hamatani-*san*'s stilted manner. But he and Michiko-*san* were kind and generous and attentive, wanting to know all about the literature I had studied in school, my family in Boston, and how I liked Japanese food so far.

Hamatani-*san* would place his palms together and lean into the table, asking each question as if opening a philosophical discussion, while Michiko-*san* spoke softly and gently, laughing as Toru tried to translate or I blurted an inelegant *oishii!* ("delicious!") in Japanese. She served a procession of small dishes— fried chicken pieces, stewed vegetables, little bread-and-cheese squares wrapped with a thin strip of nori seaweed, rice with simmered mushrooms—placing each on the table, then jumping up to pour more beer, or the wine we had brought, or tea. She barely ate anything herself, she was so busy serving.

After dinner, she walked us to the door. Then, before we stepped into our shoes lined neatly in a row, she dropped to her knees and bent so low her forehead grazed the ground. I bent with her, thinking she had dropped a contact lens or stubbed a toe.

"Stand up!" Toru whispered, his voice coming hoarse and sideways out of his mouth. I froze, confused, and it took me a second longer to realize that she was *bowing*, not searching for something missing or staunching a sudden wound. I waited uncomfortably for her to rise, certain that when she did, she'd stand with shame etched across her features: shame that as a woman she was expected to bend so low, in her own house no less, to curve her aging body in self-effacement until she was eyeing nothing but her blank and spotless floor.

Instead, she straightened in a fluid sweep, her limbs surprisingly agile, her movements calm, and on her face a gentle yet fierce pride: that she had brought me to her house; had so fully honored me and her nephew, her dead sister's only son; that this was her culture and her home and she had welcomed me so beautifully to them.

I felt lost for a moment and then suddenly released. I realized once again how imperfectly my judgments could cull meaning from this strange world, even from this group of potential new relatives. So many of my beliefs and instincts were irrelevant here. I had no choice but to relinquish the task of navigating this place—and now this family—with any real acuity, of anticipating its slights and wounds and managing them or guarding myself from them.

ALTHOUGH I FOUND an unexpected comfort in my limited ability to engage in Japanese family life, I knew that, to build a normal existence here even part-time, I'd need friends. Struggling constantly with the language and culture was already exertion enough, though: I decided I wanted to socialize with only English-speaking expats, preferably from Western countries. I recognized the provincialism of my choice, thinking back to my years in academia. I imagined former professors shaking bearded heads, murmuring under their breath about my disappointing cultural chauvinism. But I'd taken on enough of Toru's world, I decided. I'd stop short at searching out his countrymen for socializing. Besides,

I'd had a few Osakans try shyly to strike up conversations with me in random cafés only to segue into broken, red-faced requests that I help them practice English. I didn't want to work that hard with friends.

I found personal ads in the back of Kansai's two English expat magazines. Lounging in our weekly mansion studio, pale winter sun filtering through the polyester curtains, I scanned each ad in the Friendship section, squinting at their tiny font, puzzling out their abbreviations. There were posts such as 20YO WSM FROM ENGLAND, LOOKING FOR JW FOR FRIENDSHIP, DRINKS, SITESEEING, FUN. Or a headline LOOKING FOR A JAPANESE WOMAN WITH 2-5 YEARS OLD CHILD, under which appeared I, AUSTRALIAN 38YSOLD WANT TO HAVE RELATIONSHIP WITH A JAPANESE WOMAN WHO HAS A CHILD IN HOPE THAT THE CHILD FEEL I AM LIKE A FATHER AND THE MOTHER FEELS HAPPY PLS EMAIL.

Gross. Not to mention the atrocious grammar.

I knew Western men here far outnumbered Western women. I'd seen it in the glances Toru and I attracted, not just because we were a mixed couple, but because almost all mixed couples comprised white men with Asian women. We offered a surprising reversal. People would look from Toru to me, then swivel their heads back to Toru as if perhaps they were mistaken, had gotten backward what they thought they'd seen. Mostly, Toru and I found this funny. My favorite were the elderly men, sometimes small and slight, gently stooped or leaning on canes but always neatly put together, zooming through the subway or along the block with an agility rare among the aged in the U.S. They'd glance at Toru, then down to his hand clutching mine, then up to my face, then quickly back at Toru. Sometimes they'd even do a final double-take back to me. Occasionally, they'd give a little grumble or a soft harrumph. Frankly, I was charmed—although then I'd pause momentarily, wondering if they were thinking about World War II. *Do they hate Americans? Did they fight, lose loved ones, way back then? Were they in Hiroshima, Nagasaki? Or did they participate in atrocities in Nanking?* I didn't want to know.

Now I forced myself to go through all the personals in the expat magazines before giving up. Finally, in one of the narrow columns of *Kansai Scene*, I found a promising ad. A British woman in her late twenties was looking for "mates," either women or men, just to befriend. I e-mailed her, mentioning what a relief it was to find an ad that wasn't creepy or date oriented. Would she want to meet for tea someday?

The next week, Lea and I met at a café near Shinsaibashi, one of Osaka's main shopping districts, with neon signs running up and down tall buildings and an enormous cartoon poster of a Lichtenstein print on a signboard spanning one whole block. On one end, high-end department and brand stores bordered tree-fringed Midosuji Boulevard: huge, shiny windows announcing Gucci, Dolce & Gabbana, and Daimaru, a Japanese equivalent of Saks. On the other, a maze of streets coiled through the district, hemmed in by tiny boutiques, cafés, restaurants, karaoke booths, and *pachinko* places, or Japanese gaming parlors.

Lea had a funky blond haircut with pink stripes and, alongside her typical English reserve, she was warm and down-to-earth. She was younger than I and, I was excited to learn, had married a Japanese man. Like most native English speakers in Japan, she was here teaching.

She sipped her tea and in her clipped accent told me how she loved Japan, had never felt at home in England, and hoped to stay here forever. "Even if I were to divorce Shin," she said, "I'd still stay here." I was shocked to realize that some foreigners actually chose without reservation to reside long-term in Japan, as opposed to settling here reluctantly, fingers over eyes, peeking out in trepidation.

She also gave me the name of her hairdresser, who she promised could speak English and cut layers and highlights to match my hair. I wasn't sure I had enough in common with Lea that we would have been close friends if our romantic situations weren't so similar. But I admired her honesty, her sense of certainty about her life's decisions, and I was eager to keep in touch.

On one of my last nights in Osaka, Lea called me to tell me she was meeting another new friend, this one American, like me. And Jewish. Jodi was from Florida by way of upstate New York, owned a business in East Asia working with American law firms, and spoke no Japanese, hiring translators to take care of logistics. Best of all, she lived half the year in Japan, half in the U.S., where she returned frequently to manage the domestic side of her company. They were going out that night for dinner: would I care to join them?

Since I was headed back to Boston in a few days, I had a date planned with Toru that I didn't want to cancel, but I agreed to meet them earlier and have a drink while they ate. We gathered again in Shinsaibashi, outside the new Starbucks down the block from the restaurant, because I wouldn't be able to find the place myself since the streets were all labeled in Japanese. It was cold, and I exited the subway station adjacent to the café in a long black-and-gray sweater coat I had brought from Boston, flared a little at the sleeves, shaped at the waist. I saw Lea standing next to a thin, brown-haired woman about my height, faint crow's-feet tracing her large dark eyes, highlights streaking her head in a pattern just slightly chunkier and blonder than mine.

"Oh, my gawd, I *love* your coat!" Jodi gushed before we'd even concluded our requisite handshake, her New York accent betraying her childhood upstate.

I had, I knew, just found my first true friend in Japan.

SEVEN

WHEN I LEFT OSAKA A FEW days later, Toru and I had agreed on a few things. In April, I'd fly back to Japan with the frequent flyer miles I'd earned. This time, I'd apply for an extension of the ninety-day tourist visa and stay for four months or so. Then I'd return again in early December. I could still teach both semesters in Boston because my MBA writing seminars were only six-week courses. As for the prison, since the students weren't going anywhere, they let me double up on class sessions for the term's first half.

The other agreement Toru and I made was to marry.

We didn't set a specific date, and neither one of us wanted a wedding. Toru thought it was a lot of fuss for nothing. I, as yet one more political statement, was firmly against the entire "wedding industry," which I thought lured people into spending their life savings for a tacky dress, a rock derived from ethically questionable sources, and the false fantasy of a perfect day. Plus, I wanted to save for future flights home.

In Boston, my family took a similarly skeptical view, although not in support of my politics. My mother began vigorously researching Japan's custody laws, enthusiastically pointing out the country's failure to sign the Hague Convention on the Civil Aspects of International Child Abduction, meaning Japanese parents living globally have carte blanche to move their children back to Japan in the case of an international couple's divorce. I promised my mother that, if I ever got pregnant, I would hire a lawyer.

"What in the world are you going to *do* over there?" my sister Lauren asked, one of the rare times she and my mother had agreed on anything. "Are you really going to use your Ph.D. to teach ESL?"

I imagined her curled up in her shabby-chic living room in Somerville, her scruffy-bearded, stay-at-home husband making an organic whole-wheat version of SpaghettiOs for their two kids. The shelves behind her would slope under the weight of her award-winning essays and books, and above them the diploma certifying her doctorate would hang: quiet trophies from the impressive career of an accomplished woman who had come so far from such a dim place. Upstairs, her aging dogs' paws would clack peacefully across the wooden floorboards. "How can you give up so much of your life, give up your whole world, really, for a man? You, who've always been so *progressive!*"

"I'm not giving it all up," I retorted. "I'm only going to live in Japan part-time, like I've been doing," I insisted. "It's fascinating over there, and I'll only be giving up *half* of my life, of my . . ." I heard myself, too late to retract my awkward phrasing, to deny the ways it felt terrifyingly close to true.

My eldest sister and her husband raised more practical concerns. They knew me, they knew my own materialism, and they saw potential trouble down the line. My brother-in-law had come from a hard-pressed, working-class Jewish family in Queens, his father perpetually in debt, his mother toiling long hours in a retail store to send him to private school. But then he'd gone on to Wharton, earned two graduate degrees at Harvard, and become a partner at a major asset-management company. Eventually, he started his own private-equity firm in Boston and stopped flying commercial: the kind of upward mobility both my parents staunchly sanctioned.

He and my sister took me out to lunch at the country club where they, along with my mother and stepfather, were members. My sister wore pleated shorts, my brother-in-law a golf shirt and sweater, sleeves rolled up above his Chopard watch. As we threaded the way to our table, well-fed, polo-shirted men popped up from their chairs, palms outstretched to shake my brother-in-law's hand. Some clasped his shoulder, quipped about market fluctuations, deals, or their golf swings, nodding a quick greeting to my sister.

"How much does Toru actually *earn*?" my brother-in-law asked after we sat down, getting right to business as he tore into a freshly baked roll. My sister began pushing a chopped salad— no bacon, light dressing—around on her plate.

I didn't know exactly how much Toru made, but I offered an estimate, then immediately mentioned his place on a managerial track. I explained that full-time Japanese corporate employees earn considerably less and work substantially more than their American counterparts, but their jobs are much more secure, given the country's ethos of lifetime employment. "His company even sent him to the U.S., funded his exec MBA," I said, "so they must have faith in his future, his leadership potential." I felt hot, annoyed, both at myself and my interrogators, despite their good intentions. My brother-in-law's blue eyes stared evenly at me for a moment, his face like a placid lake. I wondered if he was mentally comparing Toru's one graduate degree with his own multiple Ivy League diplomas.

"Well," he said, his gaze still straight, almost tranquil, "that's less than even my secretary makes."

I sat back and blanched, wondering for a split second why *I* hadn't ever thought of getting a job as an admin in a private-equity firm. Then I thought, *God, I hope none of the waiters here are listening to this,* looking around quickly, embarrassed.

My sister jumped in. "I know you love Toru," she said, "and he really is a good person, a really good person. We can all tell . . . even though he doesn't talk that much." But the airfare going back and forth, she pointed out, would build up quickly. Would I really be happy long-term in such a tiny apartment in Japan? How would I keep up with my rent in Boston? Would I really be okay never being able to hire help if I needed it, not even if we had a baby? "Sometimes," she said, "you need more than just to love someone to make it work out."

I tried to point out that millions—billions—of people lived just fine on way less than Toru and I would earn. "Compared to *normal* people," I said snarkily, a subtle critique of their own wealth, "Toru and I are incredibly lucky, and we are doing just *fine.* We have way more money than the average person."

"Well, that's true," my brother-in-law said, gesturing to the waiter to put lunch on his tab, checking his watch for his upcoming golf game. "But you just need to be sure you're going to be happy being average."

. . .

I WAS ANGRY after our country-
club lunch, but at what specifically I couldn't tell. I knew there
was an inherent snobbery in my dismissal of my sister and her
husband simply because they had money, liked nice things, and
thought I would, too. My brother-in-law had made his fortune,
not inherited it, and he and my sister gave more money to char-
ity and so accomplished more good than I probably ever would
teaching gender studies and writing in a prison or to homeless
people. Shouldn't that make me less judgmental of them, less
disbelieving of my brother-in-law's insights about the tie between finances and contentment? Plus, part of me agreed with
my sister. *Sometimes you* do *need more than just love to build a life.*
Did Toru and I have enough between us to make it work? And
even deeper, another question pricked, a nagging sense that I
really didn't want to be average, however much I might disdain
the hubris of this admission.

Then I felt annoyed at myself all over again. If I had valued
or needed a life of wealth, I could have tried harder to earn it
myself, could have forgone the English Ph.D. and gone to law
school—or at least not chosen a job teaching inmates. Why
blame Toru for a financial future I had already basically settled
for myself?

I called my brother. He was now a doctor (much to my
mother's exuberant delight) married to a woman who had con-
verted to Judaism (much to my mother's delayed approval) and
living on Cape Cod with their two young children. He had
gone to medical school in Israel, and he pointed out the difficul-
ties of living overseas, far from family and friends. "Are you sure

you'll really be able to maintain a life, a job, and two apartments on either side of the world?" he asked.

"I know I'll regret it forever if I don't at least try to make this relationship, this life with Toru, work," I told him.

"I'm not sure how, or whether, it will work out," he told me. But still, he had no real reason for me not to try.

The only member of my family who embraced the plan fully was my father. "Living on another continent, so far away from everyone? Sounds heavenly, Trebs!" he assured me brightly, using his nickname for me. "What a life! What an adventure!" I didn't dwell on the economics. Starting with the market crash in '87, my father's family real estate business had downsized considerably. He'd never really wanted to run it anyway, and now he'd finally managed to escape it after decades of profit-dwindling deals. So I didn't want him to think I was angling for cash. Anyway, I'd been totally financially independent for years, a point of pride for me. But I did mention my greatest fear: how I'd manage to come home for any extended period of time if we lived in Osaka and had kids.

"Kids!" my father blurted out. "What would you want to do something like that for?" Then he lowered his voice a notch. "Kids. Kids are a life sentence," he confided. On one hand, he sounded like he might be joking; partly, on the other, he sounded like a man pressed to truth by a triple purpose: one part earnest reporting from the trenches, one part filial duty to set me straight, and one part delight that I was finally old enough to have these kinds of father-daughter heart-to-hearts.

A few nights later, I stayed late at my office at the university, then stopped at an Indian restaurant near campus, where I had taken Toru when he had lived in Boston. A regular, I knew the staff, and sometimes we would chat while I was waiting for take-out. A middle-aged man—dark-suited, generously mustached, and round about the torso—was presiding over the dining room that night. His white shirt strained slightly under his black jacket to cover the small rotunda of his middle. He spoke with the flint-edged rhythm of Indian-accented English, commenting that he hadn't seen me in a while.

I explained my new bicontinental lifestyle, mentioned Toru, with whom he had surely seen me the year before. I explained Toru was now my fiancé, surprising myself by feeling a little blip of excitement uttering such an old-fashioned term.

"But what will you do when you marry?" the man asked.

"Oh," I answered, tossing my head to suggest a carefree, renegade nature, "I'll just keep going back and forth. We'll live together part-time and apart part-time. If we have kids, maybe his father will help take care of them, or they'll come back and forth with me," I added, proving how well thought out the whole thing was.

"Oh, no, no, no, no, no," the man clucked softly. Then he told me in no uncertain terms how terrible our plan was. He stood behind the restaurant's small bar, cashier machine in the corner, and spread his palms wide under the stained-glass lamps. "You cannot marry and live apart!" he claimed, his tone a rising musical staccato. "You must choose one country or the other!" He had brought his wife and both her parents over from India when he moved here, he insisted, and no other family configuration made sense. Or was even conceivable.

I took my *saag paneer* and naan, clutching the take-out bag, and fled into the night. Driving home through Boston's Kenmore Square, then past Symphony Hall and finally into the South End, I couldn't shake the anxiety his words had stoked inside me, pricking at me like a pin. *Now not only my family, but even the take-out Indian guy is predicting the failure of our bihemispheric marriage,* I brooded. *And he's even from another country, so he must know what he's talking about.*

After a hasty dinner, I waited impatiently for eleven p.m., when it would be noon in Osaka and Toru's lunch break would begin. We talked three times a day: in the morning my time, before he went to bed; in Boston's early evening, when he was waking in Japan; and just before I went to bed, when he was stopping for lunch on his side of the planet. As is customary in traditional Japanese companies, his lunchtime was fixed, precise: noon on the dot until twelve-forty-five, not a minute later or earlier. He ate in the company canteen, where uniformed servers would lay out small dishes from which to choose: various types of meat, fish, and vegetables, plus white rice and miso soup.

At exactly eleven p.m., I dialed. "Tof," I said immediately, "I'm kind of freaking out."

I explained how no one thought our marriage was a good idea: not my family, not the Indian take-out guy. "You remember him, right?" I said. "From India Quality, the restaurant in Kenmore Square. With the really good *saag*."

I gave him the rough outline of my family's financial concerns. "They say we won't be able to afford the kind of life we'll need for me to come back and forth, and maybe they're right," I told him. "They pointed out how expensive it is to own a house or apartment, or to have kids. You know, schooling and stuff like that. Only my father thinks it's a good idea," I said, pausing for a moment. "But he also told me that he thinks having kids is like a life sentence."

Toru ignored my father's take on parenthood, instead countering with the observation that we didn't even know if we wanted to have kids, and we were managing just fine with me going back and forth. That the top schools in Japan were public ones, unlike in the U.S., and not expensive, although very hard to get into. I continued to lob my worries at him, and he continued to serve back measured, rational assurances. Finally, he puffed out a little sigh, a mixture of confusion and forced patience. I pressed the phone closer to my cheek, gripping it forcefully, and its heat began to make my cheek sweat. Outside my window, the hum of city traffic played on, car tires traversing smooth asphalt, syncopating out into the night.

Then, "I'm sorry," Toru said, his tone suddenly cheerful, belying the apology of his words.

Sorry?

"I'm sorry, but I can't be getting too worried about this," he continued, his voice almost melodic. "You know, your family probably would worry even if I made a million dollars in each year."

Huh, I thought. I had no ready retort.

"Maybe even *two*," he added, pronouncing it "*eben*," replacing the *v* his lexicon functions just fine without.

I stayed silent a moment longer, and I felt not just my moist cheek but my whole face hot and my body sweating from the heat of both the cell phone and our conversation, from the exertion of trying to prove all the ways our marriage was doomed.

"Well, what about the India Quality guy?" I staked one final attempt at impending calamity. "He's from another country, moved here with his wife, so maybe he really knows what he's talking about!"

"Oh, him," Toru said, his voice a swatter dispatching a fly. "Well, he should just shut up his smelly mouth!"

A laugh shot out of me, releasing all the tension I'd been holding. I'd never heard a slight like that before, and certainly not from Toru. It was base, cutting, foul. And totally hilarious. It became my new favorite insult.

CAREERWISE, Japan continued to be both a challenge and a boon. When I e-mailed my Osaka food article to the newspaper editor in Boston—leaving out the parts about my being unable to stomach anything 1) slimy, 2) raw, or 3) all that unique—she rejected it. More precisely, she failed to respond. When I tried to resend it, I got an automatic response that she'd moved on. Later, I heard that before she left her post she'd had a tendency to encourage new writers on articles she wasn't necessarily planning to run.

I already knew my success as a food writer was dubious, though. With my two teaching jobs, my Boston life in full swing around me, and the likelihood the university would continue to funnel me freelance writing, the closure of this career door failed to rankle much.

My literary series continued to grow as well. I scheduled three more events for that winter and spring, and now had a waiting list of writers wanting to read. The *Boston Globe* and other local media began reporting that people were being turned away at the door because the events were so popular, calling Four Stories the city's hippest reading series. Some people began referring to me as the bicontinental writer (with, one reporter even wrote, "the glitter eye shadow"!) who founded it. Suddenly, I had an identity known in public—albeit to a very modest circle—and it involved both Japan and Boston. My new image, on paper at least, made my multihemispheric relationship sound kind of cool, not just, or even necessarily, a doomed arrangement. *Well,* I began to assure myself, *if the cultural editor for the* Bostonist *blog doesn't bat an eye at my living half the year in the U.S. and half in Osaka, why should I?*

At the prison that semester, I was leading a course in the American modern novel, a senior seminar with students who'd made it almost all the way through the college-behind-bars program. The men sat in an uneven semicircle in front of me, stuffed into little chairs that looked like donations from an elementary school. Most of them wore faded jeans and old sweatshirts, although a few boasted prison-issue short-sleeved tops, denying the late fall air the power to make them shiver. Some sat back in their small seats, legs splayed out in front, arms crossed over chests; others hunched forward, elbows on desks, feet tapping to some internal beat.

I perched behind a scarred wooden desk, clasping fingers to fists as a cold wind seeped through the classroom's rickety panes. Every few minutes, a guard—or CO, "corrections officer," we were instructed to call them—circled the hallway, peeking through the door's cut-out window to ensure order prevailed. For the most part, the students policed themselves, knowing any serious infraction would doom the entire college program: no one wanted to face the pool of inmates who would be deprived of the chance to earn a free university degree if one troublemaker ruined everything.

We were focusing on the theme of the fallen hero in Hemingway, Ellison, Faulkner, and Fitzgerald. I placed my hands palms down on the scratched desktop, the sleeves of my floppy sweater reaching past my thumbs. Planting my scuffed flats on the old linoleum floor, I leaned forward toward the class.

"What about the theme of independence?" I asked. "The lone wolf, the hero impervious to his surroundings?" I glanced quickly at one of the short-sleeved inmates, biceps denuded, arms crossed over his chest to suggest an insouciance born of strength, not an effort to keep warm. Keeping my expression mild, I moved my eyes along the circle of men.

Students began raising hands, offering observations, and so we began a discussion one might have in any college classroom, minus the barbed wire outside our windows: of the American dream, the individual, and the ways our novels both affirmed and undermined these concepts. I rarely disclosed personal information in the prison program other than the broad outlines of my background: the region of the country where I grew up and went to college, my major, how many years I'd been teaching on traditional university campuses and in the prison system. But the students tended to talk frequently about prison culture and their lives before lockup and how what they saw in literature either reflected or seemed irrelevant to their own experiences. They also knew I was going overseas soon, that this was why we had to double up on classes for the first part of the semester, and, no, they couldn't finish their final papers late and mail them to me at my university office, because I would be gone. So today I mentioned my Japanese soon-to-be in-laws, and the East Asian view of independence as suspect, where loyalty to the group was the real test of strength and success.

"Wait, you're marrying a *Japanese* dude?" one of the men blurted out. A handful nodded sagely, as they always did whenever I said anything confirming their view of me as a radical leftist—such as questioning traditional representations of masculinity, arguing for gay rights, and now, apparently, marrying a man of another ethnicity.

At break later that day, the men milled about, some loitering around their seats, others pouring into the hallway to trade insults with students from the ESL and GED classes. Heading to the office for xeroxes, I noticed a former student coming my way. He was slight, with a fuzz mustache and a Vietnamese name I remembered from my gender-theory seminar the year before. He made a beeline for me, then stopped abruptly a foot or so away. He looked as if he had something important to say, but also as if he were bereft of either memory or speech. Settling instead on a silent grin, he turned to the men who had crowded up behind him. "Aw, shit," he said, punching his neighbor lightly on the arm before pivoting fully from me. Then, all bases apparently either covered or forfeited, he took his leave.

BY MID-APRIL, 2006, I was back in Japan for a four-month stay. Toru and I planned to spend the rest of the year researching and gathering the legal documents we'd need to marry in Osaka: a notarized Affidavit of Competency to Marry, written in English, which all foreigners marrying in Japan must use to certify their status as free and able to wed according to the laws of their own country; a second copy of this affidavit translated into Japanese; a municipal form called a Kon-in Todoke bearing the signature of two witnesses; and an official copy of Toru's Japanese family register, or Koseki Tohon, documenting household members.

That spring, Toru and I rented another studio in the same building as before. Once we were legally married, Toru's company would pay the realtor's fee for a long-term apartment, as well as the "key money" (an initial charge of three or so months' rent). They'd also cover our moving costs, the purchase of many of our appliances, and half of our rent for almost ten years: the Japanese corporate version of support for family values, a deal we would forfeit if we cohabitated before marriage. Until then, we'd make do squeezing into a tiny weekly mansion.

THAT SPRING AND SUMMER, I began spending more time with my new friend Jodi. After Lea had introduced us the winter before, we had kept in touch, making plans for when we'd be in Osaka at the same time. It didn't take long once we were both back in Japan for a close friendship to cement. Like many expat relationships, our bond came fast and strengthened quickly. Our shared sense of fascination, isolation, and at times complete discombobulation in Japan intensified our friendship, especially since we didn't know anyone else attempting to live half in Osaka, half in the U.S.

Often, expats form thick bonds before they have time to discover if they even really *like* each other or would be friends in another context. Like lovers blinded by slick surfaces, foreigners together can fall prey to a mirage of intimacy: *You're from far away and look different, too! No one will sit next to you on the subway either!*

Among a few other foreigners I'd started to meet, I already sensed how easily a relatively nice fellow expat could become an intense new friend crush. How, along with the smooth relief of having a like-passported partner in crime, a subtle disconnect could take shape, then a vague dissatisfaction. Finally came a kind of gently stultifying emptiness when you realized that, beyond geography, you and your new closest companion lacked essential symmetry.

Jodi felt like she could be a true friend, though. For one, I was fascinated by her business. She had gone to community college, and her mother had been a struggling civil servant barely able to pay the bills. But Jodi had unusual dexterity in her hands, and she became a court stenographer. She was so talented that she could do "real time" court reporting, typing testimony virtually simultaneous to its utterance. I'd never met a stenographer before; I'd only seen them on *Law & Order*, sitting modestly in the corner, hunched over some strange, square machine. But Jodi was funny and outgoing and stylish. She made a small fortune every year as a freelance real-time court reporter, being flown around the world by major American law firms taking depositions in international cases. *Who knew?* I thought.

A few years earlier, legal clients involved in international cases had started sending Jodi to Asia, repeatedly and at huge expense, because no one in the region offered the services she could. She saw an opportunity and grabbed it. With virtually no business or entrepreneurial experience, she founded the first U.S. real-time court reporting agency in East Asia.

I admired Jodi's pluck. Like most privileged American Northeasterners from education-obsessed families, I'd never met someone who had gone to community college and then founded a global organization. Nor did I personally know many people who made a living anymore from, literally, their hands.

Jodi and I also shared some similarities beyond being outsiders in Osaka. Although economically different from mine, her family was another tribe of neurotic second-generation Americans. Like mine, her mother found Yiddish the perfect lexicon to express the trauma of seeing her nice Jewish daughter in Japan. Jodi's mother wanted to know why she had to shlep all the way to Osaka every few months. "*Oy*, the kvetching!" Jodi complained jokingly, and it felt like some kind of weirdly sweet homecoming when she did.

Also like mine, Jodi's family's name had been changed when her grandfather emigrated from Eastern Europe (in my case, from Slutsky, in hers, from Chaemowitz; we laughed about both, but even she admitted my original last name had been worse). We'd sit in a bar near her apartment in Umeda, a few subway stops from mine, swilling dirty martinis that we ordered after handing a note written by Jodi's translator to the bartender. Then we'd cackle over our latest publishing idea: the launch of the *Slutsky-Chaemowitz Osaka Post*, a periodical dedicated to our misadventures in Japan. Her grandmother in assisted living in Boca Raton had already promised to be a faithful subscriber.

Later that spring, we planned a trip to Hong Kong, where Jodi had a three-day deposition. I lounged in the five-star hotel room her client had provided and tapped away at my keyboard while Jodi deposed witnesses at their law offices. When the weekend came, we went to the night markets, huge outdoor corridors lined with stalls selling brightly embroidered fabrics, little silver-threaded Chinese jackets, sweetly stitched silk purses, and ten-dollar "cashmere" pashminas I absolutely needed. In every color. We bought jade bangles and fake-jewel earrings, filling our fists with accessories, the twang of Cantonese peppering the air around us. We were stoked on a cheap-goods shopping high, fueled by an ice-thin euphoria, a kind of dizzy energy as if we'd eaten too many Twinkies.

Jodi bought a cheongsam, a tight, embroidered Chinese dress slit up the thigh. "Oh. My. God," she said as she grabbed for it, an eye-popping sheath hanging on a makeshift metal rack. "Can you *imagine* what my international *luvaah* is going to say when he sees me in this?" She was referring to her latest on-again, off-again international hookup, an American executive she only saw when he was in Asia on business. They almost always met at his hotel because she didn't like men to stay the night at her apartment. "Too much snoring." She waved her hand dismissively. "Too little space in the bed" for her not to have an easy way out.

That weekend we ate steaming plates of tofu and vegetables, bought fresh lychees at an outdoor fruit market, peeling away the rough brown skin and popping the little white mounds into our mouths, the firm flesh bursting in a rush of tang and sweet as we bit down to the pit. We had tea and pastry at a restaurant overlooking Victoria Peak, the vista of Hong Kong rising in the gauzy fog below. Then we went for fifteen-dollar, hour-and-a-half foot massages. "Heaven," I said to Jodi, leaning my head lazily toward her. She was stretched out with her eyes closed on the faux-leather recliner next to mine. *"Heaven,"* she murmured.

And it really did feel like a kind of heaven to me. I was thrilled by the newness of yet another place and culture. My cheeks felt flushed from our fits of laughter over the coffee-flavored jelly we'd bitten into at the restaurant overlooking the peak, horror spreading over Jodi's face as she realized that what looked on the menu like dark chocolate cake was really a gelatinous, Sanka-flavored Jell-O square.

I had a fiancé whose love felt both deeper and less complicated than I'd ever thought possible, even if the logistics of our relationship terrified me. I had a best girlfriend to travel and laugh with, one whose wacky bicontinental existence mirrored mine. "I feel . . . I feel weirdly . . . *complete,*" I said to Jodi after our massages ended. "I feel like I have almost everything in life I could need: Toru, you, a great circle of friends in Boston, my health, a steady income, a chance to travel, a lifestyle where I'm learning new things all the time."

"Oh, God, not me," Jodi snorted, streaking her fingers through the chunky highlights she had flat-ironed that morning. "Running the business, with Japan's red tape, is becoming a major pain in the ass. I'm not even sure I'll have enough depos scheduled to cover July." Plus, she complained, her boyfriend was driving her *"crazy"* with his inability to set a definitive schedule for his next business trip back to Asia.

"I mean," she added, "not that I'm not having a blast with you in Hong Kong or anything. But I am so *over* Japan lately." I felt a twinge of disappointment that our trip hadn't made her feel as fulfilled as I did. But then I realized I didn't really care. I loved Jodi's bald honesty, her tendency toward cranky complaint. I knew she adored me as much as I adored her. And unlike Jodi's, my work life was easy, Toru took care of any pragmatic challenge in Osaka that I might face, and I was in love. I felt happier than ever, even if the price for my new existence was the fullness of the life in Boston I'd spent years so carefully building.

After the novelty wears off, the host culture starts to intrude . . . in unexpected
and often uncontrollable ways. . . . This
sense of being different, isolated, and inad-
equate seems permanent, together with
bewilderment, alienation, depression, and
withdrawal. In extreme cases this stage can
seem to result in the complete disintegration of personality.

> • Paul Pedersen, *The Five Stages
> of Culture Shock*

Low or not low is no matter. It's just that
feelings go up, and then they come down.

> • Toru

EIGHT

THAT SUMMER, TORU'S SIS-
ter, Kei, was set to marry her longtime boyfriend, Funaki-*san*.
They'd met almost a decade earlier in their college ski club,
where in winter they'd go to nearby resorts and in fall and
spring to Tokyo's indoor mountain. A few weeks before the
wedding, Toru and I went to Tokyo for the weekend to meet
Kei's future husband. Japan's capital is considerably bigger than
Osaka, its crowds even denser, its sprawl endless. The city also
has many more foreign faces, so my light-streaked hair attracted
no attention.

The four of us gathered at a restaurant for dinner, sitting on
sleek chairs at a blond-wood table. Kei had a round, lovely face,
high cheekbones, and neatly manicured nails, and she spoke
beautiful English, as if she'd picked up a British accent at the
private girls' school she had attended. She still referred to her
fiancé as Funaki-*san*, or "Mr. Funaki," as she had done since
they had met. They had been friends, but he'd been her elder
and thus, according to Japanese tradition, deserved a formal salutation. He called her Kei.

Funaki-*san* had a wide, nervous smile, and he was sweating

at the brow a bit as he bowed formally to Toru, calling him, as
Kei's older brother, by his last name and honorific, Hoshino-*san*.
(Kei, like all little sisters, called Toru Onii-*san*, "Respected Older
Brother." After their marriage, Funaki-*san* could choose whether
to call Toru Hoshino-*san* or, like Kei, Onii-*san*.) Everyone just
called me "Tracy," pronouncing it "*To-ray-shee*."

Toru returned Funaki-*san*'s bow, inclining his head slightly
less deeply, as befitting an elder. They spoke quickly, Toru's tone
a touch more stern than usual, again befitting an elder. But they
also laughed easily, Toru tilting back his face and smiling as if to
acknowledge both Funaki-*san*'s humor and his nerves. Kei
dipped her head in a swift succession of nods as she followed
their conversation. She seemed less tense than Funaki-*san*, as if
she were both taking Toru's sternness in stride and dismissing it
as simple role-playing, all part of the expected: slightly annoying
Japanese older-brother-meets-fiancé routine.

When I interjected to ask Funaki-*san* if he spoke English, his
apple cheeks and broad forehead reddened. "Aaahh, a little,
but . . . not good, not good!" he answered, grinning toothily
and coloring even more, his hands waving in front of his face,
his eyes going wide as if this was the part of the evening he
dreaded most.

"Yes, he speaks," Kei answered with her British-inflected
accent, but she explained that he was too embarrassed to say
much. Like many Japanese people, Funaki-*san* had a horror of
shaming himself by speaking imperfect English.

"I study!" he offered, his blush now blooming crimson. "I
want improve!" he added, paused, and then, as if the pressure
was unbearable, broke down into rapid Japanese, gesticulating to
Toru, who laughed again and nodded repeated sympathies.

For the rest of the evening, Kei and Toru translated questions between me and Funaki-*san*, or I sat quietly and listened to the sharp, foreign syllables of my family-to-be. I caught a word here and there—*hai, demo, so desuka?*; "yes," "but," "is that so?"—yet mainly the stream of verbiage eluded me.

The restaurant food was perfectly prepared and beautifully presented, the room bathed in a soothing glow that softened the strict tidiness of the decor. The service, as is typical in Japan, was flawless, no hint of unpleasantness, no detail askew. My seat was plush and cozy, and I felt peaceful and ensconced in our four-some, Toru stroking my wrist when I reached under the table to grab his hand. I was happy, grateful even, to be a part of this important gathering, to be sitting by Toru's side, greeted as the elder sister-in-law. I was already becoming accustomed to my role as an integral part of the family—but one who nonetheless remained outside the fluid conversation, my face pressed to a pristine glass, so clear and light it was welcoming but for the invisible force of incomprehension sealing me off.

Since falling in love with Toru two years earlier, I'd been reluctant to learn his language. In agreeing to leave Boston at least part-time, I worried about Japan taking over so much of my life. Holding out against the language served as a kind of self-protection, a way to inculcate myself against the creep of expatriatism that flew in the face of the Boston-based academic I'd always planned on being. I didn't want Japan to make me over, to change the woman I had worked so long and hard to become. Because I was someone who loved learning, my stance made little logical sense. But neither Japan nor its language was a topic in which I'd had any interest before Toru, and now I held some hazy belief that remaining impervious to Japanese would shield me from becoming too immersed in a culture and world I still approached with ambivalence. Moreover, I stubbornly resisted the idea that Toru and I would speak his language together. So much of our relationship had become defined by *his* world, and now with him in Japan full-time, he had to make so few concessions to mine. Speaking English together—a language I loved, whose shape and expressiveness and narratives I'd devoted years to studying—felt like some small way of ensuring my world and priorities remained front and center, too.

But the limits of this stance were becoming ever more apparent. Not only could I barely understand my future family, I couldn't order in a restaurant that didn't offer picture menus or ask directions if I got lost. So late that spring, I warily enrolled in my first Japanese class. *I'll learn a few words,* I thought. *Pick up a few phrases just so I can shop more easily, go out to dinner on my own.* I planned to stop well short of learning to read or write.

One weekday morning, with Toru at the office, Tetsunobu-*san* took me to sign up for a course at the YWCA. When we had booked my enrollment by phone a few days earlier, I'd asked Toru to clarify that I spoke no Japanese. "I mean, can you make them understand, *really no Japanese?*" I added little swiping motions with my hands for emphasis, as if Toru were unaware of my linguistic limitations.

All Toru's insistence came to naught, however. In a country where protocol reigns supreme, the Y still insisted I have the usual introductory interview—in Japanese. As Tetsunobu-*san* and I sat with knees scrunched at a low table in the tidy school office, a woman came toward us from around a high desk. She had neatly coiffed black hair and a pale pink lipsticked mouth, and she held an olive green binder. Behind the desk, rows of gray filing cabinets flanked the walls. I could see another woman in back sitting at a plain wooden desk with papers stacked in a perfectly straight line. She bent over a keyboard, eyes fixed on a screen, fingers tapping evenly.

The woman with the green binder smiled as she walked toward us, bowing and offering what I took to be extended formal greetings. Tetsunobu-*san* offered what I took to be an extended formal greeting back. She sat and looked at me, still smiling. "*Konnichiwa,*" she said. I knew that word, but after a quick head-dip of apology, I blurted out, "*Konnichiwa*, but really, I speak no Japanese!"

Tetsunobu-*san* laughed, and then they spoke in one long flow. The woman looked at me and smiled some more and said a few additional words slowly to me, none of which I knew. I smiled tightly at her, my cheeks flushing, my head shaking, my eyebrows raised with my best "seriously, I have no idea what you are saying" expression. *How long is this charade going to last?* I wondered nervously, a touch annoyed. I couldn't say exactly why I was so embarrassed, but the practical American in me found this insistence on fixed procedure unnerving, as if I were caught up in a game whose rules had been explained to me but whose overall meaning I still couldn't puzzle out.

Then the woman opened her binder and passed some papers to Tetsunobu-*san*. He pointed to each line and explained what I should put there. "Your proper name here," he said, pronouncing the words *pro-paa* and then *he-yaa*. As a New Englander, I took heart hearing his Japanese lack of a final *r*. *Just like a native Bostonian,* I thought, pleased.

"Your other name," Tetsunobu-*san* said next, sounding *aah-zaa*. "Family's name, here. Here, passport's number. And birth date," he instructed, *baas-dat-to*. He waited for me to fill in each blank, his neatly trimmed fingernail slowly gesturing from one box to the next. A faint trembling shook his hand as he hovered it above.

At the address line, he took the paper and wrote out his address in Japanese and then Toru's name in the "sponsor" box. He pulled out Toru's *inkan*, his official stamp used in place of a signature, blotted it on the little black ink pad they provided, and soundlessly stamped it onto the page, then carefully counted out the deposit fee, one crisp bill after the other. When he put the money down on the table, his hand shook again, and I wondered if the walk from the subway had tired him.

I brought the rest of the payment a few afternoons later, in time for my first class. We sat in compact chairs with individualized desks spread in a small circle, a wall-length blackboard on the right. I expected to find other Westerners in the class, but when I entered, everyone else in the room was Asian. There were two young women—one Korean, one Thai, I would later learn—and two men, one a teenaged-looking boy with skinny limbs, long dark bangs, and a faintly shadowed upper lip; one a stocky man in a suit.

Our instructor was a part-time teacher, a middle-aged Japanese woman with soft eyes and hair carefully curled at her cheeks. We were to call her Fujita-*san* or Fujita-*sensei*, the former meaning something equivalent to Mrs. Fujita, the latter an honorific reserved for doctors or educators, in this case translating roughly to Respected Teacher Fujita. She smiled ear to ear, and when she pointed to herself, instead of tapping a finger toward her chest, as we do in the West, she touched the tip of her nose. She wore a high V-neck sweater, a polo shirt buttoned all the way to the top, and a pair of what my mother would have called "slacks": plain, neatly pressed, and polyester.

Everyone else besides me spoke at least some Japanese, and the two other women, married to Japanese men, used it at home with their husbands. We weren't supposed to speak anything else in the classroom. The first week, we started studying the first of Japan's three alphabets. The main alphabet, called *kanji*, consists of thousands of characters, each one a full word and based on China's writing system. Only after learning the first two thousand of these characters is a student considered proficient enough to read a newspaper or function in Japanese society; schoolchildren, starting at age six, learn a thousand by the time they are twelve. Our class wasn't even going to begin studying *kanji*, though, because we were too novice.

Instead, we began with *hiragana*, a letter-based alphabet like English of forty-eight units. Then we would move on to *katakana*, another forty-eight–unit syllabary, but one reserved for foreign words. As if in perfect expression of Japan's insularity, no concept originating from another culture should sully the purity of *hiragana*. Words such as "coffee" (pronounced *co-hee*), "wine" (*wiyn*), "PC" (*pasa-con*, a kind of linguistic shorthand for "personal computer"), and "sexual harassment" (*seku-hara*) are all garrisoned securely within *katakana*.

Along with alphabets, we spent the first week practicing introductions. "*Watashi-wa* Tracy *desu*," I learned to say, "I am Tracy." "America *kara kimashita*," "I came from America." I tried at first to claim I came from the U.S., thinking that labeling my home simply "America" might be insulting to others from the far Western continents. "U.S. *kara kimashita*," I offered, which resulted in a roomful of blank stares.

"America, *desu-ne?*" the teacher asked, a smile crinkling her eyes as her nod beckoned me on. "America, right?"

Unable to explain my political correctness in Japanese, I broke into English, the one language everyone in the room understood to some extent. "But isn't that insulting?" I protested. "To call the United States just 'America'?" I sat back, pleased to have proven myself one of my country's more sensitive citizens in the age of George W. Bush. Everyone still stared blankly at me.

"You know," I persisted, "wouldn't that insult people from, let's say Canada, or the rest of North or even South America or something?" Respected Teacher Fujita cocked her head at me, a look of utter incomprehension on her face, despite her ability to follow my words. The Korean woman stared around the room, as if searching for missing Canadians.

"*Watashi-wa* Fujita. *Watashi-wa* Nihon *kara kimashita,*" the teacher said, not unkindly, tapping her nose. "I am Fujita. I come from Japan." Then she gestured to me. "*Anata-wa* To-ray-shee-*san desu,*" "You are To-ray-shee-*san,*" she said. "America *kara kimashita,*" her smile now a promise to guide me patiently through a lesson that had clearly confounded me.

Oy, I thought.

She gestured once more toward me, and I surrendered. "*Watashi-wa* Tracy *desu,*" I parroted. "*Watashi-wa* America *kara kimashita.*" Respected Teacher Fujita gave a little celebratory clap, then hugged her hands together as if savoring some small delight before she turned to the teenaged boy next to me.

He informed us that his name was Feng, which he pronounced *Fung,* and he was from Chuugoku. Before I could stop myself, I interrupted again. "Chuugoku?" I asked. "What's Chu-go-ku?"

Respected Teacher Fujita slid her eyes in my direction, a hint of patience possibly wearing thin on her eternally kind face. "China," she said softly in English, nodding quickly in her own small surrender. Then she moved to the man in the suit. *"Watashi-wa* Chen," he said. *"Watashi-wa* Taiwan *kara-kimashita."*

Feng whipped around in his chair to face his neighbor. "Chuugoku!" he corrected.

"Taiwan," Chen countered.

"Chuugoku!" the teenaged Feng said once again, and then he broke into a stream of what I assumed was either Mandarin or Cantonese.

I snapped my head around to see how Respected Teacher Fujita was going to handle the minor diplomatic showdown erupting in her classroom. She blinked a moment, then smiled wider, as if the conversation were all part of a polite nice-to-meet-you. I turned back to the China-Taiwan conflict.

Chen grumbled quietly under his breath, but then he began to laugh. He expostulated something in some language back to Feng: I guessed a gentle scolding from an elder. Then Feng began to laugh, too, a teenaged chortle followed by a quick swipe of long bangs from his eyes, and the moment passed. Respected Teacher Fujita happily clasped her hands together once more, looking almost beatific, and turned to the Thai wife.

A few weeks later, the class moved on to the topic of hobbies and jobs. I learned that Feng was here because his mother had married a Japanese man (a fact he had to explain to me in broken English, since the Japanese explanation was completely beyond me) and that he worked in a ramen restaurant. Chen was a Taiwanese businessman whose company had sent him to learn Japanese (also a fact learned through hushed English translation while Respected Teacher Fujita was busy at the blackboard). The Thai woman, named Bhuta-*san*, provided no end of mirth for the teenaged Feng, since the Japanese word for "pig" is *bu-ta*.

"Bhuta-*san, shigoto-wa nan desuka?*" "Mrs. Bhuta, what is your work?" the teacher asked while Feng sniggered. Bhuta-*san* looked at the Chinese teen with a tight, helpless smile, her dimpled cheeks reddening, and then she turned to Respected Teacher. "*Watashi-wa shufu desu!*" she answered.

"*Shufu?* What's *shufu?*" I blurted out, as usual, in English. It was the first time I'd been introduced to the term.

"*Shufu!*" The teacher turned to me, as if I simply hadn't heard, as if it were not possible not to know this word.

"*Shufu!*" Bhuta-*san* repeatedly kindly for me, this time a little louder.

"*Shufu!*" the Korean woman, An-*san*, echoed helpfully. Chen-*san* and Feng-*san* nodded knowingly.

I shrugged.

"*Shufu!* Housewife!" Respected Teacher explained.

"Oh," I said. "*Shufu.* Housewife."

"An-*san wa?*" the teacher asked, turning to the Korean woman.

"*Watashi-mo wa shufu desu!*" "I am also a housewife!"

"*Watashi-mo, desu-ne!*" Respected Teacher Fujita said happily, "I am, too, you know!" pointing to her nose again. Apparently, despite her part-time job teaching at the Y, she still defined herself by her primary identity as married to her house.

"To-ray-shee-*san wa?*" she asked me next, nodding. "To-ray-shee-*san no shigoto wa nan desuka?*" "What is To-ray-shee-*san*'s work?" "To-ray-shee-*san wa shufu desuka?*" "Is To-ray-shee-*san* a housewife?"

I thought about my years of university jobs in Boston, my work teaching inmates. I pictured myself at past faculty meetings, sitting forward at a table flush with academics, my blazer-suited forearm supporting my weight as I leaned in to expostulate, comment, challenge, or demur. Heads would nod. Jargon would be deployed, egos would plump up like a fat bird's plumage in the knowledge that we spoke of learned things.

Now, I struggled to land a few simple words. "Oh, *shufu*, no," I said, then dutifully added in Japanese, *"iie, iie,"* "no, no." I shot a half-apologetic, half-I-hope-I-still-seem-respectful smile at Bhuta-*san*, nodded to An-*san*.

"Watashi wa . . . freelance writer," I said, then added, "How do you say 'freelance writer' in Japanese?" I mimed holding a pen over an imaginary piece of paper, pinching together my index finger and thumb, and moving them back and forth, hoping to distract Respected Teacher Fujita from my persistent use of English.

"Ii, desu-ne! Furino raita!" she exclaimed. "Isn't that great? A freelance writer!"

Bhuta-*san* smiled at me, her expression one of gentleness infused with perhaps a touch of pity, while An-*san* looked skeptical, as if, with all this freelance writing business, I was eventually bound to fail when my marriage became official and I graduated to *shufu*. Chen and Feng just nodded noncommittally. My classroom culture shock became complete a few days later when, moving on to the topic of favorite hobbies, Respected Teacher Fujita explained that hers was "cleaning house."

When I brought my first quiz home—a line of wobbly *katakana* I had written mostly correctly, earning only a few swipes of Respected Teacher's red pencil—Toru held it up for full view.

"Oh, *great!*" he enthused, nodding in silent agreement with both the crimson corrections and the bright check mark at the paper's corner. "That's *great!*" he said again, and then he put the paper down and turned to me. He smiled wide, then drew his mouth together in a more serious aspect, as if he had important news to impart. "You know," he said, nodding, "I have some information: I feel proud you." Then he nodded once more, more firmly this time, and I buried my face in his shoulder.

BEFORE KEI'S WEDDING in August, Toru told me that the event would include formal family introductions, common at Japanese marriages. The bride's family would sit in one line, the groom's facing them in another, and one by one, each member would rise and be introduced. This would happen after the main ceremony and have no witnesses outside direct relatives. "So," Toru asked me, "are you okay with being my fiancée? With being announced?"

We were in Tetsunobu-*san*'s apartment picking up more clothes for Toru to bring to the weekly mansion. His father was in the living room watching a National Geographic–like show on TV, animals chasing each other with hot, quick strides or lounging sleepily in their habitats, the hushed, liquid voice of the announcer strangely similar to American animal-show narrators even though the language was different. Every once in a while, Tetsunobu-*san* would sip cold tea from a small green ceramic cup, his right hand shaking again as he brought it to his mouth.

Suddenly, I felt a small, fluttering anxiety inside at the idea of announcing our engagement formally. *But nothing is irreversible,* I thought.

"Okay," I said. "Let's do it." Then, "What do I have to do? Do I have to say anything? In *Japanese*?" A new kind of nervousness pulsed.

Toru assured me that I only had to say one line of greeting, which he'd rehearse with me beforehand. He'd sit next to me and tell me when to rise, and then I'd stand up and do a little bow toward Funaki-*san*'s family and give my salutation, and then I could sit down again. "But how about ring?" he asked. "Do we need? Do you want it?"

"Ring?"

"Yeah, ring, like engagement ring. We don't need, though," Toru said. He'd already told me he hated wearing jewelry. I'd already told him I thought diamond rings were a waste of money and I had no desire to own one. But we still hadn't decided whether or not I would get a different kind of ring or wear anything to signify our engagement or marriage.

"I don't know," I answered. "Let's just wait and see. I don't really need a ring, but if we find one, a cheap one that we like, maybe we could buy it. We have a few weeks, right?"

That weekend, we went shopping in Osaka's Umeda District, flush with upscale malls and underground boutiques. I'd seen a ring I'd loved a few weeks earlier in a store called Beams, a sort of Japanese cross between the American shops Madewell and Barneys with a touch of the more youthful Forever 21 thrown in. The ring bore no resemblance to anything bridal, but it had a chunky sliver band that managed to look both graceful and substantial, with a dangling glass piece cut like a sweetheart diamond but as black as night, so it flashed darkly and made a delicate tinkling sound when I moved my hand.

It was the sound of that tinkling I liked best. Within the

chaos of Osaka, the bright noise felt like Toru's love: like an anchor, a little aural tether securing me in place amidst a swirling world.

"Huh," Toru said when I waved the ring at him from my right hand. Although neither one of us was superstitious and the piece was clearly not meant for an engagement, I was reluctant to place the band on my left hand while we stood in the store. A thin, lovely salesgirl watched us, her lips pursed, her hands held neatly at her front, and my cheeks felt hot under her stare. *Does she know we're thinking of this for our marriage?* I wondered. *Is she surprised that he's engaged to a gaijin? Does she think the ring is stupid?* Then, *Does she think my hips seem big compared to a Japanese woman's?*

Inside, I felt the sting of disappointment at my own self-consciousness. I tried focusing on Toru's expression, on his words rather than the useless chatter in my head. As I waved my hand back and forth, his look of concentration cracked into a smile. "Actually, kind of cool," he said. He watched my hand toggle to and fro another moment. Then, "Kind of great."

"It doesn't look anything like an engagement ring, does it, Tof?" A surge of something light washed through me, along with a smug sense of invulnerability, thinking of how the salesgirl wouldn't be able to follow our rapid English.

After we bought the ring, we went for lunch at a little Vietnamese stall tucked into a hallway of Umeda's sprawling underground. Toru sat across the table from me, grasping the shiny dark blue bag with the wrapped ring. We ordered pad thai and satay and soup, and then Toru pushed some fried rice crackers out of the way, little swirls of pink and white in a rough wooden bowl, and removed the jewelry from its box.

"Could you," he said, suddenly quiet and grave, his voice soft, his dark expression fixed and staring carefully into mine, "Could you still consider to marrying me?" He handed me the ring, and I grinned at his sudden formality amidst all our shunning of tradition. Then I took the ring and slipped my finger through its shiny silver hoop, and we listened to the bright tinkle lifting in the air around us.

NINE

THE WEEKEND OF KEI'S WED-
ding, Tokyo was a furnace. The sky was steel blue, the sun
clamping down like a vise. I stepped outside and within a minute my skin was slick: August in Japan. Osaka, when we'd left it
a few days earlier, had been even hotter.

I'd brought a thin, sleeveless, V-neck black sheath with a
little camisole to shorten the neckline's plunge. But the morning
of the wedding, I discovered I'd forgotten the right underwear.
The ones I had were visible through the dress and pinched a bit
at the waist, giving me a little fleshy swell at my hip that Toru
thought was sexy and I thought was out of the question. My
size-six frame, petite in the U.S., was already big by Japanese
standards. I wasn't inclined to further accentuate any curves.

Also out of the question were stockings. I never wore them,
and I wasn't starting in ninety-eight-degree weather. Besides, by
the time my lingerie crisis became apparent, we had no time to
buy either new underwear or hosiery.

Standing in our tiny hotel room, air-conditioning blasting, I
said, "Well, I guess I'll just go without underwear, Tof."

"Oh, great . . . ," he said, still captivated by the sheet he was studying that held directions to the restaurant and wedding space. He clasped the strong swoop of his jaw in one hand, eyes staring hard at the paper.

I held up a little compact mirror to try to see how the dress looked with me denuded underneath. We were staying in a business hotel, a no-frills place offering rooms not much bigger than our weekly mansion, but immaculately clean and about a quarter of the price of a regular hotel in Tokyo. I angled the hand mirror toward the small wall one they provided.

I moved the little mirror right, then left, then right again. The room had one night-table lamp and a fluorescent ceiling light, but I couldn't tell if my dress would be see-through where Kei's ceremony and party would be held. From one angle, it looked fine. But from another: *How much is visible back there?* I imagined standing up to be introduced as Toru's fiancée to all of Kei's new in-laws and hearing uncomfortable Japanese murmurs rippling through the room.

"Tof!" I yelled, even though he was only a few feet from me. "Is this see-through?"

"It's fine," he said, still not looking up from the printed directions.

"Seriously, Tof. I need to know."

He glanced upward, nodded, and looked back down. "No problem!"

"Because you know how embarrassed I'd be if, like, Funaki-*san*'s grandmother noticed I was naked underneath?" I shifted the hand mirror some more, angling it high, then lower, then turning to face the wall mirror so I could study my reflection straight on.

"I don't think grandmother will come," Toru muttered, no

more consumed with those directions than he could be if they held a map to Atlantis.

"Tof! Seriously! Won't you be embarrassed, too, if someone notices?"

He sighed, put the directions down in his lap. "You're enough sexy anyway," he said.

"What does *that* mean?"

"You know. Enough sexy!" he repeated.

I slanted my head and widened my eyes at him, giving him my best "in English, at least, that doesn't clarify anything" stare.

He sighed again. "You can't help but be sexy," he said, forehead wrinkling under the black spikes of his hair. "Underwear or no underwear is no matter. Still sexy, either way." Then he motioned for me to turn around so he could give my backside one final check. I wondered if the vision of Funaki-*san*'s grandmother, mother, whomever, noticing suspicious swells and valleys under my dress had finally unnerved him.

"It's fine," he said again, as I turned back to face him. "Looks good! And anyway," he said, eyes now wandering back to that beloved direction sheet, "no one looks at your hip but me!"

ONCE WE HIT the sidewalk and were swaddled in humidity as thick as gauze, I stopped worrying about panty lines. The less I had on, the better. We walked the eight or nine blocks to the wedding venue, a restaurant in the upscale Ginza neighborhood with an extra room that could be transformed into a makeshift chapel. In the heavy, heat-blasting air, I was glad Toru had studied the directions so well. I had to wipe under my eyes to keep my mascara from running down my face.

As we entered the building, cold air-conditioning hit me, licking up my arms, legs, and face. *Bliss*, I thought. At the elevator, Toru's older cousin Jiro-*san* joined us, along with his wife, Sachi-*san*. I'd never met them, but I'd heard they were funny and outgoing and, as Toru said, "a little wild." At their wedding, Toru had told me, one of their friends had gotten drunk and hoisted himself onto a table—minus pants or underwear—and lay with his legs spread up into the air.

"You. Are. Kidding me," I'd gasped through laughter. This was not my vision of staid, polite Japanese people. And Toru's aunt and uncle, Michiko-*san* and Hamatani-*san*, seemed so proper. "What did his parents say?"

"Hamatani-*san* just kept shaking head and saying, 'Too much! Too much!' But Michiko-*san* laughed a little. Maybe thought was a little funny."

"Really? But isn't that *so* not Japanese?"

"Well, kind of unusual, but not so much. When getting drunk, these things can happen. Kind of crazy, but kind of not so, for party."

In Osaka, I'd already noticed a surprising acceptance under very specific circumstances of behavior that in the U.S. would be considered outrageous anytime. Toru and I sometimes saw drunk salarymen in rumpled suits passed out on the sidewalk in broad daylight, pedestrians streaming by unconcerned; or well-dressed people weaving down city blocks late at night, leaning over periodically to retch. The first time we found a businessman asleep on the street next to his own stomach contents, I'd been aghast, but Toru had tried to convince me it was actually "sign of peaceful society": people feel safe enough to be vulnerable in public without worrying about crime or injury. I'd been both skeptical and amazed.

But I could also understand how—since Japan exerts so much pressure to be contained, controlled, rule bound—when people let loose, they can *really* let loose. In general, the society seemed to tolerate it, perfectly happy to ignore it as long as the person was drunk or participating in some other sanctioned activity for blowing off steam, as if it were all a necessary byproduct of living with such strict self-regulation. I wondered if this was why Japanese pornography and crime fiction were so violent, or the sex clubs I'd read about so outlandish: some apparently featured women dressed as kilted schoolgirls standing on mock train cars so customers could pretend to molest them. As long as a behavior remained relegated to the sphere of imagination, of fiction—or of the alcohol induced—people by and large remained unconcerned.

"But," Toru had added, when he'd told me about the naked table dancer at his cousin's wedding, "not so good to do in front of parents. Better to wait for after party, just with friends." *Well, at least my lack of underwear can't compete with that*, I thought.

Now, as we crowded into the elevator at the wedding venue with Jiro-*san* and Sachi-*san*, I felt curious to see them up close. Both were thin and smiled easily, and Jiro-*san* had short hair that tufted upward like Toru's, although his facial features were softer. Sachi-*san* wore a plain pale dress with short sleeves, her straight dark hair reaching her shoulders. She nodded up and down after we met. *"Kakko ii, ne!"* she said, gesturing toward me. I smiled, then said through my teeth, "What's that mean, Tof?"

"It means good-looking, or fashionable, or kind of chic," Toru said, and then they launched into Japanese with lots of laughter and, I assumed, catching up.

Because Toru's mother had been Catholic and Kei still identified as such, a priest officiated the wedding ceremony. I'd heard that in Japan many white men rent themselves out as "fathers," fake priests who will perform at Japanese weddings to provide a Western feel. It's an alternate way to make money that tends to pay more by the hour than teaching English. (One BBC article quotes a fake British priest saying, "People like the dress, the kiss and the image. Japanese Christians make up only 1% of the country, but now about 90% of weddings are in the Christian style."[1])

I was a touch disappointed when Kei's priest turned out to be Japanese. "Is he a real priest?" I whispered to Toru.

"Ya, real," Toru whispered back. "Not like fake whitey," he said, and we snickered. We'd been laughing about this term since we'd noticed one of Osaka's underground malls was named Whity (but pronounced as if the word included a penultimate *e*). We'd immediately taken a series of pictures of the sign along with a nearby café called Honeypot, which I found equally hilarious. Toru had stood in front of the signs and pointed, making mock-horrified faces while I cackled like a tween and aimed my camera, confused shoppers turning to stare in confusion at our mirth.

When I thought about it now, though, it made sense Kei would want a real priest for her wedding, since her religious

---

1 See the BBC News article "Faking It as a Priest in Japan," http://news.bbc.co.uk/2/hi/6067002.stm for more.

beliefs were real, too. I smiled at the father, and he nodded prayerfully at me.

The ceremony proceeded in Japanese, and Tetsunobu-*san*, sitting on Toru's other side, held up a picture of Toru's mother. I heard the priest say her name, "Eiko-*san*," and then a string of solemn words. I bowed my head, felt my silly mood condense into something softer, quieter, then sad. Up at the altar, Kei and Funaki-*san* stood still and expressionless, he in tails, she in a white gown. I glanced at Toru, who sat with his eyes down now, equally expressionless. His father looked up toward the picture he held aloft, Eiko-*san*'s framed face smiling, but he, too, remained expressionless.

I knew inside they were all rent by grief, and I felt momentarily shocked at how seamlessly they hid it. I knew Kei must have missed her mother achingly, especially at this moment. I knew Tetsunobu-*san* must have felt a cold space by his side where his wife should have been sitting. I remembered Toru on the afternoon he learned of his mother's accident, his body trembling in that taxicab in Seoul, and then again on the night he'd returned to Korea after visiting her in the hospital in Osaka, only to learn she had died just after his plane had taken off. I imagined them seeing her in a coma in the hospital before she died, gathered in the gloom by her bed, tubes hooking her to machines. I wondered if they were remembering her that way now, or thinking of other scenes: a mother's nighttime kiss, cool and soft; an encouraging hand waving on the first day of school; her back at the kitchen sink, arms moving as she peeled the skins from vegetables.

Suddenly, although I had never met Eiko-*san*, I missed her sharply. I wondered how it would have felt to be related to a woman so different from my own mother. I grieved for her, too: for her missed chance at being here with her children, her husband, at the altar of her daughter's wedding. Inside, my chest felt wobbly as I thought about her family in their silent, hidden grief. I wondered, considering the stoicism of Kei and Toru and Tetsunobu-*san*, if doing something as overt as crying here and now, in public at an event meant to be a celebration, would be judged excessively emotional: by the other attendees, by themselves, by Japanese standards in general. Somehow, that made me even sadder for them.

I wanted to grab Toru's hand but I didn't, because I didn't know if he would find it an intrusion, and I didn't want to shatter his equilibrium if he was, in fact, fighting down tears. I couldn't see the other attendees because we were in the front row, but the room was silent save for the priest's monotone intonation.

I felt a sob push against my own throat, and my eyes began to sting, but I pressed down the emotion as hard as I could. I pushed my leg alongside Toru's knee so he would know, would remember through that quiet pressure that I was beside him, with him. Quickly, I wiped a tiny tear that had leaked onto my lash line. Then Tetsunobu-*san* lowered the picture, and the priest's prayers turned to other matters.

After the ceremony, the rest of the guests went one floor up to the dining room, while the two families lined up in a room adjacent to the makeshift chapel. We sat on two long benches facing one another, Kei and Funaki-*san* standing at the end. Tetsunobu-*san*, Michiko-*san*, Hamatani-*san*, Toru, and I were there to represent Kei's side.

Now Funaki-*san* announced each of his relatives, calling

their name and, if relevant, their job or professional title. As each person stood and bowed, our side would say, *"Hajimemashite. Dozo yoroshiku onegaishimasu,"* roughly translating to "Nice to meet you. It is an honor to make your acquaintance." Then Kei repeated protocol with her side.

When I stood up, I put my hands flat on my thighs and bent low at the waist, as Respected Teacher Fujita at the YWCA had taught us was the polite way to bow. My back was to the wall, so I didn't worry what was visible through my dress. *"Hajimemashite!"* I said on my way down. Then I raised myself up and, embarrassed, forgot the rest. *"Dozo . . . gozo . . . ,"* I muttered, turning red-faced to Toru. He said something to the line of Funaki-*san*'s relatives, offering an apologetic dip from his seat, and everyone laughed kindly. I sat down abruptly, feeling both grateful and childlike.

Funaki-*san*'s grandmother nodded her powdered face, then gave a lipsticked smile, as if pleased I had made the effort but not the least surprised it had proved beyond me. After all, I was a foreigner, and this was Japan, where the language, food, and customs remain inaccessible to outsiders, even in the unlikely event one marries into a native family. I knew I was doing nothing to dispel that myth.

I also knew that in some Japanese families, a foreign relative was considered a mark of shame. I'd heard of the common Japanese practice, especially popular before the mid–twentieth century, of people hiring private investigators to research potential mates' clans to avoid a scandalous match. A *gaijin* in the family could definitely be a no-go.

I'd asked Toru if he thought Funaki-*san*'s parents were wary of my becoming, technically, related to them. "Could be," he'd said. "But probably not. We're not such high family." Nowadays, he explained, mostly only very wealthy or politically important people researched potential matches. "I have aunt who married Bhutan doctor," he'd said, so I would not be the first foreigner in the family anyway, although I would be the first non-Asian. "Besides," he'd added, "my uncle was student leader in communist movement at Tokyo University, in 1970s." At least, according to the old guard, Toru had assured me, that was even worse than being a *gaijin*.

But all throughout Kei's wedding, I thought I sensed a weird energy coming from Funaki-*san*'s mother. She was unfailingly polite but so reserved that I wasn't sure whether she was just immaculately contained or inclined to coldness. She wore a red and gold kimono, and when we met, she smiled tightly and bowed very slightly, like a wooden statue tipping down one notch. She spoke a little English, and I tried to congratulate her, comment on the beauty of her kimono, yet still she only smiled and inclined her head.

Maybe she's shy? Uncomfortable speaking English? Or I'm imagining things? I couldn't tell if her reserve meant anything or not. Was it one more sign I didn't know how to read, or not a sign at all?

"I think Funaki-*san*'s mother doesn't like me," I whispered to Toru as we made our way to the dining room. We were placed at a small table with his father, the picture of Eiko-*san* next to our plates. Funaki-*san*'s family was at their own table across the room. As is customary at Japanese weddings, Kei's and Funaki-*san*'s bosses were at tables, too, rising to make some of the first toasts.

"She probably just shy," Toru said. Later, when we went to

have family pictures taken, we all gathered in one long line, Kei and Funaki-*san* in the center. The photographer put me and Toru on one end, then went to his tripod and surveyed the group. He gave an order to his assistant, who approached the line and made some adjustments: a torso turned here, an arm or foot adjusted there. Then she came toward me. She moved me left a bit until a small gap separated me from Toru and the family chain.

"See, I told you she doesn't like me!" I said to him after the photo shoot. "I bet she told the photographer to move me aside so she could cut the *gaijin* out of the family photo!" I was more curious than upset, though. On one hand, these were technically my extended family-to-be. On the other, they were people I couldn't have a conversation with. I wasn't even sure whether they cared I was a foreigner, and I didn't have the language or cultural skills to read between the lines and find out. Like my strange detachment from Japanese gender norms that in America would disturb me, once again I thought, *This isn't my country or my culture.* My remove kept me feeling both isolated and protected from what happened here. Moreover, Toru didn't seem upset, which I figured was the best sign.

Now, he laughed at my accusation. "They just were adjusting line, making space even," he said, grabbing my hand. "Although maybe . . . maybe she will decide to cutting *gaijin* out of family photo!" he teased.

Then another thought seized me. "Oh, God," I said. "What if the photographer could tell I wasn't wearing any underwear! Could see through my dress. *In front!*" I grabbed Toru's wrist, my tone somewhere between a shriek and a whisper. "Maybe that's why he needed his assistant to separate me, so he could crop my . . . my crotch out of the photo later!" I spent the rest of the day with my hands crossed below my waist like Adam and Eve in Eden, maneuvering Toru to stand in front of me whenever I could.

FOUR MONTHS LATER, we were on a sidewalk in Osaka, layered in heavy coats and hats. It was December 2006, and a wet winter wind stung our faces as we peered at the door of the U.S. Consulate. Toru and I needed to retrieve a form claiming I was of sound mind and acting under free will, certifying that when we filed our Japanese marriage papers a few hours later, even though I couldn't read them, I'd understand their meaning.

In the cold, Toru and I looked at each other for a moment. Our hands were clasped, but neither one of us spoke.

We'd been preparing for this day for months, although I'd gone home to Boston in the interim after Kei's wedding. I'd found another subletter to rent my apartment for part of the semester, but he only needed it for two months, and I planned to be in Osaka for four. I was beginning to feel more frazzled by both the financial and practical burdens of the Boston studio, in part because my rental agreement forbade me from subletting.

I guessed my landlords knew and didn't care as long as I paid my rent on time every month and fixed anything that broke, but I couldn't be sure. "We *love* you," they always told me when we talked. They were both male flight attendants, now based on the West Coast. "Never leave us. Never." They'd been crestfallen when they heard I was marrying a man from Japan, then delighted by my plan to keep living in Boston half the year. Once, when I got stuck in the apartment because the aging lock had broken from the inside, they responded as if I'd called with news of a three-alarm blaze. "I have a mani/pedi appointment in forty-five minutes," I'd told Stu, "so if you can get the locksmith here in thirty, that would be great."

"Oh, girlfriend, *no*, not a mani/pedi," he'd said, his voice hushed. "We'll have you out of there as soon as possible." Ten minutes later, a locksmith was dismantling my door.

Wow, they must have had really bad luck with tenants in the past, I thought, having been unaware that simply paying your rent on time made you a hot commodity. Still, I tried to keep the sub-letters secret in case my landlords balked—or kept my last month's rent and security deposit after kicking me out.

In the weeks in Boston before I returned to Japan to get married, my chest felt tight and my skin a little wrong, like what should be a seamless layer threatened to gap or slip. I tried not to wonder what those feelings meant. I'd lie awake and listen to the sound of late-fall traffic on the South End streets outside my apartment, the drunken laughter spilling from the bar across the road, boys with high voices shouting into the night. In addition to all the work of finding and vetting subletters, the task of pre-paring to leave home for four months was itself overwhelming: packing my personal belongings while still leaving the apartment adequately furnished; finding a place to store my car; drumming up new freelance work; preparing to reenter a world of opposing rules, rhythms, and customs; scrambling for the best price on the twenty-four-hour trip in economy-seat hell it would take to get there. I imagined myself floating in dark, empty space at the end of a flimsy rope, like the cartoon figure from the beginning of *Lost in Space*, a TV show we watched when we were young.

Jodi and I had a name for this: the Reentry Phase. We both suffered from depression and angst in the first weeks of our transitions to and from Japan. Even the things we most looked forward to in each country felt remote or insubstantial: for Jodi, the food in Osaka or her garden in Florida; for me, the warmth of Toru's body or the utter sense of home I found in Boston. No thought or comfort could completely dispel the fog of anxiety that came on either end of our bicontinental stays. The shifts always felt tectonic: too huge, too unsettling, and just plain *wrong*.

We both took heart that the other experienced the same internal roiling, though. Neither one of us knew anyone else trying to live one life on two continents, so we assumed these emotions just came with the territory, like jet lag on a body: the mind's inability to deal gracefully with planet-sized moves. We promised each other we would never make any life decisions during the Reentry Phase. We would acknowledge but not act on any emotion within the two weeks buffering either end of our Japan–U.S. transfers.

Once I get back to Osaka, get settled, feel Toru next to me, and make it through my first two weeks there, I'll be better, I'd tried to comfort myself. The borders of my life would shift back into line. The unusual arrangement Toru and I had made, to have me living in both countries, would start to feel manageable again, normalized. If maintaining my Boston life while I was in Osaka became too much, I'd deal with that problem then. I didn't like not having a firm plan, a perfect blueprint for how to cope with this contingency. But I was learning that in real, messy life, sometimes you can't fully smooth down the future before it arrives.

Things did recalibrate eventually: the axis of my world tipped upright again, not sideways at an angle that left me feeling I might slip off reality's edge. In Osaka, I got back into my rhythm of going to one of my morning cafés and working on freelance assignments from our tiny weekly mansion in the afternoons, then cooking a few nights a week at Tetsunobu-*san*'s apartment. On the weekends, Toru and I walked around the city or went out to dinner, and the soft pressure of his hand holding mine always stilled me, as if his palm could summon gravity to coalesce once more around my feet.

During the weekdays, I sank back into my minor expat bubble, like a little glass globe keeping the real Osaka both in sight and out of reach. My orb contained the few restaurants I could go to on my own, the train stops I knew, the stores whose aisles I could navigate solo. I became accustomed once more to the background murmur of a language I could barely follow, printed signs whose messages withheld meaning.

I enrolled in another Japanese class at the YWCA and joined a gym near the school. I could now very slowly sound out words that were written in the two alphabets we'd learned. This helped at cafés: I could recognize items like *hotto cohee* (hot coffee), *ca-fe o-rei* (café au lait), or *butta toast-o* (buttered toast) even when there were no pictures. But I quickly realized that learning Japanese would prove much harder than even I'd anticipated. For one, the writing system provides no separation between words, so whole sentences run together in one long string combining all elements, including *kanji*, the primary one I still didn't know. To me, it felt similar to trying to read soMEthiNGLIkeThiSBUt withHONeextRaunrEAdAbLeaLPHabeTTHRownin.

Even apart from reading, the language seemed like Japan's phonological equivalent of China's Great Wall: an impenetrable barricade barring foreigners. In addition to regular conjugations (different verb forms for past, present, etc.), the grammar encompasses up to five forms of honorifics, each dependent on both your role and that of your interlocutor. Understanding roles, in turn, requires extensive cultural knowledge about both hierarchy and the Japanese notions of groups and boundaries: elder relatives require different forms than both younger relatives and elder nonrelatives, but speaking to the latter about the first requires yet another variation. The word for "husband" changes depending on whether you are talking about your own spouse to a family member or stranger, about a stranger's spouse in a formal setting, or about a stranger's spouse in a casual situation. And that's just the nouns.

"Why can't I just learn the most polite form," I asked Toru, "and use that all the time?"

"Actually, kind of rude to use most polite form in casual situation," he said. Employing too formal a conjugation at the wrong time suggested snobbery and an uncouth mixing of boundaries, more hierarchical no-no's, he explained.

Then there was the counting: well over a dozen different ways to say "one, two, three," depending on the kind and shape of the object being counted. Flat objects, like plates, require one word, long items like bottles or pencils another, people a third, buildings yet another, and on and on.

In school, the verb forms we were learning were not the ones people used in everyday conversation. So after months and months of Japanese class, I could order a drink, ask for a bigger size at a store, or inquire formally about someone's hobbies (which never did come in handy), but having a conversation remained well beyond my reach: once someone responded, it was usually all over.

The gym proved equally challenging. One week, I summoned the courage to try a yoga class—or what I thought was yoga. I knew which studio held the classes, and I looked on that room's schedule to see which time slots contained notations. Where a time slot has writing, that must mean a class, I reasoned.

On the day in question, I arrived at the gym early. At the threshold to the locker room, I removed my "outdoor" sneakers, as required, and stored them in a cubby, then walked in stocking feet to my locker. After changing into yoga pants and a T-shirt, I carried my "inside" sneakers to the edge of the locker room before putting them on. I didn't understand the logic of inside and outside sneakers, since we wore both up and down the stairs to the locker room, but I knew enough to follow protocol.

When I got to the yoga studio, a number of women were already lying on their mats, wispy hips encased in stretch pants and matching tops, indoor sneakers removed and set neatly beside. Some lay with their eyes closed, and two had their faces pointed toward each other, whispering softly. Lying down myself, I alternated gazing up at the ceiling and looking around the starkly tidy room: wooden floor shiny and dustless, mats and blocks stacked in their corners, edges aligned. I tried not to stare at the other women, but I wanted to keep watch, knowing I would need to follow their movements once the class started.

When the teacher entered exactly on the hour, sat lotus style in one fluid swoop, and began to talk in Japanese, everyone closed her eyes. *Must be some kind of beginning meditation.* I squeezed my eyelids together, then cracked them open to check for signs of stirring, maybe a transition to Downward Dog pose. No movement.

Fifteen minutes later, we were still prone on our mats. Sometimes the teacher murmured in Japanese, and sometimes she went silent. Straining to move soundlessly, I toggled my head from left to right and back again, anxious to catch the beginning of the first yoga posture. *This is the longest intro meditation ever.*

Twenty minutes in, and still no change. On the ceiling, I thought I noticed little puffs of steam or fog coming from tiny apertures, but their outlines were indistinct. *Good God, is there a gas leak? And when is the damn yoga flow actually going to start?*

By thirty minutes in, I was taut with exasperation. I wondered if the subtle puffs of vapor coming from the ceiling were meant to be part of the meditation. *Or is this an aromatherapy class?* I never did find out. After fifty minutes of quiet commentary from the instructor alternating with periods of silence, my head flopping right and left on my mat as I tried to peer through pinched eyelids at what was happening around me (which was always nothing), the other women began to stir, sitting up, rolling their mats, nodding thanks to the serenely smiling teacher.

My cheeks burned as I gathered my indoor sneakers and replaced my mat. I imagined the other women trying to discern if I was fluent in Japanese or just hopelessly confused about both the class schedule and what had occurred over the past hour.

"Poor my love!" Toru said, a laugh breaking through his

frown, when I told him that night. He offered to get a copy of the schedule and translate it for me, but I declined. I'd had enough of group activities. I'd just exercise on my own, on the treadmill I knew how to program or the cross-trainer whose controls I'd figured out.

Still, I was hopeful that my world might expand once Toru and I were officially married, or at least that life in Osaka would become more normal. With a spouse visa, I could come and go from Japan as I pleased, not worrying about travel restrictions for tourists. I'd have health insurance through his company and could give up my U.S. coverage to save money. Plus, we'd move into a real apartment, and I might have a place in Osaka that felt like some kind of center.

As part of my increasingly settled half-life in Osaka, I'd begun making a few more friends. I met Jessica, a poet, through a group called the Association of Foreign Wives. I'd known about the organization for a while but had resisted joining: the name sounded disturbingly like the TV show *Desperate Housewives*. Eventually, though, I gave in and signed up, knowing I'd need a community around me if I was ever going to have a quasi-normal life in Japan.

Jessica and her Japanese physician husband lived in Kobe, a twenty-minute train ride from Osaka. She was about my age and had striking red hair, gray-blue eyes, and a round, lovely face. She'd first come to Japan years ago when she'd decided to quit a Ph.D. program at Caltech and, not knowing what else to do, came overseas to teach English. As a kid, she'd grown up in a conservative Mormon family with seven siblings in Pennsylvania, but she had stopped going to church when she married her husband.

Jessica fascinated me: Who gets into a Ph.D. program at Caltech and quits midway? Who starts off as a Mormon and ends up a funky foreign wife in Japan? She had gravitas, I decided, and the integrity to make hard decisions. Plus, she'd gone to high school with a lot of Jewish kids, she'd told me, so she totally got my kvetching.

Like me, Jessica was ambivalent at best about living in Japan. She'd come here for her own reasons, but she'd stayed for her husband. She also felt much more comfortable in the U.S. and struggled with all she'd given up by marrying a Japanese man whose career was not transferable. Moreover, like Toru, Jessica's husband was the eldest son and designated caretaker of a widowed parent.

At lunch one day at a Southeast Asian restaurant in Kobe, Jessica ordered us pho noodle soup from a Japanese waitress in a Vietnamese dress. She spoke quickly, even adding little native-sounding fillers, quick pitter-patters of *"ano"* ("umm") and *"et-to"* ("so . . ."), and her ease with the language made me momentarily wistful.

Bent over our soup, we gossiped about the expat scene, marveling at how different we felt from many of the foreigners we'd met. "Those *gaijin* who dress up in *yukata* robes, or who insist on only speaking Japanese? Like if someone speaks to them in English and they still respond in Japanese?" I rolled my eyes.

"I know!" Jessica shrilled. "As if it's not totally, one hundred percent clear that they are *not* Japanese, as if everyone can't see that they're foreign. Um, hello, you're *white*!"

"The thing that I find most incomprehensible is when people

say they feel more at ease in Japan than in their own countries. I don't get it! How, in *Japan* of all places, can any Westerner feel more at home than in their real home!"

"Especially," Jessica said, leaning forward, "when Japanese people are constantly reacting to you like you're some kind of bizarre alien?"

"Frankly, I really think you've got to be a little screwed up to move halfway around the world and make a home in a country as completely different as Japan," I confided, as if both Jessica and I hadn't ourselves done the same thing.

Then Jessica confided a revelation of her own. She'd read something—she wasn't sure where: an online forum? an expat magazine?—that supposedly could predict perfectly whether a foreign woman would find contentment long-term in Japan. The answer depended on three criteria: "Whether she was unhappy in her own country and came to Japan as an escape," Jessica said, counting the first item off on her forefinger. "Whether she came to Japan for her own reasons, and not for a man," she ticked her middle digit, "and whether she's fluent in Japanese."

Jessica tapped her third finger as she listed the final requirement for, I realized, my own future happiness. The platinum band of her wedding ring caught the afternoon sunlight, and then as she lowered her fingers to her lap and nodded at me with her gray-blue eyes, I felt my chest sinking with her hands. *Strikeout*, I thought as I stared silently back at her, my heart boring into my stomach. *I've failed on all three counts.*

Jessica smiled at me, unaware of the panic her "*gaijin*-girl" quiz had shot through my torso. I didn't bother considering the source of her information, didn't question whether online forums or expat magazines always offered airtight information. Instead, it felt as if my failure of the future-happiness exercise confirmed my own hidden suspicions: *I knew I'd been kidding myself that this whole arrangement could sustain itself. And now I have the test results to prove it.*

WHEN THE END of December presented itself and the day arrived that Toru and I were to file our marriage contract, I woke with a slight sore throat, my skin oversensitive. Toru had taken the day off of work so we could get to the U.S. Consulate during business hours to retrieve and notarize my Affidavit of Competency to Marry. After the consulate, we would file the affidavit at the Osaka Central Ward Office, along with an official copy of Toru's family register and a statement signed by two other witnesses (Tetsunobu-*san* and Michiko-*san*) acknowledging our nuptials. Once we'd filed these, we could fill out our license and have it processed that same day. Signed, stamped, wedded.

But at the door to the consulate, a Japanese guard stopped us. He wore a blue officer's uniform, a gun in a black pouch snug at this side. He held up one hand.

He and Toru spoke in flat-sounding Japanese. Toru paused for a minute, looked down and examined his shoes, then raised his head and addressed the man once more. The guard responded, neutral-toned, disinterested.

Toru turned to me. "Terrible!" he said. "Document section is closed!"

The major New Year holiday wasn't set to begin until two

days later, when offices, stores, and government facilities would shut for a week or so. When we'd double-checked the consulate's website that morning, it said they were open. But the guard now explained that the American staff in the document office had decided to start their holiday early. Toru nodded as he told me this, part emphasis of our misfortune, part confirmation of his countrymen's stereotype about mine: when it comes to Americans' work ethic, these slipups were bound to happen.

We stood on the sidewalk under a bony row of tree limbs and wondered what to do with our day now that we weren't going to get married during it. We'd have to wait until after New Year's before both the consulate and the Osaka Central Ward Office would be open again.

So we grabbed a bowl of hot noodles and went to the movies—some Hollywood blockbuster with Japanese subtitles and too much noise—and tried to enjoy our unexpectedly free day. In the darkened cinema, I shivered, my head feeling thick and cottony. My mood had slipped along with the theater lights as they'd dimmed. I felt weary, overwhelmed, and pricked raw by a realization I couldn't shake: when I'd learned that morning that we couldn't sign our marriage papers, my first feeling was disappointment; my second was relief.

TEN

I WOKE THE NEXT MORNING achy and low. Toru had gotten up earlier, and now he came to the side of our narrow bed and knelt. He stroked my forehead lightly: he'd sensed my anxious mood from my restless shifts throughout the night, tangling the sheets around his tranquil sleep.

We looked at each other silently for a few moments, neither one of us moving. "Poor my love," he muttered.

"I feel low, Tof."

"I know."

"I think. I'm not sure."

Toru's gaze held: direct, steady, waiting.

"I feel kind of freaked out. And yesterday, after the consulate was closed and, and I felt relieved, and now I'm wondering what that means. Or if I can really go through with this."

Toru looked down. Swallowed a moment.

"So you mean," he said, his eyes rising back to mine, "you don't want to marrying now?"

I felt stuck, bog-heavy.

"I don't know," I finally said. "I don't know if I *don't* want to get married. I mean, I do want to marry you. But now I don't know if we should wait, or put it off for a while, or what. I mean, I know we have a week before we can do anything anyway, with the New Year holiday and all."

Toru looked down again, his jaw clenching in tight little pulses.

"So I'm not saying we need to *do* anything, or rather *not do* anything right now because of the holiday." My words came in a rush. "But I just feel like I need to tell you, to be up front, that I'm not a hundred percent positive that next week, when the consulate reopens, I can still go through with this."

He shuddered then, a quiet shaking beneath the usual equipoise of his body, as if it might take all his strength to call that stillness back once more. Then he just exhaled slowly. "Okay," he said finally. "But please just think on it."

For the next few days, indecision plagued me, jabbing me like a bully. It wasn't that I didn't want to marry Toru. I just didn't want to make a decision I was supposed to be sure about forever. I felt trapped, not by Toru, but rather by Japan. Like the country was a prison I could never fully escape if I married someone who called it his home. Our home.

Screwing up my brain, I tried to imagine if I'd ever fall in love with Osaka the way I'd fallen in love with him: the strange rhythms of the city, its rushing crowds and jigsaw buildings, its housewives and same-suited salarymen. Would this ever be a place where I felt at home? I couldn't wrap my heart around the vision. I saw an endless sweep of days with unreadable signs and blank stares, smiles covering or conveying unreadable emotions. Doors with strange shapes printed above their handles. *Is this* PUSH? *Is it* PULL?

I tried next to imagine going back to Boston to build a life without Toru. I envisioned the safe, familiar sidewalks of the South End. Neighbors with broad, easy smiles offering greetings, trading expressions. Yet also a hollow space by my side, an emptiness even more gaping than the vacuum of life as a displaced American in Japan.

Something else nagged at me, too, a realization hidden beneath my struggle over Osaka versus Boston, pushed down even farther within my chest. When I tried to picture Toru moving to the U.S., my anxious indecision wouldn't cease. Not because I couldn't imagine Toru leaving his career, abandoning his father, and still remaining at peace, but because some things *I* most treasured in our relationship were tied to Japan. I loved how confident and *fluent* Toru was in Japan, not just linguistically, but professionally, culturally, logistically. I wanted to believe I was an independent woman, but deep down I wondered if, even more than autonomy, I prized how completely Toru took care of me, especially in his country.

Nothing had ever made me feel as safe and loved as Toru navigating me through an entire world both fascinating and impenetrable. I knew I would love him no matter where we were. I'd already loved him just as fiercely in Boston as I had in Kobe, Beijing, Seoul, or Osaka. But I had to admit: a part of me loved our *relationship* most when we were in Japan. If I was trapped by this country, it was a trap of my own construction.

I didn't know how to solve this conundrum or even if a solution existed. But I knew what scared me most. It wasn't even the dual reality of my desire for independence scraping up against the comfort I found in someone taking care of me; instead, what terrified me was the permanence both Japan and marriage would assume in my life if I became Toru's wife. *If I could just marry him for, like, three years or something. Just make a shorter-term commitment, I think I'd feel less freaked out.*

I thought back to our earlier decision to build a life both together and apart, to have me live in the U.S. and Japan. People said it couldn't, shouldn't be done. But we'd done it anyway. And so far we were happy. Why not make our own rules about marriage then? Why not try our own form? Try marrying on a three-year term?

I wasn't sure Toru would go for it. I didn't want to get divorced, and I was loath to repeat a mistake similar to my parents'. But I was more loath not to give my relationship with Toru the most earnest attempt I could.

I imagined being old and bent, and looking back—if I was lucky enough to survive to such an age—and feeling the deadweight of an avoidable regret. A life whose potential gifts I had shunned. Sometime during the next few days, a realization coalesced: becoming family with Toru was one of those gifts. So was our freedom both to wed and to make our own rules. In my mind, I nodded to that gnarled-handed woman. I was not necessarily prepared, but I was still willing to risk trying marriage, despite my confusion and ambivalence. At least for three years.

When I presented the idea to Toru, he grinned, but to his credit he didn't laugh. He smiled as if my zany mind was one of the things he might love most about me, as if he was thinking, *Who else would suggest, in all seriousness, a three-year marriage— across two continents?* I loved him for that, and even more for what I read in the steadiness of his grin: he felt compassionate about my fear, charmed by my neuroses, and completely unthreatened by either.

. . .

A WEEK LATER, we filed our marriage documents and were handed a paper at the Osaka Central Ward Office declaring us a legal unit. It was now early January 2007. Because we had created our own nuclear entity in Japan, we were required to make a new family register, removing Toru from the one he'd always shared with his parents. Toru showed me the form before he filed it: a white sheet of columns next to long vertical lines of Japanese characters. He pointed to his name and our address (or rather his father's address, which we would list as our main domicile until we signed a lease on our own apartment). Along the bottom edge, in a field resembling one for footnotes, sat a space with letters in *katakana*, the ⌐et reserved for foreign words. The letters looked ⌐es I'd learned to write my own name. ⌐t?" I asked Toru. "Down there?" ⌐!" ⌐am I down there? Why aren't I on the main part ⌐it's our family register? Why aren't I listed as

"You are listed. As wife," he assured me. "But only listed in note field. Listed as wife down there."

Foreigners, Toru explained, were not permitted to appear in the main body of the family register. So although I was now legally Toru's wife, I was also apparently the family footnote.

When a little while later I obtained my official alien registration card (which I was ordered to carry at all times), I was heartened to see my name written prominently in English along with my nationality and place of birth: BOSTON, MASSACHUSETTS. The latter was listed in both fields, as if my nationality extended down to my city and state.

"What's that?" I asked Toru, pointing to some Japanese characters that looked like his name on another part of the card.

"That? That's me."

"And what's that line in Japanese above it, introducing your name? What does that say?"

Toru peered closer at the tiny black font. "Oh that? That say 'master of the house.'"

THE WEEKEND AFTER we married, we went to a hot-springs resort for an impromptu mini honeymoon. We stayed at a *ryokan,* a traditional Japanese inn with lacquer-wood furniture and shoji screens. We slept on soft futons rolled out each night over a floor of straw tatami mats bordered with silk stitching. During the day, we wore thin, patterned *yukata* robes, and in the evening we were served dinner in our room, course after course of tiny elaborate dishes. The only entertainment besides eating and lounging involved *onsen:* dipping into natural thermal waters bubbling up from underground.

Except for rooms with private *onsen* baths—out of our budget—most hot springs in Japan are separated by gender, switching once a day. In the morning, women will use one side and men the other; in the afternoon, they switch. Toru and I chose our *ryokan* because although the baths were single sex, they shared a low wall on one end over which a bather could see the neck and face of someone sitting on the other side. We could soak separately in the steamy water and still see and talk to each other if we perched in just the right place.

Entering an *onsen* is a detailed affair. After taking off your clothes and storing them—usually in little wooden baskets— you enter a shower room lined with individual handheld showerheads, each featuring a little stool and bucket in front of a tray of soaps and scrubs. Then you crouch on one of the tiny seats and scour every bodily plane and crevice. Arms and chest, face and neck, thighs, calves, and torso. In between each toe. Hair and scalp. A surreptitious rinse between the legs.

Not until you are pink with careful scrubbing should you approach the actual *onsen* water, walking naked from the shower room to the thermal pool. At our *ryokan*, a good fifteen or twenty minutes had elapsed between the time Toru and I parted at our separate entrances and when I approached the hot spring on the women's side. I'd dutifully lathered my body with soap, shampoo, and conditioner, then chosen among the different facial exfoliators, or what I figured were such by their varied cartoons of women rubbing circles on their cheeks.

Entering the *onsen* itself, my skin felt rosy. I waded into the shallow pool, the hot water swirling slowly around my legs as I crossed the main expanse, then turned left slightly toward an alcove bordered by the low wall separating the gendered sides. I saw someone already sitting there, his head resting back, a small towel thrown over eyes and forehead, black hair sprouting from its edges. *Toru's already here!* I thought happily.

"Hi, *kakoii!*" I sang out, using one of my nicknames for him, a cross between "handsome" and "cool." He didn't answer, but I smiled hugely as I strode toward the little ledge, snug against the rough stone wall just inches from where he sat. "Was there anyone else in the men's side?" I called out, as I waded forward.

Still, no movement.

He must be so relaxed he can barely move. "I was the only one in the women's!" I didn't bother crouching down to hide my torso in the water: his was the only figure visible.

It wasn't until he removed the washcloth and gave a little scream that I realized, no, this wasn't Toru. It was another Japanese man, his face a mask of shock before the naked white woman striding, mid-conversation, toward him. Taking in the full scene, his jaw dropped even faster than I did, and by the time I had crouched under the waterline, his eyes had widened into horrified saucers.

Like a synchronized swimmer on steroids, in one jerky movement he turned, half stood, and began hurling himself through the water to the exit, the hot spring leaving small tornadoes in his wake. I could still hear his antic swishing when Toru came into view, his head turned back to watch the fleeing bather.

"Huh!" Toru said, as he approached me, turning for one more glance behind him. "Guy is in kind of rush." Then he swiveled fully toward me. "Why're you hiding so low in water?"

WE LEFT THE hot-springs resort the next day, our cheeks scrubbed smooth, limbs heavy, as if the *onsen* had leached all torsion from our bodies. Sitting side-by-side on the express train, watching the landscape rush by in streams of color, I felt a jolt of joy. Toru laid his hand over mine, warm as the water we'd just left. He made me laugh with jokes about the other passengers: a man dozing openmouthed like a soprano in mid aria, a grandmother chatting away while her oblivious husband, head buried in *manga*, emitted strategically timed grunts.

My love for Toru is actually increasing, I thought, now that we'd signed our marriage papers. Such a simple feeling, such a common, unremarkable truth, but to me, it came as an utter surprise: that you could love someone even more after you married him than before you pledged to wed.

Suddenly, the idea of marriage's permanence felt safe, not threatening. *Toru's my partner, and I'm his.* I couldn't believe such a thing had happened to me. It was like having a perpetual buddy in one of those systems from summer camp where they pair you up so someone saves you if you start to drown. I'd always fretted as a child during these assignments: "What if my buddy is drowning, too?" I always asked the counselors, and they never had an answer beyond throwing up their hands or ordering, "Enough already. Just get into the lake."

But I knew Toru. He'd never drown unless human survival was impossible. He'd tread water for as long as it took to figure out a way to save us both. I'd been fortunate enough for the universe to assign him to me. And if luck held, I might even love him more and more, not less and less, now that we'd signed up to either sink or swim together.

Then I realized, as Toru drummed his fingers against my palm and Japan rushed by outside the window, that maybe this wasn't just great odds in a cosmic buddy system but something more basic. Maybe this was what it meant to find a home. Although Osaka would never be my home, it was Toru's, and now, in addition to Boston, he was mine.

ELEVEN

AFTER OUR TRIP to the *onsen*,
I fell into a rare spell of optimism. I was still relieved that my
marriage had begun to represent security (at least so far), not a
slippery slope toward disillusionment. Toru's own approach to
depression and anxiety also soothed me. His attitude diametri-
cally opposed my native family's. For us, depression was considered less a feeling than a dreaded guest whose very existence
caused endless hand-wringing, actual arrival brought intense
agitation, and occasional loitering spawned an all-out expectation of the end times.

Once, soon after we were married and his father's hand had
been shaking again at dinner, Toru seemed down. I peered into
his face. "Are you low, love?" I asked, carefully surveying the
landscape of his cheeks and brow for hollows unduly deep. He
admitted that he was, but then looked confused as I assaulted
him with questions and potential avenues for analysis.

"Low or not low is no matter," he said, when I'd quieted.
"It's just that feelings go up, and then they come down."

I stopped and stared at him a moment, uncharacteristically
speechless. But I kept his perspective wrapped inside, and it felt

like a little shiny pebble of wisdom, all the more brilliant for its simplicity. *Imagine that. Depression could be something you just feel, not something you end up choke-holding yourself with while trying to wrestle it away.* Suddenly, my twenty-plus years of therapy seemed like . . . *a lot?*

I started to focus on happier future plans. Now that we were married, Toru's company would subsidize both our move to a new apartment and half our rent for ten years. We'd claim a place we could call our own, and later in the year, Toru would come to Boston for two weeks, bringing his father, sister, aunt, and uncle to meet my family. These prospects dangled like a perky promise: a fresh sense of completion to my life, a new symmetry to my two worlds.

For our new apartment, Toru and I chose the third place we saw, an eighth-floor unit in an eleven-story building. A plaque carved into faux marble stood just outside the entranceway. In slanted *katakana* letters, it read RUI SHATORE: a Japanese approximation of Louis Châtelet, as if the property were a minor cousin of Versailles. Above the name, the tablet boasted the building's confused monogram, two entwined, cursive *L*s. Around the corner stood an art gallery marked with more English letters. GARRELY, its sign proclaimed.

The apartment was just a few blocks from Osaka Castle Park and about a quarter mile from Tetsunobu-*san*'s. It was listed as a three-bedroom, but the place totaled around six hundred square feet, and one bedroom was so small you couldn't fit a double bed into it, so we decided to use it for laundry and storage. The second bedroom was actually a sweet little tatami room with a shoji screen over the windows so hushed sunlight filtered through and straw mats with pretty stitched borders covered the floor. Toru explained that in traditional Japanese houses, the family would sleep in this room, pulling out their futons every night and during the day storing them in the large sliding-door closets at one end.

Instead, we moved the TV along the wall facing the living/dining room, which had just enough room for a modest-sized table and a two-cushion couch. Over the next couple of months, I bought candles and small Japanese and Chinese paper-covered lamps as well as a yoga mat. Then I claimed the room—when Toru wasn't watching soccer on TV—as my workout/relaxation/excuse-for-buying-knickknacks space.

Purchasing our other household goods, however, was a more challenging affair. We tried to complete most of this task before our move-in date, and I was happy to shop for furniture and sheets, although I sensed some irritation on Toru's part when I kept detouring off into clothing and shoe stores. "I'll be just a sec!" I'd swear, and then Toru would grumble and start tapping out "one, two, three, four" with his foot at the threshold of the shop, as if in useful illustration of my tendency to use a "sec" nonliterally.

When it came to buying dishes, I focused more successfully, at least eventually. At first, I'd been uninterested in acquiring the essentials for home-cooked meals. But then Toru's father took most of his own dishes out of his listing kitchen cupboards, lining them up neatly on his small table, leaving only a lonely single set for himself. "Otōsan!" I said. Now that Toru and I were married, I'd begun calling his father by the Japanese term "Respected Father" rather than his proper name, as tradition dictated for a daughter-in-law. Tetsunobu-*san* had told me I could call him whatever was most comfortable for me, but when I proclaimed I'd call him Otōsan, he smiled really wide.

Now, as he took his dishes out for us to have, my voice caught in my throat. *He thinks Toru and I won't be coming over for dinner anymore; that now that his son is officially moving out, he'll be left alone.* "Otōsan," I said again, "you can't give these dishes away!" I tried to explain that we would still be coming over a few nights a week for dinner, that I'd still cook and we'd eat together. But I felt my heart squeeze with sadness. This man had never lived alone in all his sixty-seven years. He had lost his wife recently, and now he'd simply laid out his housewares for us to take as his son left, too.

"Ah, but you may need!" he insisted, gesturing to the bowls he'd stacked for us, his hand shaking in a slight quiver. It would be another year or so before the tremors got much worse.

"Oh, no, we're fine," I insisted. "We're buying new dishes, and in the meantime, we'll just eat here with you." I searched his face to see if he understood. I'd begun putting the dishes back into the cabinets when Toru walked into the kitchen from his old bedroom, where he'd been packing clothes. "Tof!" I turned to him. "Your father is trying to give us his dishes! Can you please explain that he still needs them, that we won't stop coming here for dinner altogether?"

Toru spoke to his father, a quick string of sentences that sounded edged by irritation, and Otōsan simply grunted. I couldn't tell whether Toru was annoyed because he thought his father was being dramatic or impractical, or if his own guilt was feeding his agitation. I paused, thinking I'd ask him later, then cautioned myself not to indulge in my tendency to probe painful places in search of understanding when I knew Toru found more safety in silence. Disappointed to realize I'd probably never get a full translation of what had just transpired, I picked up another small pile of plates to return to their rightful cupboards and began planning time to buy at least three sets of dishes.

Within a few days of our move, we still hadn't finished purchasing our appliances: washing machine, dryer, air-conditioning units, vacuum cleaner, microwave, and toaster (our only means of cooking besides the stove and tiny fish grill since, like Otōsan's apartment, ours came without an oven). The first hint of trouble arose with the vacuum cleaner.

"Let's just buy a cheapo one," I'd said a few weeks earlier. We were in the Midori Denki—Green Electronics—superstore, where we passed a salaryman in a suit and an overcoat reading a book while he bucked up and down on a sample mechanical bull. "Tof," I said, straining to block out the weirdness of the suit in the fake saddle, "I really hate vacuuming, and besides, we can hire a housekeeper to come in once a month or something to do the heavy cleaning."

"Housekeeper?"

"Yeah, a housekeeper, you know, like a cleaning person or a maid service. What I have in Boston. They come in once a month and it's great, only about fifty dollars to clean my whole studio."

"No, we don't have this in Japan. Too expensive. Only very rich people has maid."

"Well, how expensive could it be, just for once a month? Like more than a hundred dollars an hour?"

"More." Toru's rapid nod left no room for doubt. "Anyway,

I don't like housekeeper. Don't want to having someone in house. Someone not family. Someone strange."

"Seriously?" Then, my voice going flatter, "Seriously, Tof, I really hate vacuuming."

"Not so bad. We'll do together. It's kind of what adults does, keeping own house clean." He leveled his stare at me, raised his eyebrows slightly.

On one hand, I figured he was right: if I was old enough to have my own place, I should be mature enough to handle occasional vacuuming. I wasn't surprised that Japanese people avoided housekeepers, since privacy was so important here. On the other hand, I was still thinking that this was an argument we could save for later. *So we buy a vacuum. That doesn't mean we can't also hire a housekeeper sometime.*

I couldn't help sniping a bit, though, when, after much research, Toru picked out a brand costing thirty thousand yen. "Three hundred dollars, for a *vacuum*?" I still noted everything in dollars, just lopping off the last two zeros of yen, even though the exchange rate didn't always line up neatly—just one more way to pretend I was still shopping in the U.S. "That could buy almost a quarter of a year of monthly housekeeping service," I said, sulking.

"Okay, but what about after quarter year? We'll still need to clean house then!"

I had to concede he had a point.

As for our washing machine, microwave, air conditioner, and other large appliances, Toru approached these purchases with similar gravity. He spent a startling amount of time on his computer with an Excel file, listing each big expenditure and the different prices offered at every major store and Web vendor. He'd check and recheck the list with each new shop we visited or place he researched online, then recombine and recalculate the items according to different sales, purchase packages, delivery charges, and "frequent-shopper-point" offerings. He even color-coded the thing according to some obscure schematic.

His enthusiasm for his Excel file caused me both vague annoyance and grudging respect for his thriftiness. *If he wants to spend hours in deep communion with his color-coded appliance list, what's it to me?* But the copious amount of time he wanted to devote over a series of weekends dragging me through actual appliance stores: a different matter altogether.

For one, Japan is an incredibly crowded country, especially in its main cities. Although strangers rarely touch or make eye contact, navigating the sheer human onslaught of weekend shoppers was grueling. Moreover, although the big electronics and appliance vendors differed in their names, branding styles, and marketing strategies—all of which I was sure was thoroughly accounted for in Toru's color-coded list—their stores all shared one distressing tendency: nonstop noise over diabolically loud sound systems. Since I'd arrived in Osaka, I'd been unnerved by the platform-shoed, miniskirted young girls standing outside hipster clothing shops, yelling at inhumanly high frequencies *"Irasshaimase!"* "Welcome!" But now in these mammoth appliance places, I was flat-out alarmed by the sound system backdrop. Blaring musical interludes alternated with rapid-fire announcements in Japanese, Chinese, Korean, and a clipped British English. Salespeople dressed as wobbly-headed cartoon characters clutched megaphones and hollered about special deals. Adolescent women in white polyester minidresses and shiny go-go boots stood on carpeted blocks holding model cell phones and screeching about, I assumed, their latest dialing plans. The effect was like fingernails down a blackboard—in IMAX surround sound.

Then, as if the cacophony was not bad enough, Toru wanted to spend hours in the actual presence of every available appliance model, taking notes, pulling out his tape measure, double-checking the little pad of paper where he had carefully recorded the dimensions of each bathroom corner or kitchen counter. "Um, love," I tried, "it's great that you are being so conscientious about stuff for our new apartment, but why don't we just pick the store with the best general prices and buy everything there all at once?"

He scoffed at my woeful lack of strategy. Next, I tried pointing out that if I was to add up all the time we were spending comparing appliances and instead devote that time to working, I'd probably earn more as a freelancer billing hourly than we'd save through his complicated purchasing plan. But Toru remained impervious to my logic.

I managed to tamp down my growing frustration and keep my voice mostly even until he steered us toward our fourth appliance place in one day, our second visit that weekend to a superstore called Yodobashi Camera. "Tof," I said, my tone creeping higher as he ushered me through the electric doors, shoppers whipping past, a raucous Muzak version of "The Battle Hymn of the Republic" torturing the air around us. "You. Are. Kidding me." Then, hysteria on the horizon, my voice pitched higher still: "*Again* with Yodobashi Camera? *Seriously?*"

Toru turned to me. He grabbed my hand, stopped, and searched my face as if gauging the likelihood of spousal meltdown. Then he gave one of his definitive nods, stroked the wedge between my thumb and forefinger, and prodded me toward the escalator. I followed dumbly, wallowing in private misery.

Silently, when we had gone a few floors up, Toru turned the corner and led me to a theater of model massage chairs. The gaudy faux-leather recliners were displayed in long rows and tipped back at various angles. Some had matching foot massagers at their base, and many had capped retirees or suited salarymen in full repose, eyes closed, mouths thrown open, ties aslant, a few emitting little bleeps of slumber.

"Sit," Toru said. I obeyed.

He picked up the control console attached to my chair and pressed a series of keys. Then he motioned for me to lie back, and I swung my legs up along the smooth Naugahyde cushioning, trying not to think about how often these sample recliners got wiped down. "Okay," he said, leaning over me. "I program chair for thirty minutes. Stay here. Don't move."

A half hour later, I was floating in semisleep: drowsy, soothed, and feeling such renewed respect for my husband's striking wisdom that even "The Battle Hymn of the Republic" failed to rile me. When Toru returned, he held a receipt for all our new appliances, bought in bulk and bargained down to the best available rate.

A FEW DAYS LATER, we moved into our apartment. It was tiny, ovenless, and big enough only for a washing machine without a separate dryer, with a kitchen sink—made for a Japanese-sized woman—so low I had to bend over it. But it was ours.

I toured our neighborhood looking for a new favorite café, settling on a Starbucks just two blocks away when I couldn't find a unique alternative. There was something appealing about sitting at the table I claimed for my regular perch just inside the wall-length windows, the display shelves full of mugs and thermoses with the American Starbucks logo and a swish of Japanese text below. The staff wore Starbucks aprons but they bowed when you entered and again when you left. The menu had familiar pictures but the descriptions were in Japanese, and some of the items were unique to Japan: cherry-blossom cookies, roasted-tea lattes. When I ordered a soy cappuccino, the cashier handed me a card to give to the barista in exchange for my drink. Under a line in Japanese, it said in English, WE SINCERELY SERVE OUR SOYMILK BEVERAGES TO OUR CUSTOMERS BY USING THIS CARD TO PREVENT MILK ALLERGY INCIDENT.

The entire scene felt like my quirky bicontinental life in miniature. I was still nervous about how I'd afford my rent at home if I ran dry on subletters, whether I'd have enough energy to maintain two lives in two hemispheres. But at least now I had an official address in two places. Maybe a real sense of rootedness in both would follow.

4.

T
H
E

R
E
I
N
T
E
G
R
A
T
I
O
N

S
T
A
G
E

The third stage is both the beginning of recovery . . . and also the most volatile stage in the culture shock process. . . . It is ironic that persons in the early reintegration stage will display a strong rejection of the host culture . . . [and] will perceive herself or himself to be vulnerable or under attack.

• Paul Pedersen, *The Five Stages of Culture Shock*

No one loves Japan, my dear.

• Donald Richie, long-term American expat and distinguished Tokyo author

TWELVE

FOR MUCH OF THE WINTER
and spring of 2007, I felt suspended in limbo. On one hand, I welcomed the easy harmony Toru and I shared, the relaxed pace of my life in Japan. On the other, I'd go through periods where I'd obsess again over how I could have ended up in a lifestyle and identity I could barely recognize. The memory of Jessica's quiz about foreign women's longevity in Japan kept shuffling behind my eyes. My U.S. freelance writing work had winnowed to part-time, and it was hard to drum up new business from across the globe. My conscience sometimes prickled as I thought about my official Japanese bank account and health insurance papers listing me as *shufu*, since I kept what little money I now earned in my Boston bank account and contributed no income to our Osaka household.

One day from my Starbucks roost, I put down my *International Herald Tribune*, pushed back my soy latte, and tried objectively to evaluate my regrets. When you live overseas, it becomes easy to mythologize your native life: all the things you imagine you'd be doing if you weren't an expat in a foreign land, all the ways you could be thriving. Maybe I'd have a tenure-track job as a literature professor in an English department, not a half-year lectureship teaching communication strategy to MBA students supplemented by some freelance writing gigs. Maybe I'd be making a name for myself in the prison education world, coauthoring a book with a gifted inmate.

A hazy fantasy filled my mind of my work making such a splash it moved Congress to fund more college-behind-bars programs. I'd yet to fill in the details, but it sounded fantastic in my head. My coauthor would secure a promising job waiting for him upon his release; I'd give quick but eloquent interviews tastefully plugging the book while lauding some new study proving college education in prisons reduces recidivism—and, of course, my outfit would be perfect.

But the truth was, I'd had basically the same amount of anxiety, longing, and regret in my "real" American life as I did in Japan. Boston, after all, was where I'd given up trying to get a tenure-track job. My South End apartment was where I'd spent semesters wondering if teaching gender studies to men behind bars really made a difference, or if it was mostly just a way to assuage my guilt about my own easy access to education while providing a convenient ruse for my students to rack up points for good behavior. At home, I'd brooded over whether I should be making more money, succeeding more spectacularly, dressing better. There were lots of times when I'd felt alienated, discouraged, or like I didn't quite fit in. *It's called being human,* I suddenly thought, *not necessarily a human overseas.*

You make sacrifices and admit failures no matter where you live; but for expats, sometimes it's too easy to believe the grass was actually greener on the side you'd already left. In your new country, feelings of longing and regret magnify easily, but are they really just falsely sharpened by the occasional isolation of being a foreigner? From the other side of the world, it becomes all too easy to let slip your gimlet-eyed view of home.

Now, in the Osaka Starbucks, Johnny Cash's song "Ring of Fire" began playing over the café's sound system. "I went down, down, down and the flames went higher," Cash crooned, while the kilted Japanese schoolgirl next to me slumped over, asleep atop her table, head bent until her forehead rested next to her half-full mug of coffee, sequined cell phone glittering beside her. As my mind tried to parse my own two contrasting worlds of fantasies and disappointments, I thought, *Sure, my life in Boston was easier: no getting around that. But was ease my ultimate goal?*

I pulled a spiral notebook out of my bag and began making a list of What I Really Wanted in Life. Some kind of lasting, familylike bond or bonds. An existence where I wasn't unduly suffering or lonely, with close friends who mattered. Fulfilling work. Time to read and travel, to exercise and stay healthy. Enough money to eat out a few times a week and buy sweaters at the Gap. The chance always to be learning, never losing my curiosity about the world. Great shoes.

So, yes, ease would be nice. But was it most important? Wasn't a life of wonder more rare than one of comfort? Surely, meaning held more value than simple convenience—or even happiness.

Could I really claim Osaka was stopping me from achieving my most cherished goals? I wasn't getting anywhere anguishing over how much my current setup looked—or didn't look—like the existence I'd always imagined. Instead, it was time to figure out how to make my actual life into the best one possible.

I started in on specific objectives: Check out more of the

expat literary scene in Japan. Try writing for some of the English-language magazines and newspapers. Run some Four Stories events in Tokyo. Accept that life as an expat was going to be uncomfortable and alienating at times and then accept that this didn't make it wrong—or even necessarily worse.

The Starbucks soundtrack changed to a Bob Dylan song I didn't know, but I recognized the voice, its raspy twang a smoky contrast to the sharp shapes of the *kanji, hiragana,* and *katakana* letters on the café signboards around me. I committed to one final plan: despite my dismal track record with the YWCA language classes, it was time to sign up for another semester of Japanese.

THE MOVE to our new apartment behind us, our kitchen shelves stocked with basic pots, plates, and cutlery, I started cooking three nights a week for Toru and Otōsan at our place. I made pastas, grilled fish or small steaks on the fish grill, or served dishes I could cook in a wok, looking up recipes online. Otōsan would come over at eight, always neatly dressed, in cooler weather wearing a sweater vest or cardigan, his graying hair tidily combed. If Toru wasn't home from work yet, I'd pour his father a beer and turn on the Japanese news. Sometimes, Toru would text saying he'd be later than nine and we should start without him.

Otōsan didn't talk much, a man whose disdain of waste encompassed unnecessary conversation. Even when Toru had dinner with us, the two of them ate mostly in silence, his father approaching each dish separately, finishing his meat or pasta before he'd move on to the salad or vegetables. Toru ate with more energy, his cheeks puffing out as he chewed. If either of them wanted more beer or something from the refrigerator, I got up to pour or fetch it, and sometimes for a moment, I'd think of Toru's aunt and how, when she made dinner for us at her house, she served while everyone else just sat and ate.

Occasionally, Toru would say something in Japanese to his father, who would grunt in assent or acknowledgment. But after he finished everything on his plate, Otōsan always smiled and said, *"Gochisōsamadeshita,"* to me: "Thank you for the good meal." Then he'd sit back in his chair and wait calmly for Toru to finish and me to serve green tea. If I'd actually managed to avoid overcooking the cashew chicken or burning the steak, his eyes would light up and he'd flash me a grin that fell somewhere between surprise and delight. *"Mmm, tori-niku wa umai!"* "The chicken is tasty!"

Sometimes the stoicism between Toru and his father was too much for me to bear, and I piped up with conversation. "Otōsan, I'm thinking of making a new fish dish next time," I offered, showing him a recipe I'd printed out. "Do you like salmon?"

"Of course!" Otōsan nodded. After a few times of his replying "Of course!" to food-related questions, I realized he was using the phrase to mean "Yes, very much."

I knew it was rude for Americans in Japan to broach the topic of World War II, but I was curious about Otōsan's experience as a young boy then, and I asked Toru if he thought his father would mind my queries. "Probably okay," Toru said.

So sometimes at dinner, I asked Otōsan directly about that era, or other times it would come up in a roundabout way.

"Otōsan," I said one night, "did you have ice cream in Japan when you were little?" He told me he hadn't really tried ice cream until he was almost a teenager, although the war had ended when he was just six, because food was so scarce for many years after the armistice. "Really?" I said. I hadn't realized that the food shortages had lasted so long or would have affected families with sufficient money. But Otōsan explained that money wasn't the issue: there was no food to buy.

"How about chewing gum?" I asked, and he told me how the first time he'd tried gum, he'd been given it by an American soldier handing out candy on a train. I tried to call up the image: a khaki-suited late adolescent, colored pins on his lapel, light brown hair waved to the side, his capped head inches higher than the car full of wary passengers around him, his fist full of pink Bazooka bubble gum. "Did you like it?" I finally asked.

"Of course!"

When I inquired if his family and neighbors felt weird or threatened by the presence of American soldiers, Otōsan told me that, really, people were just relieved the war was over.

After Toru finally finished his food, I cleared the dishes, stacked them by the sink to wash later, and boiled water for tea. The men sat at the table, silence alternating with brief staccato comments or more soft grunting, neither of which I could decipher, and then I brought the cast-iron pot full of *sencha* and poured them each a cup. When Otōsan had finished his tea, he carefully pushed back his chair with a "*Sore, jaa,*" "Well, then," and finally another "*Gochisō sama deshita,*" inclining his head to me.

We both walked his father to the door, where he steadied himself and slipped into his shoes waiting in the foyer, a black pair of those thick-soled loafers designed for senior citizens. In my new semester at the YWCA, I'd just started learning *keigo*, the most formal set of honorifics, and now I tried to bid him farewell in proper fashion befitting a daughter-in-law. *"Itte kudasatte arigato!"* I called out, bowing palm to thigh. Otōsan stopped mid-turn toward the door, Toru shooting me a wide-eyed look. Then his father let burst a toothy laugh, his smile spanning rosy cheeks.

"What?" I asked, pivoting to face Toru. "What did I do? I tried to say, 'Thank you very much for honoring us by coming!' You know, '*Itte kudasatte arigato!*'"

"'*Kite kudasatte*' is 'You've honored us by coming,'" Toru said slowly. "'*Itte kudasatte*' is 'You honor us by leaving.'"

My brother called on Skype later that night while I was washing the dishes. It was early morning on the East Coast, and he was driving to work at the hospital, his voice sounding muffled, the noise of the highway throbbing in the background. "Well, I just served dinner and tea, and now I'm washing the dishes," I said, the cord of my headset wobbling as I bent over the sink. "No dishwasher. It sucks. Or I guess the dishwasher is me, the good Japanese wife," I quipped.

"What's Toru doing?" Scott asked.

"He's watching TV. He offered to help clean up once his father left. When his father is here, though, they sit at the table and I serve."

"Huh."

"I don't really mind, actually. Strange as that sounds. I feel like it's just something I do a few times a week out of respect to Toru's father. Like it's his culture, so this is what I do to respect him in it."

"Yeah . . . ," my brother said. "I don't really see you hopping up and serving and doing the dishes all by yourself for some American guy. But still." He paused. "It doesn't bother you? *You?* To assume such a traditional role?"

"That's just it," I admitted, trying to arrange more neatly the items I had already washed, now piled at haphazard angles in the drying rack. "It feels almost like an act, just a role I'm *playing*. Like this isn't my culture, it's just something I pretend at."

"But it *is* your *family*, right?"

I couldn't explain it to my brother, nor to myself for that matter. But Japan remained so opaque to me, its rhythms and customs so different that playing a traditional "housewife" role here felt unthreatening. Especially since I still had access to a whole other half of my life—the American half—that bore no resemblance to my identity in Osaka.

"Well," my brother grumbled before he got off the phone, "I just don't get it." Then he repeated, "I just don't see you jumping up and serving some American dude."

"Neither do I," I admitted.

But after we hung up, I wasn't sure what I had told Scott was entirely true, at least not anymore. Ending up in a life with Toru that seemed so . . . so *retro*, where he gave me money because I couldn't communicate with bank tellers, where he handled all the logistics of our existence while I played housewife, had made me reconsider what it meant to be independent. Sometimes, I was learning, what mattered most wasn't the category of our roles, or even the limitations we confront and the sacrifices we make, but whether we've chosen these roles or sacrifices and have some way to shape them ourselves, whether we've been given alternatives and still found a way to make the more traditional scenario fit us. Instead of always needing to be a completely autonomous woman in total control, maybe I could even be a housewife, at least part-time—as long as I chose that existence and could mold it as my own. As long as I could find a way out if I needed one.

Later, my stepsister called. I replayed the night's events for her. "Who *are* you?" she asked, laughing.

By the time I organized my first Four Stories event in Tokyo, I'd started believing that I could build a worthwhile life—even one I could be proud of—that didn't perfectly mimic my long-held image of success. But I was still troubled by that malingering question, *When will I fall in love with Japan the way I've fallen in love with Toru?* After all, I loved Boston. Wouldn't I need to love Osaka before I could finally let go of my regrets about the faraway life I'd chosen?

Sitting on the bullet train to Tokyo, I was surrounded by salarymen eating bento lunch boxes, while outside my window, Osaka streamed into Kyoto, then Maibara, then Nagoya, our pace thrilling as we sliced through landscapes blurred with speed. Electric poles along the track morphed into solid streams of white against green rice paddies spread like shagged quilts.

I thought about one flip side of expat life: how easy it could be to impact Japan's small foreign scene. After one of my first Four Stories a few months earlier in Osaka, the *Japan Times*, the country's largest English newspaper, ran a piece about the series on the front page of their national section. The editor, an Osaka-based American married to a Japanese woman, had been easy to contact and kindly receptive to stopping by one of the events, and a few months later, he agreed to be one of my future readers. For the Tokyo evening, I'd been contacted by an editor at another major English paper, the *Daily Yomiuri*.

The authors I'd found for the Tokyo event tended to publish with smaller, more regional presses than many of the writers at Four Stories Boston. But they were just as gracious and eager, in some ways more so because nothing like Four Stories existed in East Asia. They were also more distinctive because Japan had so few authors publishing in English. As a foreigner here, it wasn't unusual to track down another expat and just e-mail him or her (whereas in the U.S., it could seem a bit *off* just to e-mail one of the country's most widely published writers and ask if they'd like to read, for free, at your local literary event). Frequently, you found friends in common.

In Tokyo, I was staying with my new friend Ariel, another American writer who was married to a Japanese dentist. I'd met her through the foreign-wife grapevine, easy to navigate, especially compared to the much larger community of white men married to local women. Ariel had long blond hair—mussed and a little wild—and an offbeat fashion sense. She reminded me of Botticelli's Venus emerging from a shell in frayed jeans and cowboy boots. Like I did, she made a living as a freelance writer and editor, although she worked on textbooks for English as a foreign language. Ariel took to the expatriate life more easily than I, had sought it out when she went to South Africa for graduate school, but she was liberal and funny, funky and kind, and like Jodi and Jessica, a woman with whom I knew I could build a lasting friendship.

My other new friend, Leza—a Jewish vegetarian from Berkeley, married to a Japanese man, and the owner of a Tokyo-based yoga studio—was going to read at the event. She had published a number of books through small independent co-ops and presses, and had won a translation grant from the National Endowment for the Arts. She'd also been the longtime editor of author and film critic Donald Richie. He wasn't well-known outside of the circle of East Asian scholars, but he presided over the Japanophile literary and academic scene like Oscar Wilde, Michel Foucault, and Lafcadio Hearn rolled into one. Leza had convinced Richie to read along with her at Four Stories Tokyo opening night.

Leza also introduced me to the venue I'd found, called the Pink Cow. The restaurant was popular with the Western expat crowd and owned by a Californian, named Traci. She'd been in Japan for decades, and her hair was even longer, blonder, and more tousled than Ariel's. Traci bopped from the bar to the restaurant floor throughout the event, passing out drinks, flinging Japanese here, English there, like a boisterous bilingual surfer girl who had washed up in downtown Tokyo. That night, I read something I'd researched and written about a prison reform activist from America named Stephen Donaldson, who in the 1970s was the first man raped in a U.S. prison to speak publicly about sexual violence among male inmates. It was edgy, but it apparently appealed deeply to Traci, who every once in a while during breaks in the readings would scream across the floor to me, "Oh, my gaaad! I feel like we are sisters! Like spiritual sisters or something! With the same name!" Sometimes she followed up with a bear hug.

The crowd in Tokyo was, not surprisingly, smaller than the

ones in Boston, but opening night drew about sixty people, and I was pleased. Among both the attendees and readers, Donald Richie fascinated me most. He was in his early eighties, and he wore a dark suit and round black-rimmed glasses and had thinning gray hair whose wisps strained to escape a light pomading of his head. He read a passage from his classic travel book *The Inland Sea,* contrasting Japan and the West. When Richie smiled, he revealed a line of slightly crooked teeth. Altogether, he emitted an air both erudite and mischievous.

Richie had arrived in Japan as part of the U.S. occupation forces after the war, and except for brief trips back to the U.S., he'd never really left. I couldn't get over that he'd lived here for more than half a century. *He must really love the place,* I thought.

After the readings, when we were mingling and drinking, I put my burning question to him. "When did you actually start to love Japan?" I waited a beat, then said, "I mean, how long did it take after you arrived to really feel like you fell *in love* with the country?"

"My dear," Richie drawled, looking down at me from behind his owlish glasses, "*no one* loves Japan." He threw his arm out as if for dramatic effect. "It's just that the country is so endlessly *fascinating. That* is why we stay." His voice sounded gravelly and grand, like an Oxford don addressing a toddler.

I felt the shock of one who has spent hours searching for an object, only to realize she was holding it in her pocket the entire time. *No one loves Japan!* His words upticked gleefully in my head. Riding back to Osaka the next day on the bullet train, I continued to turn Richie's proclamation over in my mind. Mount Fuji peaked in the distance on the right, white-capped, immortal. Nagoya, Maibara, Kyoto. The country no longer felt so insurmountable, and relief rushed through me as the ground outside flew by. I may never love Japan, just as I had always expected— and feared. But, apparently, I didn't need to.

I RETURNED HOME for the fall. In October, Toru came to Boston for two weeks, bringing with him his father, Michiko-*san*, Hamatani-*san*, Kei, and her husband. Our families together, we provided my mother with her first chance to find her own unfettered joy in my marriage to a Japanese man: we agreed to have a wedding blessing at Temple Israel, complete with a bimah (a raised platform where the Torah is read), a chuppah (the makeshift structure under which a betrothed Jewish couple stands), and Rabbi Friedman.

Temple Israel was Reformed, the most liberal strain of Judaism, and Rabbi Friedman was known to perform weddings for gay couples, rendering moot one of my main objections to the whole Judeo-Christian tradition, its homophobia. Besides the religions' historical intolerance of homosexuality, I also disdained both their bibles' attitudes toward women. But I'd already wed a man in whose language "husband"—*shujin*—technically meant "master," so now was no time to take a symbolic stand on gender in the Old Testament.

In preparation for Toru's presentation at the temple, that summer, while we were still in Osaka, my mother had mailed him a collection of books. One was titled *What Is a Jew?* while another covered "four thousand years of Jewish history" and spanned almost six-hundred-fifty pages. Opening the box she'd sent, we found one of her yellow sticky notes embossed at the top with her usual monogrammed script, now bearing her name from her second marriage, FROM THE DESK OF CHARLOTTE ROSEN, and below that, a large smiley face she'd penned along with an encouraging "Enjoy!" Although her enthusiasm was sweet, neither one of us could help snickering over the title of the first book. Then we took the whole stack and stuffed it at the back of a bookshelf.

Before he even got to Boston, though, Toru charmed my mother by saying he wanted to wear a yarmulke ("one of those little Jewish hats") at the temple. Privately, he joked to me that he was planning on perching it sideways in homage to a rapper's cap, but my mother thrilled to his choice of headgear. "You know," she said to me later, after I'd arrived home in mid-August, her voice hushed with gravity, "he's doing this out of respect to me." Then she nodded, her blond hairdo dipping in her own apparent homage to Toru's Confucian values.

That fall in Boston felt golden. I decided not to teach at the prison, and I scheduled all my half-semester MBA writing seminars for the two months before Toru and his family would arrive. Otherwise, I spent the semester on some small freelance projects.

Back in my South End studio, I hung up copies of old pictures I had found at Otōsan's apartment along with more recent photos: Toru as a baby in his kimono-clad grandfather's arms, the garden in the background faded around the edges from age; a series of before-and-after snapshots Toru and I had taken on the winter day we were legally married at the Osaka Central Ward Office, our cheeks stung with cold, me in a white faux-fur hat, Toru in a knit ski cap, in the last picture his mouth open and eyes widened in mock horror; some old photos of Toru and his sister as toddlers at the beach, Kei's little red bikini askew, Toru's chest puffed out in older-brother pride. His mother was beautiful in her sunglasses, his father standing in the water with a touch of Elvis Presley in the dark sweep of his hair.

At home, I'd sit in bed leisurely reading a novel or *Vogue* or watching TV, newly enamored of *Gossip Girl* and *Criminal Minds*, and then I'd turn my head and see the pictures of Toru and his family, the roots of my Osaka life, and I felt full. Toru and I talked on our usual three-times-a-day schedule. Although frequently the conversations involved lists of what he'd eaten for lunch or dinner, our brief connections built a structure of intimacy around my independent Boston existence. I wondered sometimes whether I should be more worried about the banality of these discussions, whether their lack of intellectual banter meant something serious, but then I'd tuck these thoughts away behind the warmth I felt at knowing for certain that my solitary days would always be enclosed by the reliability of his three calls.

I spent nonteaching days at various cafés in Central Square, sipping spicy chai or peppermint tea and reading the *New York Times*, then grading assignments, the leaves turning yellow along Mass Ave. At night I'd go out to dinner with friends: my favorite linguini with Seth and Robert at the Franklin Café, garlicky grilled chicken salad with lime-cilantro dressing at the Miracle of Science with Jenna and Megan or Stacey, all the foods and people I missed in Japan.

On Saturdays, I'd make no plans and spend the day shopping or just walking along Newbury Street, a geography I knew perfectly. International students from nearby colleges milled around me wearing designer clothes, hopping out of sports cars, calling to one another from their early alfresco cocktail hours on restaurant terraces. Tourists loitered near sidewalk vendors with bad hair selling art. Teenagers in cutoffs and flip-flops walked and squawked on cell phones. We were all languid, unhurried under a crisp blue sky, watching one another lazily as the sun bounced off smooth store windows. I wandered in and out of boutiques, picking up knickknacks or clothing I knew would fit, turning each item over in my hands while I listened to the voices around me: the novelty of conversations I could understand completely.

At Crate and Barrel, I found ceramic rice bowls in the Asian food and cookbook section. They were slightly larger than traditional Japanese ones and embossed in a modern black-and-white cherry-blossom pattern. I brought four to the register and asked the twenty-something clerk to wrap them carefully. "I live overseas and need to take these back in my luggage," I explained.

"Cool, where?"

"Oh, in Japan, actually. My husband is from there."

"Oh, wow, cool!" the clerk enthused, and I felt proud and more smug than I knew was seemly with my veneer of multiculturalism.

THE WEEK BEFORE Toru arrived, I turned forty. My mother and stepfather took me out to dinner at an expensive restaurant in Back Bay with perfectly al dente pasta, a wine list I couldn't read, and paper-thin filets of veal. In no uncertain terms, my mother warned me that my idea of wearing a black dress to the wedding blessing was "unacceptable."

"But I always wear black when I dress up. And besides, this

isn't like a traditional wedding. And I am *not* wearing a white gown." I staked my claim. "Toru and I can't afford some expensive dress; that's just not how we live," I admonished, signaling to the waiter for another fifteen-dollar glass of malbec. "Plus, white's the color they wear to funerals in Japan." I had no idea whether this was still true, though I knew they used to wear white at traditional Shinto funerals. But I also knew my mother would have to back down at the threat of a cultural faux pas. (Eventually, I'd learn that most people in Japan wear black or dark colors to funerals today, just like we do.)

A few days later, my mother took me shopping at Saks. Despite my snarkiness about the wedding industry, my mother seemed happy at the prospect of shopping for a dress with her daughter, her smile regal, her eyes rolling along with the saleswoman's, all of which secretly I found touching. We finally both agreed on a little knee-length cream-colored cocktail dress with a black border cinching the waist, marked down to one hundred fifty dollars, so I could still maintain my opposition to the commercial rip-off of contemporary nuptial rituals.

I'd also been playing phone tag with my sister Lauren, which quickly devolved into a battle, waged over voice mail, about who was failing to call whom back in a timely manner. "Are you coming to the wedding blessing or not?" I said in a huff on her recording. "I really need to know soon, because we have reservations for dinner at L'Espalier afterward."

When we finally reached each other, we argued some more, rehashing a variation of the same fight we always had. Something was said about her not getting my voice mails and why I hadn't just called back. Something else was said about her never, *ever* returning calls like a *normal* person. A surprising amount of energy was expended, on both ends, about the likelihood of Sprint's voice mail system failing as well as the exact definition of the word "soon."

"Okay," Lauren eventually said, the word floating through the night on a little jet stream of agitation, "I agree to take fifty percent culpability for the misunderstanding. . . . But now," she added levelly, "I want you to take—to make very clear that you take—at least fifty percent culpability, too."

"Well, I take some responsibility, but fifty percent, no. Maybe forty percent. *Maybe* forty-five," I counteroffered.

"That's not good enough. I want it understood—I want it very clearly agreed upon—that this is not my fault. I refuse to have this go down in the family narrative as one more time I screwed up." Then for good measure, she added again, "I refuse that."

"Well, I refuse to be lumped in with the rest of the family. This is between you and me," I added, feeling pleased at the simple calculus of my rejoinder, "and I don't believe, if we're going to define it precisely, that your stance is as logical, as reasonable, as mine."

Then I stopped. Replaying my words in my head, I realized why we always rehashed this argument: it was how we bonded. We listened to ourselves fight, secretly claiming points for the elegance of our barbs. As sisters from opposite ends of the family spectrum, never mind children of first- and second-generation Americans who strived to belong by attaining advanced degrees, we'd loved each other largely through the struggle to make meaning. What we really longed for was to reach precise designations upon which we could all agree. And because this had always been a losing battle, and because we knew this but couldn't stop trying to deny its inevitability, we fought all the more furiously.

I knew then that underneath our traded recriminations were the real questions we'd never ask or even understand. About how I ended up my mother's favorite and Lauren the child shunned, or why parents sometimes choose so clearly among their children. About how Lauren had gone to live with another family, and how any of us could have let her. About why I hadn't done a better job protecting her when we'd all lived together, and how she could have expected such a thing from me, terrified and not yet ten. And about why there was always some damn Holocaust movie looping in the background anyway.

As Lauren and I hung up the phone in mutual frustration, my bond with Toru started to make better sense, too. Although our relationship frequently skirted the verbal and our life in Japan left me stranded both linguistically and geographically, I'd found solace in a world that expected no eloquence from me.

The next morning I called Toru, who was packing for Boston. I complained about my fight with Lauren, telling him I was reluctantly going to meet her for breakfast.

"I'm still annoyed at her." I sulked.

"You know, this is okay," he said. The rhythm of his syllables rose and fell with his accent. "Just remember to be generous," he told me. "Just remember how you have the love of her."

"Yes," I said. "I do."

THE DAY OF our wedding blessing, Toru and I spent the morning at a café having scones and tea, then jogging along the Charles River. Later, while Toru napped off some of his jet lag, my friend Demaris came over and straight-ironed my hair as a wedding gift. "Wow, looks great," Toru said, when he woke up. "Such a cute!"

That afternoon, we took a taxi to the temple. Holding hands on the sidewalk, we saw a small handful of picketers. When they began protesting the West Bank settlements, although I found their noise annoying, I silently agreed with them. Then Toru's father, sister, brother-in-law, and aunt and uncle showed up, piling carefully out of a van-sized taxi. They'd arrived only the day before, and now they bowed to us from across the sidewalk. The protesters watched for a moment, and as if invigorated by the diversity on display, one pointed out, "Israel oppresses Asians, too!" (which I conceded could technically be correct, as Israel sits at Asia's western edge). Then another clarified, "Including the Chinese!"

Toru's family stiffened almost imperceptibly, a split-second pause in each of their formal bows. I knew Hamatani-*san* and Kei understood the protesters' English perfectly, but even Michiko-*san* and Kei's husband, though far from fluent, could easily translate the "Chinese" part. I widened my eyes and turned toward Toru. But then we both just laughed. His family straightened one by one, none of them betraying any other sign that they'd just been mistaken for people from an entirely different country and culture by a group of angry white liberals.

Inside the synagogue, I introduced Toru's family to my father and stepmother, my siblings, and my stepgrandmother. I'd only met Nippy, my Texan stepmother's mother, once, but she seemed delighted to be included, smiling a huge red-lipsticked grin and drawling greetings to Toru's family as they each bowed again. Kei's husband, Funaki-*san,* remained pink-faced, as if ter-

rified someone might ask him a question in English. My oldest
sister, Robin, colored along with him. Nonnative speakers made
her nervous, I knew, left her afraid she'd laugh during some
awkward pause of mutual incomprehension.

My mother and stepfather had met my new in-laws the night
before at a dinner they'd hosted at their apartment in Brookline.
I'd been alternately anxious and amused at what Toru's family
would make of the two uniformed caterers my mother had hired
for a dinner of nine people, but they'd been so jet-lagged I wasn't
sure they'd even noticed. "Your father will probably think, 'Of
all Tracy's sisters, I liked those two who stayed quietly in the
kitchen and just served dinner,'" I joked to Toru. But Toru just
seemed relieved that at the dinner my mother forbore mentioning "his country's" empress again and the Japanese public's reaction to the lack of a male heir.

Now at the temple, my mother nodded her approval as she
noted Toru's dark suit and the yarmulke perched on his head.
From outside, the chants of the protesters echoed softly through
the synagogue's thick walls, like voices in a faraway schoolyard.
Under the chuppah, Rabbi Friedman smiled beatifically, then
turned to Toru's family and, still smiling, his arms now outstretched, acknowledged the beauty and inconvenience of America, where everyone could speak their minds, at volume. Toru's
aunt and uncle bowed again.

When the holy man began intoning the marriage prayer,
Toru started nodding in time. I remembered that his executive
MBA program had taught the importance of providing verbal
cues of understanding when communicating with native English speakers. Now, Toru deployed this practice faithfully. "In
the name of Abraham, Isaac, and Jacob . . . ," the rabbi chanted,

Toru interjecting with "un *huh*, un *huh*," then dutifully nodding again to confirm he was following.

Finally, Toru stamped the wineglass, binding us together in the tradition of my forefathers. As the goblet snapped under his heel with a cold, clean crack, I knew, despite all my cynicism, the day was perfect.

THIRTEEN

In December, I returned to Osaka. Over the next few months, I tried to arrange a few double dates or participate in social events with some of my new expat friends and their Japanese husbands. I remembered how uncomfortable Toru had been in America going out with groups of my friends, but I hoped with other Japanese men—especially ones married to foreigners—he'd be more relaxed.

One night, a woman I'd recently met named Helen had people over to her apartment above the ramen shop her Japanese husband owned. Helen had come to a Four Stories event a few months earlier and told me she was a regular reader of the food-and-foreign-life column I'd just started for one of the expat magazines, about the city's best restaurants for squeamish eaters. My miserable failure at writing about Japanese cuisine for the Boston newspaper a few years earlier had prepared me perfectly for the gig. Helen was outgoing and friendly, and we'd both gone to Tufts for college, although she was young enough to have missed me there.

It was a Friday night, and Toru texted me from work telling me he was going to be late to Helen's gathering. That morning, he'd been reluctant to join, but eventually he'd relented. "Why don't you want to come, love?" I'd asked.

"I don't know. Just seems tiring after long day at work."

I'd brushed aside his lack of enthusiasm, thrown on some sparkly eye shadow, and headed to Helen's. The plan was to have cocktails at her apartment and then head around the corner with a big group of people to an *okonomiyaki* place—inexplicably named President Chibo—that made savory Japanese pancakes with shredded cabbage, pork, and a choice of fillings such as cheese, spicy Korean cabbage kimchi, and *mochi*, a kind of sticky rice cake.

At the party, I gave Helen a quick hug, handed her a bottle of wine I'd bought at an import store, and sat down next to a woman I'd never met. "Hi, I'm Lisa!" she said in a loud American accent, her big blue eyes shiny, her hair and dress both solid black. She held out her hand, and then she smiled a mouthful of the whitest teeth I had ever seen.

"Hi!" I said, blinking into the wattage. "How'd you get your teeth so white!"

Lisa laughed, raised her glass of red wine, and told me she guessed she was just lucky in the dental department. I liked her immediately. I told her my name and learned she was from Montana, was single, had been in Japan off and on for almost fifteen years, and was an assistant professor at a nearby university.

Around us was a collection of other people I'd never met. A few were Western women with Japanese husbands or partners, and some were friends of Lisa's from her university or the American consulate in Osaka. A mix of languages tangled in the air.

Toru showed up just as we were about to leave for dinner. I

introduced him around, waiting for him to strike up a conversation with one of the Japanese men. But after quick greetings, he stayed quiet, sipping his beer and looking relieved when Helen soon announced it was time to leave.

At the *okonomiyaki* restaurant, Toru and I sat at the end of the long table holding our large group, an American woman named Jesse and her ponytailed Japanese boyfriend, who was a musician, to our left. It was loud, and the corner end where Toru and I sat abutted a wall to our right. I tried to lean across Toru to ask Jesse and her boyfriend questions over the background din. "Where are you from? Have you been in Japan long? Is music your career, or do you have another job as well? Where do you play?"

Then, turning to Toru, "Love, have you ever heard the name of that club?"

"No, never heard," Toru said, looking down and arranging some food with his chopsticks. The conversation plodded on for another minute or two, then spluttered, Toru smiling tightly into the awkward silences. Soon Jesse and her boyfriend turned to the couple on their left.

Later that night, walking home, I asked Toru what had happened. "Why didn't you want to join the conversation?"

"I don't know. Just tired after long day at work." Then he said, "I'm not like you. I'm not so social. Not so good at talking to people I don't know."

I tried, not totally successfully, to understand: Toru's long hours at the office where he had to project formality, politeness, and eagerness at all times; the fact that Japanese couples tended to live very separate lives, with work, home, and friends divided into firm boundaries that husbands and wives didn't cross together. I thought about how I'd never been invited to Toru's office, not even for their New Year's parties, since company events were employees only. Once, when Toru had a friend from college getting married in Tokyo, I'd assumed I'd go with him, but, no, Toru told me, spouses weren't invited. "Why would they be?" he'd asked.

I was still frustrated with Toru, though. I was a social person, and in *my* culture, partners spent time with each other's friends. The other Japanese men at the restaurant were more willing to blend into their partners' social expectations, or at least have a conversation.

"Okay. I know you don't really like socializing," I said, "and I know how tired you must be after work. And I know this is Japan and maybe it's unusual for couples to go out together with other people. But I'm *American*. You married an *American*. And I need my spouse to at least *try* to make an effort with my friends."

"I did try," Toru said, staring at the sidewalk.

"So, I need you to try harder. If you can. I mean, I moved to Japan for you, and I need a little of my own life, my American life here, as much as possible." Listening to myself, I thought about how I'd once hoped not to become an expat spouse who harped on the refrain "But I moved here for you!"

"Okay," Toru said, after a moment, as if he'd just agreed to attend a Saturday seminar on the history of the widget.

Over the next few days, I turned our conversation over in my mind. Maybe Toru would be more comfortable one-on-one, with just one other couple. It *had* been noisy at the restaurant, and Jesse and her boyfriend were younger and obviously a little more funky, Toru in his suit sitting next to the long-haired musician. Maybe he'd just felt out of his element.

I called Helen and asked if she wanted to have a double date. We'd eat at her husband's ramen place—how could that not be interesting?—and I could write a column about Hiro's family's restaurant business. We chose a weekend night so Toru wouldn't be tired from work. On the day of our plan, he spent much of the afternoon sighing as if stricken by some deep personal woe, but he agreed to come.

The restaurant was open-air along one whole wall, and we sat on little straw tatami mats, steam from our kimchi-laced bowls rising in the cool air and reddening our cheeks. Helen and I gossiped and laughed while Hiro and Toru spoke stilted English, even to each other. "Um, love," I finally said, "you can speak Japanese to Hiro, you know. Helen and I don't mind."

"Seriously, Hiro." Helen rolled her eyes at me and we laughed again.

Eventually, the men eased into a flow of their own tempo, talking rapidly in Japanese, grinning now and then, and even letting loose an occasional laugh. *Success!* I smiled triumphantly at Helen.

Later that night, Toru and I walked home again through the neon-splattered Osaka streets. "Did you have fun?" I asked. "It seemed like you did! They're nice, right?"

"Yeah, pretty fun," Toru answered, a lilt of surprise in his voice.

"So, do you want to get together again with them sometime?"

"Oh . . . no," Toru said, as if one idea bore no connection to the other.

I laughed at first, mostly at the sheer unexpectedness of his response. Then I stared at him, disbelieving. I was running out of ideas about how to make him want to join me and my friends, and forcing him to socialize was failing to produce the results I'd hoped for.

A few days later, I called Helen in frustration. "I know!" she said. "Hiro had the same exact reaction. Had fun. Has no interest in doing it again. What's with these guys?"

I hung up, staring into a situation beyond my control. I thought again about the separate lives of most Japanese husbands and wives, the supposition that spouses would not—even should not—be everything to each other. Though Toru was nontraditional in some ways, I needed to accept that, socially, we'd remain divided. I felt a little lonely at the idea and unsure once again about what limitations and differences one was supposed to accept in a marriage. What's too much to sacrifice? And how to even know?

Then an image came to me of a former therapist I'd had. She'd recalled what her mentor, an elderly psychologist, had once told her: "The most important part of a good relationship," she'd said, as I leaned forward, "is not the symmetry, but what you do with the disappointment."

I BEGAN MAKING more plans alone with expat friends: afternoons at a chocolate café in an antique Japanese storehouse with wooden beams across the ceiling and dense cups of liqueur-spiked hot chocolate; dinners during the week at new Italian or Spanish restaurants I wanted to try. I appreciated that Toru was always enthusiastic about my own socializing, urging me to go out whenever I wanted. "It's not even that I necessarily *have* to have you join us," I told him.

"It's more that I wish you didn't seem so uninterested in the prospect. For instance, if you could just say something like 'Well, it sounds like fun and another time I might really want to come, but tonight I'm just really tired from work.'"

Toru considered my objection carefully. One evening, when I told him I was planning a girls' night out that weekend at a new wine bar, he looked me in the eye and nodded. "Well, it sounds like fun, and another time I might really want to joining," he said, perking with enthusiasm, "but, you know . . . ahhh, it's girls' night out!" Then he beamed me the confident smile of a husband secure in his own supportiveness.

Most weekends, when I wasn't going out with friends or to a restaurant with Toru, we spent an evening at Otōsan's apartment, where I'd cook for both of them. Preparing dinner there for Toru and his father filled me with a simple contentment that both surprised and intrigued me. The apartment was so tiny. The kitchen so old and cramped. But Toru's father seemed so easy to please. I'd bend over the egregiously low kitchen sink, chopping scallions or rinsing rice, the muffled sound of Japanese news or their version of Animal Planet coming to me from the living room, where Toru and his father sat on a sloping couch. Then I'd remember my parents when we still lived as a family, before I was ten. My mother's voice taut and severe as she tried to corral all four of us kids, my father, and our shih tzu onto the plane for our summers in France. We'd be dressed formally for travel, the dog neatly groomed in his cage before the airline attendant took him off to cargo while both my parents looked on, tight-lipped. Or our winter skiing weekends in Vermont, groceries loaded in the station wagon trunk to restock the house in Stowe, my father absently holding the wheel, my mother staring furiously out the window while we kids silently flipped through Mad Libs in the backseat. The only time I remember the entire family laughing together was the day the dog woke from between my parents in the front seat, shook off the sleep from his tiny furred torso, ambled over to my father, bit him, and lay back down. Or at least my mother and we kids laughed.

In Osaka, Toru's father would smile when I laid out the fish, rice, and stir-fried lotus root on the old kitchen table. He'd nod or laugh at my questions about Toru growing up or my miserable attempts to speak polite Japanese to him. When I handed him printouts of a few new recipes I wanted to try, urging him to pick his favorite, he read through each one slowly, looking the pictures up and down, running his finger along the list of ingredients in English, sometimes sounding them out under his breath. Finally he'd grin and hand me his choice. After dinner, he'd pat his stomach and accept his cup of tea, saying "Shank you, To-ray-shee." Then he'd shuffle back to the living room couch, turn on the TV again, and settle in with an easy sigh.

There was nothing more he really wanted in the world other than dinner at home with his family. Toru had once told me that even when his father was working he'd insisted on coming home for dinner in time to eat with his wife and children despite the Japanese expectation that businessmen work late and then go out drinking with colleagues. He'd probably limited his corporate advancement by so unapologetically choosing family over work, but he hadn't cared. Now, though sometimes I worried about the potential impact on Toru's career, I admired that he tried to repeat his father's precedent whenever possible.

Later, after he'd watched some TV, Otōsan would flip on the

gas water heater, run the tap until it steamed, and then wash the dishes, methodically scrubbing plate by plate. When eventually the weakness in his legs made standing harder, I'd wash up instead. Cleaning was my least favorite part, but even then, I felt a warm rush of gratification go through me, knowing I was helping banish Otōsan's loneliness and boredom a few times a week.

One night, Toru and his father stayed at the kitchen table drinking the tea I'd served while I went into the living room. Earlier, I'd found more old family photo albums, and now I plopped down on the floor to page through them. Toru and his sister appeared in little yellow kindergarten caps, presumably from "sports day," an annual school event that still continues: Toru's legs pumping during some sort of race, Kei's face upturned in song. In another album, the pictures were older, from before Kei was born: Toru as a baby at the beach, covered upright in the sand to mid-torso, pudgy arms resting on a soft shelf of grainy white, a huge complicit grin on his face as if he were actually the author of the prank; then Toru again, sitting in a red model car, fist outstretched as if to shift into gear, face and cheeks impossibly round and self-satisfied. Finally, I stopped and lingered over a photo of my husband as a newborn cradled in his mother's arms, her gaze fixed on his little bow mouth, her expression as serene and full as I'd ever seen it.

I felt a tug then, an unexpected hunger rising not in my stomach but higher, my heartbeat more a squeeze than a pump. The baby looked just like Toru still did, only rounder and quieter and his hair more sparse, his cheeks curved like fat, smooth stones. I suddenly longed for Toru not as an adult but as an infant, and then not as a wife but as a mother. The longing wasn't so much a thought but a jolt of feeling, an ache in my arms, a twitch in my fists and in my teeth, as if I wanted to grab hold of his pudgy limbs, as if I even wanted to bite his baby flesh.

My cannibalistic response shocked me less than my maternal one. I'd never really felt a longing for a child before. I thought about waking up alone in my apartment in Boston, the late-morning light across my bed, the utter luxury of lazy silence after deep sleep. Or doing yoga for ninety unbroken minutes in our tatami room in Osaka, candles flicking shadows on the wall. Booking tickets home, the long trip from Japan to the East Coast manageable only thanks to wine, movies, and the uninterrupted white noise of flight.

An echo of my father's voice came to me then, *"Trebs, kids are like a life sentence!"* and a memory of my mother staring blankly at her middle child. I'd always doubted I had a maternal instinct; maybe it just wasn't in my genes. The responsibility of parenthood usually sent a shiver of fear and dread through me, my fiercest protective instincts trained not on the dream of an infant but on my own freedom from a lifelong commitment I had no guarantee I could keep.

That night on the floor of Otōsan's living room, neither the fear nor the dread left me. But they were joined by an unexpected yearning for Toru-as-baby. I wanted to hold our infant in my arms, to gaze down into the pudgy face of our flesh made one.

TORU AND I had only ever discussed having a child in passing, never as an imminent endeavor, and the conversation always focused in part on how much time his father could devote to babysitting, even whether Toru and Otōsan could care for a little one themselves in Osaka if I needed to go back to Boston without the baby or we couldn't afford regular flights for two. But that spring and summer, we began questioning parenthood more realistically. Toru knew my reluctance, had understood it well before we were married, and we were both aware that my age could render the whole point moot. He wanted us to have a child but said he'd be content either way. "I love you first in world and always will," he told me.

One day we stopped for lunch in one of Osaka's vast underground malls. We sat by a large window separating the café from the subterranean thoroughfare, eating rice bowls while torrents of people flowed past beyond the glass. Lingering over a cappuccino and remembering my own family, I gave voice to my deepest fear. "What if I have a baby and I don't bond with it?"

Toru tilted his head in thought a moment. He told me he was pretty sure I'd love a baby, especially if it came from me and him together. "Especially if it has your pea head!" he said, recalling how Japanese people would frequently comment on my "small face." He would sometimes tease me that the Ph.D. in my professional title stood for "pea head."

The idea of a baby with my pea head failed to move me much, but I could still feel the tingling in my fists, that visceral itch to snatch and squeeze the baby in the photo at Otōsan's apartment. A little Toru. *My* little Toru. I felt a hot possessiveness. Then a jolt of something resembling joy rode along the current of that heat. I couldn't tell if it was the caffeine from my coffee or the comforting rush of pedestrians streaming past us beyond the café window, a wave of noise buffered and made soothing by the large glass pane protecting us. Or whether I really was starting to feel joy at the prospect of having a child with Toru.

"But I'll be forty-one this year. That's pretty old to have a baby. So we'd probably need to start soon."

"We have time. Not good to start until you're ready."

Toru thought even though I was a few months past my fortieth birthday, waiting another three to six months wouldn't make much difference. "Maybe too long to wait a year," he said, but he urged me to take my time deciding whether I was actually ready to try.

The rest of that year passed in periodic agitation, my temporary peace with Japan replaced by a new obsession: whether this whole house of cards, this whole bicontinental setup, would come crashing down if we procreated. I had so many questions beyond my bone-deep fear of not bonding with a child. Could we afford a kid? Forget about the cost of flights back and forth; was there even space in my tiny South End studio for me and a child? My mother's warning to me before I got married ran through my head: *you'll be a foreigner half the year and a single parent the rest*. I wasn't confident I could handle a baby *with* Toru. Handling one on my own seemed insurmountable. Plus, I was pretty sure I didn't have either the internal or external resources to maintain my freelance writing career part-time, take care of a baby, and find subletters or pay rent every month in Boston.

When I flew back home that spring to teach writing again in the MBA program, the trip was extra long and tiring. I tried to imagine holding a baby on my lap in my tiny economy seat for the ten-hour-plus flight to San Francisco and then the six-hour leg to Boston. Going the other way, I knew, would be even longer. Something about the headwinds, I'd read, added an extra hour or two to the Asia-bound itinerary. On some flights, I saw couples with infants in the bulkhead seats, airline-issued bassinets tucked into the extra legroom in front. But that would only buy me a year or so.

At baggage claim in San Francisco, I saw a blond couple with an infant. The father held the baby in a chest carrier, and the child tipped its towhead back as if it were a Chinese circus performer entering a backbend. Then the infant flopped forward into its father's chest and gave a little shriek, legs kicking the air. The mother joined them, pointing to the luggage carousel. I couldn't have said whether or not the baby was cute. All I saw was the look of pure exhaustion running shadows down its parents' cheeks.

I felt tears well up in my own eyes then. I was already tired out from the long, cramped flight, anticipating a two-hour layover followed by another cross-continental leg. Lugging a baby along with me? By myself? The entire idea struck me as demonic.

THAT SPRING in Boston felt idyllic, more so even than before as I began comparing the luxury of my single life to the severe limitations parenthood would surely spawn. My small apartment seemed to stretch out, spacious and peaceful. Even the sound of cars flowed evenly outside the tall, rickety windows of my ground-level unit. But could that soft static soon transform into something else? Traffic that would wake a sleeping baby? Infant screams shattering the night?

Still, when I lay in bed reading or watching TV and I turned my head to the wall next to my long windows, I saw the pictures I had hung the previous autumn. Toru's little newborn limbs always sent tiny sparks through my fingers, up my arms, across my chest. Sometimes, my teeth would hurt again with longing.

Increasingly, I began imagining having Toru's baby growing inside me. At my Boston gym, I ran extra hard on the treadmill. I'd raise the speed and pump my arms and legs and stare out at downtown Back Bay, the sun wrapping around the corners of Copley Place, and I'd feel my heartbeat climbing, climbing. I knew the more I worked out, the lower my resting pulse would become, and I thought about a tiny little being tucked inside my belly, absorbing, listening to the slow, steady hum I had made for it.

In winter 2009, I was back in Osaka. That October I'd turned forty-one, and I knew Toru and I couldn't put off trying much longer. Moments of terror over having a child would somersault into yearning, then back to terror again. The duality rubbed a raw friction in my chest. *Is everyone this terrified of having a kid, even if they kind of want one?* I wondered. *Or is there something wrong with me?* Other women I knew, most of whom were younger, were also thinking of having babies. Some seemed a lot less ambivalent. *What's wrong with these people that they aren't more afraid?* I'd think next. *Who goes into such a momentous life change and doesn't feel even a little terror, at least if they have their eyes open?* I couldn't tell if I was more limited or more enlightened than my peers.

That February, the quandary over whether I could afford both my Boston studio and a baby was settled for me. I was in Tokyo again visiting Ariel when my landlords got in touch. They were putting the unit on the market. Because the apartment was old and needed a lot of refurbishing, they were offering a low price, especially for a South End property. Still, even with Toru's company subsidizing half our Osaka rent, coming up with a down payment for the studio would come close to tapping us out. I'd always known we were priced out of buying in Boston. But since the current real estate market was so unstable, I assumed I'd have some time to figure things out. Even at a low price, I doubted my landlords could sell the unit quickly.

I was still holding on to this assumption when I got a message a few weeks later telling me the apartment had sold. When I clicked open the e-mail, I read its words with shock. Then a graver thought formed, about how right I'd been months earlier when I'd feared that my whole bicontinental setup was just a house of cards waiting to collapse.

5.

主婦

THE AUTONOMY STAGE

The persons who emerge from the detachment of stage one, the self-blame of stage two, and the hostility of stage three are in a position to build a new perspective between their former identity and the new host culture. . . . As in previous stages [though], it is likely that the individual will regress to earlier stages from time to time.

> • Paul Pedersen, *The Five Stages
> of Culture Shock*

Smile, Think Positive, Let Yourself Relax, and Ready for Conception.

> • Slogan from IVF Namba
> Clinic in Osaka

FOURTEEN

THAT WINTER, I MOURNED THE loss of my Boston studio. Jodi, who was back in Osaka by then, tried to convince me that losing the rental was really for the best. Ariel reminded me how stressed out I'd been, needing to find subletters every time I came to Japan. Over Indian food one night, Jodi pointed out that not only had the rental situation been stressful lately, it would only become more so if I had a baby. "Seriously," she said, stabbing a vegetarian samosa with her fork, "you want to worry about trying to get knocked up, and then maybe having some screaming infant, while either paying into someone else's mortgage every month or trying to scrape together the cash to buy your own place?" She urged me to just give myself a break, take a year, and see what it was like not having my own place in Boston. "You can always stay with friends, or your mother or siblings."

Honestly, I wasn't sure my mother would let me stay in her apartment, especially if she and my stepfather were away in Florida. Between them, there were ten adult stepchildren, although all the others had their own homes in the U.S. But I guessed my parents were reluctant to open their apartment to the sprawling next generation. When I admitted such to Jodi, she flared her nostrils, then stabbed another samosa. "I'll never understand your family," she muttered. Anyway, my friend Louise had a two-bedroom apartment in Jamaica Plain, a grittier neighborhood than the South End, that she was constantly struggling to afford alone on a new assistant professor's salary, and I figured I could always sublet a room from her when I went home.

A few weeks later, my friends Jenna and Matt packed up my beloved studio and moved my belongings into storage. Matt was in freelance construction, so the job gave him a chance to bring in some extra cash, although Jenna kept trying to lowball me. "You don't need to pay us. Just pay for the rental truck and storage space!" I e-mailed Matt to ask what his hourly construction rate usually equaled, then sent a check, although I suspect he lowballed me, too.

Toru tried to comfort me by telling me we could look for a cheaper apartment in a less upscale neighborhood when I went back to Boston next. "Well," I said, "I guess especially if I don't end up getting pregnant we may be able to afford that." Over the next few months, even though I felt sad about losing my studio, the release from the responsibility did leave me with a clean new space in my chest that used to be filled with worry.

By now, Toru and I had started trying to have a baby, or at least had stopped using protection. If it turned out I couldn't get pregnant, we'd accept living childless. No invasive treatments, no medical acrobatics, we agreed. Still, I told Toru I thought I should get checked out, just to ensure I had no cervical cancer or other health issues that might complicate a pregnancy. I took a deep breath and scheduled my first visit to a gynecologist in Japan. Or rather, I found a women's clinic reported to have English-speaking doctors (but not nurses or receptionists), and asked Toru to make an appointment for me.

When I arrived for my checkup in late February, the receptionist handed me a questionnaire. *In English!* I noted with relief. She wore a dark blue uniform, straight skirt to the knee, with a white blouse and little blue handkerchief knotted at her neck. She looked identical to the other two receptionists busy filing paperwork and smiling, down to the clinic's logo pinned to their collars, as if the women were flight attendants for the gynecologically inclined.

"What seems to be a problem today?" the questionnaire asked. Then it gave me my choices: "infertility," "gender selection," "timing intercourse," "IVF," "AIH," or "others." I wasn't sure what "timing intercourse" was, and I had no idea what "AIH" meant. I checked "others." At the top of the form were fields for my height and weight in centimeters and kilograms, measurements I'd never used. I hesitated, then just filled in five-foot-five and 118 lbs. There was no mention of my blood type, but at the bottom of the questionnaire were boxes for "husband's name," his occupation, and *his* blood type.

When the pink-and-white-uniformed nurse finally called me into the examination room, she motioned for me to remove everything below my waist, put on some pink fabric slippers, and seat myself in a large padded pink chair that monopolized the small space. It looked like a recliner with a polyester yellow curtain hanging over what turned out to be leg rests. I shuffled toward the contraption, the communal slippers uncomfortably humid around my toes, my midriff covered with a tiny pink towel. Once I extended my legs beyond the curtain, everything from my navel down was obscured, but I heard voices coming from behind the yellow expanse.

"Um," I called into the vacuum, but there was no answer. I peeked my head around and could see the nurse looking down the hallway beyond. There were no walls or doors blocking the view from my lap to the thoroughfare. "Open *wa daijobu*?" I asked quickly, in some kind of weird Japinglish, "Open okay?" pulling the polyester curtain aside.

The nurse nodded, smiling, and then called down the hall, "Inoue-*sensei*!" "Dr. Inoue!" A white-coated woman came hurrying to my pink-chaired alcove. The nurse approached the recliner and stepped on some levers, and suddenly the top portion of the seat tipped back while the leg rests extended farther and opened into a wide V, the whole contrivance rising up to eye level. "Good morning, Mrs. Tracy!" the doctor greeted my splayed repose. Then she snapped on a pair of rubber gloves, pulled the little towel from my lap, and began her exam. The entire time, more pink-outfitted nurses clutching charts rushed back and forth down the hallway behind the doctor's back while my naked feet flopped toward them.

When I returned to the clinic to get my results, Inoue-*sensei* assured me I was healthy, but she clucked over my age. If I wanted to get pregnant, she urged me to get my hormone levels tested. By now, Toru and I had gone a couple of months without protection. "I'm not worried," I told two foreign friends who went to the same clinic, but I agreed to have more tests "just in case." Returning once again for the results, I was relieved when the nurse called me into a room without a mechanized pink recliner. I sat between the blank white walls of the doctor's office and waited.

"I'm sorry, Mrs. Tracy," Inoue-*sensei* said, looking down, and she pushed a sheet with green and white boxes of lab results toward me. "I'm sorry," she repeated, still staring at the paper, "but your hormones are . . . out of range."

Apparently, I had a significantly depleted supply of eggs, the doctor explained in broken English. "Every month, it's precious now," she said. She advised Toru and I start IVF immediately. She warned my chances of having a baby at all, even with medical intervention, were very slim.

I felt pierced by the news. Drawing a line at "no treatment" had felt different when deep down I'd assumed the cards were in my hands. I was fit, ate well, exercised daily, and had never smoked. *I was carded on my fortieth birthday, with my parents!* I thought, remembering the night in Boston when my mother and I had argued over my wearing black to the wedding blessing at her temple. At the time, she'd smiled proudly when the waiter had asked for my ID, temporarily forgetting her frustration with my poor sartorial choices. We'd all laughed at the irony, someone questioning whether I'd reached drinking age when I was entering my fifth decade. Now, though, it felt like the joke was on me, my young face and bottle-blond highlights apparently masking my shriveling insides.

Over the next few weeks, Toru and I batted the idea of medical treatment back and forth. Following the clinic's advice, he went in for testing, too. Unlike me, he was in perfect procreative shape. "I worry you," he said, as we reviewed the physical rigors in vitro would require of me. But he, too, was shaken by our sudden poor prognosis.

We decided we'd wait until mid-spring, and if I still wasn't pregnant, we'd give IVF a try.

I BEGAN MY first round of treatment in mid-May. My confusion and fear about having a baby hadn't dissipated, but somehow they didn't staunch my growing resolve to try IVF. I couldn't explain the paradox even to myself, but my brain shifted into autopilot, as if a new determination was rolling through the landscape of my ambivalence. At times, it felt like our potential baby was waiting for us to claim it, or at least to give it a chance to arrive, and something inside was compelling me on as if a homing pigeon had set up residence in my chest. Other times, I simply felt bewildered.

My period started on Mother's Day, two days after an actual pigeon showed up at our balcony door, a sort of harbinger, it seemed later, of all that would come next. At first, Toru and I watched warily as the bird began hanging out behind our air-conditioning unit. Sometimes another pigeon would join it, and they'd flap around with antic jerks until we banged on the sliding glass door.

"Stupid pigeon," Toru would mutter, as they lifted in hurried flight.

But the birds always returned, and when the pigeon couple began depositing twigs and scraps of underbrush behind the air-conditioning unit, Toru became even more annoyed. "Doesn't stupid pigeon know he's trying to build nest in terrible place?"

It wasn't until Mother's Day proper that we realized the female had laid an egg, depositing her future offspring on our balcony as if she'd been specially chosen to symbolize the miracle of life on this Hallmark holiday. I took it all as a personal affront.

My period had started a few hours earlier, and when I saw the offending orb, I couldn't believe the audacity of that fertile bird. *Procreating on my property! When I'm reproductively challenged!*

"Terrible!" Toru exclaimed, when he saw the egg sitting roundly on the concrete.

Earlier that morning, I'd come out of the bathroom shaking my head, and he'd kissed my forehead. He'd assured me once more that if I didn't want to go through with the IVF, that was totally okay. The most important thing was that we were together, Toru had reminded me, calm, unhurried.

But he really kicked into action when he saw the pigeon egg.

He immediately got online and within an hour learned everything there was to know about 1) the pigeon reproductive cycle, and 2) what to do if a pigeon tried to complete that cycle on your balcony.

"We have two choice," he reported, closing his laptop and turning to me. "If we don't do something, stupid pigeon will get a mess all over. And when baby hatches, it will walk around and make an even more mess."

He eyed me aslant. "So . . . we can throw out egg—and there will probably be another soon, because pigeons usually lay more than one." He could tell I wasn't won over. "Or we can build cardboard box and put egg inside, and stupid pigeon will be sitting on egg in there."

I've never been a nature lover, but the idea of chucking out a future chick felt too mean—and too inauspicious, especially on this of all days. "We have to at least try to save it," I said, "even if that evil bird did steal my eggs."

"Still, it may ignore egg after a human touches it," Toru warned. But I didn't budge. "Oh, okay," he finally sighed. "That's the chance we take if you want to try to saving the egg."

He went to the futon closet that we used for storage, pulled out old Sanyo and Panasonic boxes, and began to fashion a makeshift nest. Then he put on rubber gloves and a mask. "Don't get bird flu!" I yelled stupidly as he stepped onto the balcony, the pigeons flapping away in a riot of feathers. He picked up the egg and some twigs and arranged them in the box.

"Stupid pigeon," he grumbled again as he stepped back inside. He threw out the gloves, pulled on a clean pair of jeans, then went back to the glass to spy for the birds' return. "Huh," he said, after a few minutes of watching the vacant balcony. I came and hovered by the curtain. The sky was empty.

Toru sank onto the couch and picked up a magazine, and I got online. I was signing up for a new "Over 40 and Trying to Conceive" forum on an infertility chat site. I wanted to learn what other women, particularly Americans, were going through during their IVF rounds, since so much of my treatment would unfold in Japanese and, I feared, remain incomprehensible to me.

In the living room, Toru and I looked up frequently to check the window, then turned back to our tasks with feigned nonchalance. After ten minutes or so, he gave up the charade, drawing back the curtain liner for a better look. "Has she returned?" I jumped up to join him.

When one of the pigeons finally flew back (the mother, we both assumed), she walked around for a while behind the air-conditioning unit, looked at the box, made a pigeon noise. Then she hopped in and sat on the egg. I looked at Toru and smiled.

"Stupid pigeon," he said. "So dumb. She doesn't even know

she's in box, that I picked up egg myself." He gave his head an exasperated shake, belying the relief around his face.

BEFORE I COULD begin trying to produce my own eggs with the clinic's help, I had to supply a copy of our marriage license. Toru and I then had to sign a paper saying we understood that, in the event of our divorce, the clinic would automatically destroy any unused embryos we may have produced, regardless of our desires. I also learned that the Japanese Society of Obstetrics and Gynecology prohibits the use of donor eggs. Surrogacy: also a no-go in a country so conservative about heritage and bloodlines.

But when the clinic asked us to sign another sheet providing permission to use any embryos we discarded for stem-cell research, I quickly agreed. I expected Toru to share my support for scientific discovery, especially since he was completely irreligious, yet he shook his head. "Why not?" I asked.

"Don't like," he said, stern. "That's private." I puzzled out his response, finally realizing that his reaction stemmed from the not uncommon Japanese discomfort with mixing private and public, with crossing boundaries meant to be kept sacred. So, no, not a religious objection, but one still rooted in an ideology that always caught me a little off guard as an atheist in a secular culture. In America, tradition always seemed to derive from piety, and even after all this time in Japan, I was still surprised by dogma divorced from religion, as if I had found a couch in a kitchen or glimpsed green where I had always seen red.

Our embryos' potential futures now safely codified and documented, I spent the next two weeks shuttling back and forth to the clinic to get my morning shots, which they insisted a nurse administer. I read on the Internet that in the U.S., patients could do their hormone shots at home. I guessed grumpily that in Japan infertile women were not to be trusted with sharp objects.

Every day after my shot, I'd come home and sit in my living room marking the calendar: depending on whether or how fast my follicles grew, the egg retrieval would be on this day, the transfer on that. Then I'd settle down to try to work.

By now, the pigeon and I were passing time side-by-side. She'd sit in her little cardboard box just outside the glass door, warming her two eggs. (Toru was right; she'd laid the second twenty-four hours after the first.) I'd sit on the couch just inside, tapping at my computer keys. Every so often, I'd put down my laptop, slide open the glass, and look out, hoping to see what was happening beneath her. Sometimes she'd cock her head and stare back at me, blinking her beady eyes.

We're both creatures strangely out of nature, I told her one afternoon, not saying the words out loud but thinking them as I watched her fidget, weighing whether I posed enough of a threat to inspire flight. *You're just a silly bird trying to hatch your babies behind an air-conditioning unit in a huge polluted city, inside a Japanese salaryman's discarded cardboard box.*

And I'm a forty-one-year-old woman with "poor ovarian response" trying to get knocked up by a petri dish and an army of doctors who barely speak my language. She cocked her head away from me, stared into the bowels of the air conditioner, rocked lightly on her genetic loot.

About five days after I started my shots, I climbed back into the pink mechanized chair for an ultrasound, inspiring the doctor to report that my follicles were growing at a slower than average pace. "But still, some are growing," she said. "I thought maybe they would not be able to grow at all . . . because of your age, and your own hormones being so much out of range. So this is good." She nodded, smiling me out the door with an expression more tentative than reassuring.

"Well, *my* eggs are growing. Slowly," I told the pigeon that afternoon in my daily soliloquy. "But better than they expected," I added quickly. She blinked blankly at me. Later, when she flew away to get food or more twigs or to complete one of her pigeon errands, I peeked out at the box. The eggs lay there, bald, promising, and white, an ovoid taunt.

"Stupid pigeon," I muttered.

A FEW DAYS before my egg retrieval, a nurse handed me an instruction packet to prepare me for the minor surgery of sticking a needle into each ovary and sucking out the five follicles I'd managed to grow after fourteen days of shots. Most of the papers were in Japanese, but she pointed importantly to a few that had been translated into English. "No makeup. Don't put nail polishl [*sic*] or perfume before coming to our clinic," one sheet said. "Clip your fingernail. Take antibiotics every after meal for four days. We welcome your husband's attendance." Another page, titled "Restriction on the Number of Embryos," explained, "Transferring high numbers of embryos may have high rate of pregnancy, but may bring multiple pregnancy. Multiple pregnancies are high risk to woman's body and fetus." One more difference between IVF here and at home: Japanese doctors were very reluctant to transfer more than one embryo. No Octomoms here.

The morning of my procedure, I opened the sliding glass door to check the pigeon. In the box lay one broken shell, the other egg hidden somewhere beneath the bird. *Did the mother somehow know the egg was bad and crack it?* I wondered. *If not, where's the baby?* I turned away from the balcony, reminding myself that I'd never been superstitious. If the little chick met an untimely end before it had time to hatch—if the mother somehow rejected the egg because in her animal wisdom she knew it would not thrive—this had no symbolic resonance for my life.

Later that day, I met Toru on the subway platform. He'd taken the afternoon off from work so he could go to the clinic with me. "Did you see stupid pigeon?" he asked immediately. "Did you see egg?"

I grabbed his hand. A middle-aged woman and some salarymen in dark suits like Toru's shifted slightly from us, as if noting the public affection without doing anything that in the Japanese lexicon of manners would be as gauche as staring.

"Yes! What did she do? Did she smash the egg herself?" I was secretly a little comforted that perhaps, after all, she wasn't going to prove the better mother.

"No." Toru laughed. "It hatched. She's sitting on it."

"Oh." I was both relieved and disappointed. "Well, that doesn't seem like very good mothering, to sit on your babies once they're born."

"It's what all pigeons do to keep them warm, like with eggs." Toru rubbed my palm with his thumb. "Fathers sit on chicks,

THE GOOD SHUFU 251

too," he said. And then the signal for the oncoming train began to sound, followed by a woman's voice over the loudspeaker, crisply offering direction or warning, although I couldn't tell which.

TWO DAYS AFTER they removed my follicles, the doctors deposited one fertilized embryo inside me, the only potentially viable one I had managed to produce. After the transfer, I lay down at the clinic for a few hours until Toru guided me home on the subway, holding my elbow, my head like packed cotton from the anesthesia. Then I began the notorious Two Week Wait, as they called it on the forums; I christened it the "Too Bleak Wait." I rested around the apartment, trying not to knock about too much, waiting to see if our embryo would take hold.

Within a few days, the second pigeon egg hatched, and I'd hear Toru every morning before he went to work, standing at the balcony door. Still in bed, I imagined how he looked, handsome in his pressed suit, his dark hair shining in the early sun as he drew the living room curtains, slid open the glass. He thought I was still asleep, but I could hear him tsking softly to the baby pigeons, who had just started to peep out from beneath one parent or the other.

One day, I heard the mother pigeon, or maybe the father, fly away in search of something. I stood at the door so I could see the chicks in their box, unobstructed. I watched their sparse yellow hair tufting over pinkish gray skin, little bodies puffing out with each quick breath.

They learned to fly a few weeks later. They were practicing taking off when I took a home pregnancy test on the twelfth day after my transfer and saw a faint double blue line.

"Congratulation, Mrs. Tracy!" the doctor said in broken English the next morning at the clinic, confirming my pregnancy with a blood test. The nurses were all giddy. Although they spoke no English, I knew what their delight said: *Forty-one! Getting pregnant on your very first try with IVF! With your own eggs!* They smiled happily and bowed enthusiastically, and they repeated these effusions every week when I came in for ultrasounds. *"Ii, ne,"* they would say—"It's great, isn't it!"—and their eyes would sparkle as they clasped their hands against the bright pink of their polyester uniforms.

I felt somewhat removed at first from the life force gathering in my belly. I was enthralled that a little being was tucked just inside my belly—half Toru, half me—but also a little numb, overlaid at times with a kind of quiet shock. The progression from deciding to try to have a baby to starting IVF to becoming pregnant had unspooled so quickly, as if I had been looking out the window from the bullet train to Tokyo, the world around a blur. I also still felt scared of what becoming a mother would do to my identity and my connection to Boston, but as I did when I started IVF, I followed a clear pull to continue my daily shots and pills, now a different kind of hormone cocktail, and adhere to each and every clinic direction about sustaining the flicker inside me. Every week after my ultrasound, I'd stare at the black-and-white photos they handed me, tracing the outlines with my finger: first a tiny dot, then a larger spot with a white blink inside where the embryo's heartbeat had appeared, and then a little bean-shaped figure, curved against a dark and hazy background.

Although the action was all taking place inside me, Toru seemed both less removed and less shocked. He'd guide me through stores with his hand against my lower back, a proud smile playing at the corners of his mouth. "Take rest and keep warm," he'd tell me. At night, he'd lean over in bed and whisper in Japanese against the skin of my stomach.

THE PIGEON CHICKS from the balcony were long gone by the time our embryo's heart stopped at nine weeks. The doctor, a man this time, told me at my weekly scan. What had appeared vibrant and growing seven days earlier now proved dormant on the screen. He never actually explained any of this; instead, he tried to make me know, with his splintered English and his Japanese insistence on politeness at all times. He didn't ever actually say, "I'm sorry, your baby has died." He just kept shaking his head and sighing, sucking in his breath, moving the ultrasound wand around inside me with the embryo's measurement—"eight weeks, five days"—printed along the bottom, the moon-shaped figure in the middle now bereft of its blinking center. The doctor shifted the screen back and forth as if to draw my eye to the stillness splayed across it, waiting for me to say something.

But I wouldn't. Grasping on to whatever meager fragment of control was left me, I kept my mouth clamped shut.

For the next week, the embryo inside me stayed put despite its loss of heartbeat, my body refusing to accept that the beginnings of our child had come to an end, refusing to relinquish its hold. But my belly felt like a mausoleum. The day was hot and clear when Toru brought me back to the clinic, holding my

hand the whole way. Then the doctors knocked me out completely so I wouldn't hear them speaking words I couldn't understand while they scraped the embryo out of me.

My earlier emotional remove from my pregnancy now began
to shatter, although my numbness stayed, but it felt colored by a
different, sadder shade. Songs that had once made me think of
painful breakups now reminded me of the embryo, suddenly
gone, and I wept as I had when I was an adolescent over the loss
of some infatuated future. I lay in bed and looked out my bedroom window at the hot gray sky, Osaka's buildings a jigsaw of
the same dull hue. "So you're leaving / If you have to go / Then
go / But my heart's going with you," the words to a British pop
song echoed through me, and I thought of the bundle of cells
that had blasted to life then faded inside me. While I was still
pregnant, I'd been so confused about what parenthood would
mean, and there was still a lot that remained confounding. But
one thing I knew now: motherhood was a whole new way to
break your heart.

FIFTEEN

THE MISCARRIAGE CHANGED
me in other unexpected ways, too. On the July day when the
clinic doctors cut the dead embryo from my belly, I'd awaited
the procedure on a cot in the surgery prep room, struggling to
understand the Japanese nurse administering my IV. I had one of
those moments where the mind separates briefly from the body
and we stand outside our experiences looking in. *I can't believe this
is happening,* I'd thought. Not because I hadn't known miscarriage was a possibility or because I believed my story was sadder
than anyone else's. Millions of women miscarried—or didn't—
every year in situations far worse than mine. Rather, the whole
experience seemed so surreal. The barren prep room walls. The
once-life inside me. The nubby blue curtain pulled around
the sides of my cot, the barely decipherable commentary from
the nurse. The laminaria sticks made from seaweed that the doctor had inserted into me that morning to dilate my cervix, after
which I was told to go home, rest, and come back in the afternoon when the sticks had expanded inside me, hour by aching
hour. I imagined the doctors now in the next room, laying out a
tray of sharp instruments, waiting for me to fall asleep.

Then another thought slid into my brain, and with it, I slipped fully back into my body. *If this is what we have to go through to meet our baby, then it's where I'm supposed to be.* The conviction felt clean, strong, pure.

As I mourned the miscarriage over the next few weeks, that determination stuck, then dug in deeper as the months wore on. With each cycle that I felt my mastery over my body wane, my ability to conceive recede further, my focus grew on finding something I could control. When Toru asked if I wanted to go back to Boston for a break, I told him no. I was committing to Japan full-time now, only willing to go home if I had a month where the doctors told me I couldn't try conceiving—and then, only for a few weeks.

Although Japanese insurance doesn't cover IVF, the procedure here costs only about a third of what it does in the U.S., so we weighed what we could afford and agreed we'd either try four more rounds or quit when I turned forty-five in a little more than three years, whichever came first. I grasped on to the plan as if it were a lifejacket in a tide I couldn't turn. The night after we'd learned our embryo's heart had stopped, I'd seen Toru shudder and then break with grief for the first time since his mother's accident, but now he took to reminding me that "no matter what, we are together in always."

My fears still hadn't dissolved about whether motherhood would overwhelm me so much I wouldn't be able to bond with a child. Yet like a runner in a race, what ultimately pulled ahead was that sense our baby might exist in some way or place, be waiting for us. I didn't know what this feeling meant or how someone who had so little belief in fate or the spiritual could be driven by such urges. But I'd married Toru without understanding in my brain how our relationship worked when we were so very different, when for years I had striven for a life that looked nothing like the one I'd chosen. Maybe I didn't need to get it; I just needed to go with it. Because the alternative was worse.

While my infertility was challenging my preference for logic over instinct, it also changed my feelings about being in Japan. For the first time, Osaka was a place I was choosing for my own reasons, not because of Toru's career or family obligations. I knew we could never afford five rounds of IVF in Boston, especially not at my age with my poor prognosis, when insurance would be unlikely to cover any of it there, either. Our setup in Osaka, with me working freelance writing jobs part-time from home and Toru earning enough for me to work fewer hours, would also make it much easier to manage the fatigue of treatments.

At the fertility clinic, the doctors declared my uterine lining too thin for a new embryo transfer. I'd heard that acupuncture could help, so I found a Japanese practitioner of Chinese medicine around the corner from our apartment. Neither he nor his receptionist spoke English, but I muddled through an attempt to explain my situation. First, I tried detailing my predicament to his receptionist, a whippet of a young woman at a high, bare desk. On the wall behind her hung a diagram of a man's body facing front and then back. He had blue and red dots snaking up and down his limbs and torso and over his skull, each energy point connected by a web of black lines.

"I'd like to do acupuncture. I had a baby inside, but it died. Nine weeks. Soon, I'll become forty-two," I stumbled in broken Japanese, arcing my hand over my abdomen to mime pregnancy while the receptionist nodded and smiled and then nodded and narrowed her eyes and said *"Aah, so desuka?"* "Oh, is that so?" I didn't know the word for uterus, and I couldn't remember the one for thin, but I thought the term "narrow" or "skinny" might work, explaining in more broken Japanese, "I do IVF now. But the doctor says my stomach is too skinny."

The receptionist eyed my torso. She may have even raised an eyebrow. *"Chotto-matte!"* she said, "Please wait a bit!" then called out, *"Sensei!"* "Doctor!" A tall muscular Japanese man stepped out from behind a curtain to the side of the desk. My attempts to explain my diagnosis didn't go much further with him, either, despite repeated hand signals toward my belly and then holding up my thumb and forefinger and placing them a few millimeters apart in an attempt to mime "thin." *How the hell does one mime "uterine lining"?* I thought, as I felt my face go hot.

We finally managed to book me an appointment for the following week. I'd made it clear that I wanted to get pregnant, that I was doing IVF, and that I was forty-one, and I figured we could at least go from there. When I got home, Toru wrote a note in Japanese. When I gave it to the acupuncturist, he nodded as he read it, then laughed with his head tipped back, repeating my "too skinny" comment a few times before he pulled out a new pack of needles.

After the clinic finally declared me ready to complete my next round of IVF, I tried not to get my hopes up, despite our earlier good luck. "Keep warm your belly," Toru would remind me when we went to bed, sometimes adding, "And keep warm your foot." We told Toru's father I was doing another attempt at in vitro and now had a new embryo inside me that we were hoping would take hold, and every night at dinner, he would peer at me carefully, then ask in English, "How is your baby?"

. . .

BY 2010, I was forty-two and my third embryo transfer had failed. Late at night, while Toru slept next to me in bed, I'd lie teary-eyed in the dim pool of light from my bedside table and troll online for books about holistic approaches to fertility, particularly for women of "advanced maternal age." During the day, I mined the forums for advice from other women. I started different fertility diets and then stopped running, walking my four-and-a-half-mile route instead to conserve my energy and "nourish my blood," although I had no idea what that actually meant.

Where I drew the line, or to be more accurate, admitted an ambivalent defeat, was with "positive thinking." A lot of the books I read and the women on my Over 40 IVF forum promoted the importance of visualization and happy thoughts. "Love your embies and imagine them snuggling in for nine months!" ran one such commentary. I couldn't stomach the idea of calling my embryos "embies." They were invisible cells, not cartoon characters, and even though I longed for the future they might hold, I couldn't honestly say I "loved" them when they were mere two- or four-unit blobs. *What if that's my problem?* I sometimes wondered. Maybe my inability to be a positive thinker was preventing me from getting pregnant. *Or my continued ambivalence about motherhood.* On one hand, I knew these fears were illogical and ridiculous. On the other, I felt guilty and afraid they were true.

Walking my route around Osaka Castle Park with six hormone patches stuck to my stomach, I seethed over some of the forum comments. One woman, newly forty-three and pregnant, suggested that every single time you went to the store or strolled down the sidewalk, you should imagine pushing your future baby in a carriage. "Never, ever stop thinking positive thoughts!" she admonished, and I imagined her rubbing her growing belly with a triumphant smile. *Of course she's saying that; she's pregnant!* I fumed, my arms pumping by my sides while the patches on my abdomen chafed against my shorts. Above me, Osaka Castle rose on its hill, all white walls and grayish-green scalloped roofs, gilded figurines flashing late-afternoon sun from its peaks. I barely noticed.

When my forty-third birthday and the fourth failed treatment passed, I found myself confined within yet another bubble. In addition to the remove of being an expat in Osaka, I'd become encased in a new kind of limbo. I was the only woman I knew doing years of failed IVF in Japan, while around me everyone else moved on. Like a rough wooden Russian doll inside a collection of nested glass *matryoshkas*, I could stare out and others could stare in, but each layer separated me further.

By this time, Jodi had moved permanently back to the U.S., and almost everyone else I knew in Japan had young children. Most of my Boston friends were still childless or never wanted kids, and I'd Skype with them sometimes, but they were so far away. Meanwhile, I'd watch my fellow Osaka expats jiggle their infants up and down, and wipe their mouths, and check their diapers, and I felt both bored with their babycentric conversation and removed from the whole group. My energy depleted, I closed down Four Stories in both the U.S. and Japan. Every day became consumed either by where I was in my cycle, hope for the current or next round of treatment, or efforts to positively impact the unknowable workings of my body, as if my insides held a supply chain of eggs on an assembly line that I was stalling each time I tried to fix it. I imagined those eggs tucked inside my organs, once clean, white spheres now going dusty and sluggish.

Meanwhile, the frustration of not knowing whether we would ever have a child, where my life was headed, made me ache, and a new fear began to haunt me: Will I spend four years in the prime of my life trying to get pregnant and end up with nothing but failure and lost time? I tried to write about my sense of suspension, but I couldn't call forth any meaning from it. I tried to work more freelance jobs, but I didn't have the energy.

Toru was sad each time an embryo transfer failed, but he bounced back more easily than I. His outward life had barely changed: he still got up every morning, ate his white toast with butter and milk tea, put on his suit, and took the train to work, slowly advancing in his career at the pace he had pretty much expected. Meanwhile, my life had telescoped until it was hard for me to see much beyond the imagined mirages of what was happening at any given moment in the organs twining through my belly. The whole time, I had a quiet soundtrack looping in my head: *How did I become this person obsessed with my ovaries?*

One night, Toru told me that his company was considering moving us to San Diego, where his unit had an office. I tried to imagine us starting over in a new place: the relief of trying medical treatment, if somehow we could get sufficient insurance, "at home"—even though San Diego was thousands of miles from Boston. "But what about your father?" I asked.

Over the last year, Otōsan's movements had gotten even shakier, and he now needed a cane to walk. He'd also begun to stutter sometimes, ever so slightly, like the words got tripped up on his tongue for a moment before they resumed their usual course, a stream with a small pebble in its flow. We tried to get him to see a doctor, and after months of shrugs and other quiet resistance, he agreed to go. A series of appointments and brain scans yielded a diagnosis: Parkinson's syndrome, a kind of degenerative constellation of muscular and nerve failures. The condition looked like Parkinson's disease, but it responded less well to medication, and it usually progressed more quickly.

When Toru told me about San Diego, I knew if Otōsan came with us it would be strange living together with my father-in-law, especially in America. But the idea of leaving him alone in Osaka was worse. I imagined him sitting on the couch in our living room in San Diego watching Japanese TV on satellite, like I did with CNN and *Law & Order* in Osaka; walking to the corner convenience store, dapper in a thin sweater vest. I saw him tapping his cane to each shaky step under a bright California sky, dipping his head in polite greeting to neighborhood teenagers skateboarding by. "Do you think your father would come with us if we asked him?"

Toru took my hand. "Thank you," he said quietly.

A few nights later, Otōsan came over for dinner. "Are you going to ask him about San Diego?" I whispered to Toru in the kitchen alcove while he grabbed a beer and I tried to finish the stir-fry. But Toru said nothing about the potential move during the meal. Finally, after I served the tea, I raised an eyebrow, and Toru nodded to me. *I guess I'm going to have to be the one to broach the subject,* I thought. In broken Japanese, I managed something equivalent to "Otōsan, maybe Toru's company moves us to San Diego. If we move, Otōsan also wants?"

Toru's father stared at me placidly for a moment, as if trying to sort through my mangled syntax. He sipped his tea, then put down the cup and turned to his son with a quiet string of words that I knew was a question by the way his tone ended higher. I expected their discussion to last a few minutes and include at least a modicum of emotional expression, especially on the part of Toru's father as he absorbed the surprising news. I wasn't holding out for tears or hugs or a frantic hour of questions, but I was bowled over when just a few moments later, Otōsan nodded his head once, took another slow sip of tea, and then turned to me, still utterly unruffled. He pushed back his chair, delivered his usual *"Gochisōsamadeshita!"* in thanks for the meal, grabbed his cane, and shuffled to the door.

Toru got up to see him out. I was too flummoxed to move. *"Kitte kudasatte arigato,"* I called weakly, thanking Otōsan for honoring us with his presence. "What happened!" I asked Toru when he returned. "What was that all about? What did your father say?"

"Nothing," Toru said, reaching for the pot to pour more *sencha*.

"Nothing? What do you mean nothing? Did you explain what I was trying to say? Did you tell your father about the move?"

"Ya, I told him."

"Well, what was his reaction? Is he coming with us if we go? Did he seem upset? Or excited?"

"Oh, no reaction," Toru said, turning for the couch with his teacup still in hand.

"What do you mean *no reaction*? Or is he in shock? Is that why he didn't react?"

"No, not in shock," Toru said. "Just no reaction. Not yet."

He looked at me, and I shook my head and raised my palms, squinting my eyes as if the invisible explanation might become clearer that way. Toru sighed.

"We don't know if moving yet," he said simply. "So no need to really making any plan. I explain to my father, and he's glad if we want him to come." But, Toru told me, since this was all still just speculation, there was no need for his father to think too much about it. "We'll worry the logistics later," he said.

Over the next few days, I replayed the scene in my head, calling friends in Boston and Osaka to share my shock. "So his father just pushes back his chair, gets up, thanks me for dinner, and leaves without a word!" I narrated, "and I'm going, 'Tof, what just happened?'"

But the more I thought about it, as I walked my endless loops around Osaka Castle Park, the idea of "worrying the logistics later" seemed kind of brilliant. *Imagine,* I thought, *not trying to sort out future what-ifs until they became present realities.* I knew I'd never achieve the equanimity of either Toru or his father; it just wasn't in my wiring. And I knew just because they weren't yet hashing out a potential future move—weren't trying to solve its challenges before it became fact—that didn't mean they didn't have feelings about it. They weren't perfect Buddhas, after all; they were human. But they didn't need to fix all the angles of a situation before they knew there was really something to address.

There was a lesson here, a counter to my fear that I'd spend four years trying to procreate and end up empty. There would be no way to know what the outcome would be, and struggling against this truth would do nothing to change or solve it. No one can tell you whether your body, in the end, will be capable of producing a child, or whether you'll regret what you've lost in the process. All you can do is try to take care of yourself, to stay as healthy and engaged as possible.

I didn't require positive mantras envisioning future babies. I just needed to live the life I had now as fully as I could and know that wherever I ended up, I'd tried my hardest in the time I'd been given. For now, I'd just do the best I could and worry the logistics later.

THAT FALL, Toru and I switched IVF clinics to one nearer our apartment. The new place was more expensive, but I was tired of going back to the old one, where our early good luck had bled into years of failed attempts.

The new clinic had a large, bright café where I could bring my laptop and sip hot *rooibos* tea while I waited, sometimes all morning or afternoon, for my turn to see the doctor or have blood tests or shots. The English-speaking head physician, Okomoto-*sensei,* was always dressed exactly the same: white medical coat and white polyester pants that stopped just above his ankles, with thick white socks and soft black shoes, his thinning hair swept sideways across his skull. When we met with him together, Toru and I always traded secret smiles over his outfit.

The clinic's overriding philosophy called for banishing stress—a futile goal for women undergoing IVF. In one of our first meetings with Okomoto-*sensei*, he summed up his anxiety-free approach to infertility by describing their post-embryo-transfer protocol: I should remain calm at all times, he instructed; "Of course, you can cook and do light cleaning. But you should stay quietly around the house. And no running to busy department store sales!"

The clinic sold meditation CDs, had their own acupuncture center, and even offered a marine-themed "relaxation room" with large recliners facing a wall-length screen showing calming underwater scenes. Toru and I never went into it, but we liked to peer inside and laugh over the spelling on the door—a Japanese rendering of *"reraxation roomu"*—and compete over who could come up with the most inappropriate screening for their atmosphere of forced tranquility. Toru suggested *Seed of Chucky*, I the anti-dolphin-hunting film *The Cove*, and then we'd cackle about hacking into their AV system while we waited to see doctors who would suck in their breath and clutch my charts, muttering, "*Sō, kana? Do shimashyo?*" "So, then, what is there to do now?"

Many women came into the clinic without their husbands but with their mothers, which struck me as odd until I got used to seeing these unlikely pairs. One day, I saw a woman in stilettos, skintight jeans, and a white T-shirt with a black Playboy bunny across the back. I couldn't tell whether I admired her or thought she was barking up the wrong tree. A little of both, I finally decided.

One of the clinic's most popular offerings was their Monday morning "fertility stretch" session, which Okomoto-*sensei* led himself. On Monday afternoons, a group of women would gather in the café after class, wearing loose yoga wear. They'd push long tables together, pull out their bento box lunches, and eat their *onigiri* rice balls, gossiping and comparing protocols, I imagined, for hours. I'd sit near them, tapping away at my keyboard on one freelance assignment or another, and wonder about them. I knew that far fewer than half of Japanese women worked after marriage, even if they didn't have kids, but I was still struck by the idea of spending a whole day at an IVF clinic when you weren't waiting for an appointment. Then I realized I was a lot like them. This is basically what we did with our lives: sit at the clinic, hope for two blue lines on a pregnancy test. They just did it communally, with rice balls.

One afternoon, I went to pick up my medicine in preparation for my treatment cycle. At the clinic's pharmacy window, a woman in a white-and-blue uniform handed me a pink envelope. In cursive English letters across the top, it said SMILE, THINK POSITIVE, LET YOURSELF RELAX, AND READY FOR CONCEPTION.

BY THE MIDDLE of that spring, six months after we'd started at the new clinic, Toru's company had decided against moving us to San Diego. In the meantime, I'd managed to grow one egg that the doctors removed, fertilized, and froze. I'd produced no more with all the tests, preparatory cycles, and stimulation shots than an average woman would have on her own in one month, and I would turn forty-four in less than half a year.

Just before the clinic could transfer my lone embryo, I woke one morning with burning in my stomach. When the hot spells kept coming for a week, Toru booked me an appointment with a GI specialist. "Ulcers, two!" reported the doctor, after instructing the nurse to bring in *Gaijin-san,* or Mrs. Foreigner, for an endoscopy. He stuck a camera up my nose and down my throat, Toru stroking my head while I choked and tried not to vomit, tears leaking down my cheeks as the doctor explained eagerly to

Toru and the nurse how my "narrow foreign nose" made shoving in the camera even harder. When he found two blisters side-by-side in my stomach, he announced in English, "Kissing ulcers!" seeming happy at the term. Then he scraped the lining of my gut, and a week later, he diagnosed a bacterial infection causing susceptibility to GI sores. The cure: two months of antibiotics and other medications, contraindicated for pregnancy or, by extension, an embryo transfer. Another long delay.

"I worry you," Toru said again, shaking his head. The bacteria had left me vulnerable to ulcers, but he feared the stress of infertility treatment had also contributed.

I cried over yet another stalled step, each day ticking closer to my forty-fifth birthday and our cutoff date to stop trying for a baby. Then I called the airlines and booked a quick trip home. I hadn't been back to the U.S. in more than a year. In Boston, I still felt numb and lost, but I drank wine and ate steak and French fries despite my ulcers, and I saw my closest friends.

When I flew back to Japan a few weeks later, I had a fresh plan in my clutches. I knew I couldn't control the outcome of these years of treatments, but at least I could prevent myself from looking back at forty-five and regretting I hadn't tried everything to conceive, every single month.

I went straight to the clinic in Osaka. "I want to try naturally this month, even though I'll still be on antibiotics for another few weeks," I told the doctor, a woman this time, Noguchi-*sensei*. She was younger and less authoritative than Okomoto-*sensei*, but she also spoke a little English. "I want to have ultrasounds to see if an egg is growing," I explained. She nodded slowly, her straight black chin-length hair shaking in time with her head, then pointed to the room next door, where I got into one of those mechanized chairs—blue, this time—and prepared to be hoisted, splayed, and wanded.

A week or so later, Noguchi-*sensei* gave me a shot to try to force my body to release an egg. Then I waited at the long white reception counter to pay. The clinic was busy that afternoon, a line of patients building up behind me as I rubbed my stomach where the nurse had injected me with hormones. When I got to the front, the receptionist pulled out my treatment sheet. She tried to explain a handwritten line Noguchi-*sensei* had added. "Huh?" I kept saying. *"Mō-ikkai onegaishimasu?"* "Once more, please?" The receptionist's face began to redden, the crowd behind me shifting restlessly as she continued to repeat whatever she was attempting to communicate, finally blurting out something that sounded like *"Timingu! Timingu!"* I had no idea what she meant. Finally, I offered the one line in Japanese that I knew perfectly by now: *"Shujin wa* Nihonjin. *Ato, shujin wa watashi ni oshiemasu!"* "My husband is Japanese. Later, he'll explain to me!"

The receptionist nodded, looking like I'd just handed her a jug of water at the far end of a sweat lodge. Then she ran my credit card, handed me the sheet, and hastily bowed me farewell.

That night, I showed the paper to Toru, who laughed. "What?" I asked. "What does it say?"

"It says tonight we should have fuck!"

I realized what the receptionist had been trying to say: "Timing," for "timed intercourse." On the sheet Noguchi-*sensei* had worded it more medically, of course, than Toru. But I imagined that, with the long line of patients behind me at the desk and the receptionist's increasingly panicked attempts to explain, the effect at the clinic that afternoon had been barely more discreet than my husband's.

A few days after I finally finished my last antibiotic, two weeks since seeing Dr. Noguchi, I woke around five a.m., my abdomen heavy. I went to the bathroom to check for blood. Then I went to the closet where I kept my tampons, razors, cosmetics, and pills, rifling through the contents piled in plastic boxes.

Five minutes later, I flew into the bedroom, an early pregnancy test in my hand. It was positive.

TORU MADE a clinic appointment for me that same day. Neither Okomoto-*sensei* nor Noguchi-*sensei* was available, but there was one more doctor who could manage some English, another woman. Yamamoto-*sensei* was older than Noguchi-*sensei* and had a more forthright manner. She ordered me a blood test "to make sure pregnancy is . . . real," she said haltingly.

I spent the next hour and a half in the café, unable to concentrate on anything, trying not to dwell on the doctor's use of the term "real." Women filtered in and out, the glass doors opening and closing, little trays of tea or coffee in their hands, but it all felt underwater to me. Nothing penetrated the cottony feeling in my mouth and the thrumming inside my chest.

When Yamamoto-*sensei* called me back into her office, she tucked a cowlick of hair behind her ear and smiled, pushing some test results toward me. She told me I was due March ninth, almost four months after my forty-fourth birthday.

My head continued to feel underwater for the next few days. I had no ambivalence about being pregnant now, only a happy kind of shock. Toru walked around with a quiet smile on his face, but still, he told me, "We should stay cool." That weekend, we wandered around Umeda's enormous underground in the center of the city, moving slowly through the anonymous crowd, as if speed might somehow dislodge the tiny cells growing in my abdomen. I felt a spike of awe-tinged joy, thinking, *It's the three of us here, walking around together.*

I had a day or two of slight nausea, when the smells at my morning café made me clutch a handkerchief to my face. But then the feeling started to wane. I went home and took another pregnancy test, my heart pounding so hard in my ears I could feel it thump while I tried not to stare at the stick until three minutes had passed. When I looked, I still saw two blue lines. But was one even fainter than it had been before? I couldn't tell.

The clinic put me on so much medication to prevent another miscarriage and protect my ulcerated stomach that we told Otōsan I was pregnant again, though naturally, not with our frozen embryo, Toru explaining while I laid out my series of pills one night after dinner. Otōsan smiled wide, his eyes bright, but then he turned pensive and asked Toru a question in Japanese.

"What did he say?" I wanted to know.

Toru shook his head at me, and I knew once again his father had annoyed him. Otōsan was never judgmental about our doing IVF, but he didn't really get what it was all about. Toru rolled his eyes like he did when his father couldn't figure out how to turn on the computer, then said, "He wants to know, which baby do we want? The one in your stomach now or the one in freezer?"

The next morning, my nausea still seemed on the wane. I was scheduled to go in for another blood test in a few days, but I texted Toru at work. "I think I should go back to the clinic now, as soon as possible," I told him when he called back. "I took another test this morning, and I really think the line looks fainter. It's still there. But faint."

I saw Yamamoto-*sensei* again, and she sent me back for a second blood test. I spent another hour or so in the café trying not to cry, flipping listlessly through a Japanese magazine from the waiting room, seeing nothing. When Yamamoto-*sensei* called me back into her office, she had another sheet of test results in front of her. She pushed them toward me again, but she didn't meet my eye.

"I'm sorry, Mrs. Tracy," she said, "but your baby is not growing up."

I tried to keep my voice as steady as possible, swallowing hard and glancing around the stark walls before I worked up the nerve to look near her face. In the end, I only managed a shaky question about what to do after the inevitable miscarriage. "I mean, I know we still have the frozen embryo," I croaked out. "But if that . . . if that one doesn't work either, can we try naturally again?"

Yamamoto-*sensei* tucked her black hair behind her ear again, then looked straight at me. "It's a miracle you even got pregnant naturally at all," she said, her English sounding perfect just this once.

Six weeks later, after I'd miscarried, I had my last embryo transfer. It failed, too.

"FOR GOD'S SAKE, you're not going to get pregnant, Tracy." My mother—never one to mince words—tried to level with me a few months later over Skype.

She worried we were wasting precious time. Toru and I had stopped the IVF treatments, but I insisted we still try every month with ultrasounds and hormone support from the clinic, plus new twice-a-day injections of a blood thinner for a "clotting disorder" the clinic had diagnosed, which they claimed could cause early-state miscarriage. My stomach bloomed with red and purple welts from all the shots, but I was undeterred.

"Why don't you just adopt?" my mother demanded. My eldest sister said she cried for me, she was so sad that I wouldn't have a child with Toru, but she also couldn't understand why we didn't "just adopt." "I mean," she said, "if you're still not willing to do egg donation." Both she and my mother pointed out that with adoption, too, we needed to hurry, since many agencies had age cutoffs.

Then my mother took to telling me about her friends whose daughters had used surrogates. "I can't even produce a normal egg, Mom," I said in frustration. "How is hiring a surrogate going to help?" To Toru, I complained ungenerously that, as usual, my mother thought hiring someone would solve the problem. "As if she doesn't even realize how expensive having a surrogate would be in the first place!" I said, my eyes fixing him with annoyance meant for her.

"Poor Charlotte," Toru said, as he usually did when I complained about my mother. Then, "Poor my love."

I worried about Toru holding in his own sadness and frustration, but when I tried to talk to him about it, he insisted he was "okay." "Sometimes, a little sad," he admitted, when I pushed, telling him how I'd read that men often think they need to stay strong for their female partners during infertility treatments. "It's not fair for you to have to always be the strong one," I said.

But I remembered how he never liked to talk about his mother after she died, how discussing painful things proved harder for him than staying silent about them, despite all my Western psychoanalytical beliefs in the dangers of repression. I thought about the Japanese tendency to show love and support not through words but with actions that increase interdependence. I adored Toru's father, but our bond was built on hardly any conversation: I cooked for him and he helped me with my Japanese, teaching me new words and reading directions and filling out forms I couldn't decipher. Now, with Toru, I tried to make his favorite foods or run a nightly bath for him, or insist he go for a shiatsu massage after every failed fertility step or night where his father was especially unsteady on his feet. Eventually, I found comfort in these simple, practical actions. I knew Toru's heart hurt for me, and he knew mine hurt for him, and we didn't have to pretend words would fix anything.

As for my mother and sister's advice to "just adopt," I saw on the IVF chat boards and from friends or friends of friends that the adoption process is frequently as heartbreaking, as filled with delays, false starts, and disappointments as medical treatment. Often even more so. Despite their good intentions, when people urged adoption as the obvious Plan B, I felt angry. *If they are so proadoption, with their brood of biological offspring, why don't they go ahead and adopt?* I thought crabbily. Moreover, I was suspicious about this Plan B concept. It seemed potentially belittling to both adoptive parents and children. Many parents who adopted, I saw, did so because they longed to adopt, to become family with a life already in existence, not because it was the second-best choice.

Still, I knew people on the IVF forums who were fine giving reproductive technology one or two tries and moving on to adoption. I also knew women who were willing to put their marriages at risk to become parents. They would spend life savings, leave their husbands or partners if they couldn't agree on options like egg or sperm donation, or adoption.

"A therapist once told me," a woman wrote on my Over 40 forum, "that if what I wanted most in the world was to be a mother, then I would be one; I would find a way, no matter what." The writer found deep comfort in this truth, and when I read her post, I admired her, but I knew that wasn't true for me.

What I wanted most in the world was to be with Toru, and then to have his biological child. Before marriage, before babies meant anything to me besides a frightening threat to one's freedom, I'd always thought in an abstract way that adoption was one of the loveliest choices a person could make: to decide to become family with another little person. I'd never put much stock in genetics. After all, my sister Lauren had found more comfort and safety with her foster family than she'd ever found with the parents whose DNA she shared. Even when my friend Jenna, who'd adopted her son, told me that the ideal of the adoptive parent "was total bullshit," that people who adopt do so because they want to, not from some innate altruism, I still secretly harbored admiration for parents who welcomed a lone little one in from the wide open world.

Yet when Toru told me that he wasn't open to either egg donation or adoption, I felt an unexpected relief. Since adoption in Japan is so rare, I wasn't surprised by his stance. But after we'd begun the process of trying to have a baby years before, I'd realized that my own growing longing to parent our biological child didn't necessarily translate into a yearning to be a parent in general. Wanting to have your biological baby isn't the same as wanting a child in general.

By now, the experience of going through years of treatments had confirmed another surprising truth to me: just because you think you are open to certain possibilities in the abstract—such as adoption—you never know where your true limits lie until you're faced with actual, lasting choices. Rational or not, I felt safest in my gut with the idea of a baby who was half Toru. I believed it would be harder for me *not* to bond with, *not* to love a child whose every cell contained half of him. And if Toru and I couldn't make a baby together, I'd still rather be together and childless than a mother apart from him.

Sometimes I wondered if that made me less deserving of parenthood, or of mourning its elusiveness. I didn't know the answer, but I knew the whole issue of my fertility would become obsolete soon, with my forty-fifth birthday looming just past summer. Most major studies don't even consider women giving birth at forty-five or beyond, when the average chance of someone having a baby with her own eggs drops below one percent. The latest U.S. National Center for Health Statistics report defines women of childbearing age as between fifteen and forty-four. I'd already entered the territory of a statistical nonentity.

A FEW MONTHS LATER, just days before my forty-fifth birthday, I lay curled in bed past midnight, sobs shaking through me. Toru lay beside me, wiping strands of wet hair from my cheeks. "You know," he said, locking his steady eyes to my teary ones, "if we can have baby, that would be like miracle. But it will still only be like dessert, because you will always be main course."

I couldn't believe we weren't ever going to meet our baby. It felt both so obvious and so inconceivable. How I could mourn something I'd never even had, grieve the loss of something that had never actually existed? The tension between my fear of parenthood and my longing to have Toru's baby began to transmute now into a new emotional torsion, a swirl of missing and nothingness, numbness and nostalgia.

But as my birthday came and went, I reminded myself of my enduring good fortune in other ways, and I knew it was crucial to remember such a fact. The previous January, Toru and I had celebrated our fifth year of marriage, and we'd laughed when we remembered my original "three-year nuptial plan," long forgotten once I'd gotten over my initial nerves. The night of our anniversary, sitting at our favorite Italian wine bar, bubbles rising in clear flutes, we'd toasted each other, and then Toru had turned momentarily serious. "Thank you for marrying with me these five years," he'd said, and once again I couldn't believe my luck that somehow we had found each other across cultures, continents, and half the world's wide curve. I hadn't been able to have our baby, but I'd still been given one of life's rarest gifts. I'd already gotten my number-one desire: to be family with Toru.

I thought back to him saying we were "together in always." I had no idea where I was in my life, how I would start rebuilding after fixing my existence on a dream that never came true, how I would emerge from the limbo of the past four years. But I realized now that those years wouldn't be wasted—and I wouldn't even choose to do them differently after learning where they'd led—because they would remain a testament of our love for our baby, even if we never got to meet that baby. It was a testament that felt precious to me, despite the failures that accompanied it. Really, there was no better place to be, I knew, despite the sadness in my chest, than together where we'd been, and now where I was still, with Toru in always.

The last stage . . . aims at the goal of a bi-cultural or multicultural identity [where] the individual has moved from alienation to a new identity. . . . The emotions of the previous four stages will be integrated and synthesized into this new identity with each stage contributing its own essential perspective to the development [and] an unfolding of the new self. . . . This fifth stage then is not the end point or culmina-tion of development but a state of dynamic tension between self and culture that opens new perspectives.

> • Paul Pedersen, *The Five Stages*
> *of Culture Shock*

But that's okay, that's good. Because then I can send you.

> • Toru

SIXTEEN

WHILE I'D BEEN WATCHING MY body's stasis, its unbending refusal month after month to let a new life grow inside it, Toru and I watched another life begin to teeter. One morning during the spring before my forty-fifth birthday, Otōsan bent over to pick something up from the floor of his apartment. Then he slipped to the ground. He lay quietly on the hard threadbare rug of his living room, his head curved at an angle against the legs of the couch, the cellular we'd pleaded with him to wear always around his neck now nowhere within reach, while the sun made its slow arc from the balcony floor to the living room wall and then began to fade.

As usual, I was "on call," ready to be summoned by phone. Kei was coming home that night from Tokyo. When she arrived, he'd been floorbound for some nine hours. Sometime between the folding of his body and the eternity he spent supine staring at the ceiling, he'd either broken or bruised his hip. He refused to go to the doctor to find out which.

Within a few days, he sat in a wheelchair from which he'd never fully escape, at least not until he was forced supine once

again, a year later, against the rough white sheets of a hospital ward.

After his fall, Toru and I tried to keep Otōsan living in his
apartment for as long as possible. We'd talk late into the night
about what would happen if we threw out the bookshelves and
laundry lines and small desk from the extra room in our apartment and squeezed in a twin-sized hospital bed for him. Would
the wheelchair even fit?

"I wonder it," Toru said.

But mostly, he shook his head at me. "You'd become constant nursemaid, with no privacy, and I don't think you could
stand it," he said, more willing to face the facts than I. The diaper pads his father now needed but only rarely agreed to wear;
the way I'd have to dress him and lift him and sit at the dining
room table trying to work while he sat next to me all day in his
wheelchair watching TV. I knew whenever I suggested ways we
might move Otōsan in with us, I was making Toru feel his guilt
even deeper than he already did, forcing him to protect me, to
recognize my limits more truthfully than my own guilt let me.

Mornings, a helper-*san* provided by the state would visit
Otōsan's apartment, help him dress, move him from the hospital
bed Toru had ordered to the wheelchair and then take him into
the kitchen, where she'd heat the breakfast I had laid out the
night before. Then she'd wheeled him back to the living room,
where he would sit and watch TV and strain to hold on to his
dignity in an empty room. He would stay alone until I came
over in the afternoon to take him for a walk and fix his dinner,
although three or four days a week I wouldn't even come for his
walk, and he would sit there silently until I arrived to prepare his

food. He refused to have a helper-*san* in the apartment except for in the early morning, after Toru told him it was too much for me to get up at six-thirty every day and bike to his apartment. I blushed and looked down when he told Otōsan this, and then I looked up and said, *"Gomennasai,* Otōsan," "I'm sorry." After, I added, as if it could erase his anguish at having a stranger handle him each morning and then spending his days all alone as a prisoner in his own body, "But I can come every evening and some afternoons, too, and we can take a walk in Osaka Castle Park!"

When we did walk, I'd push his wheelchair and Toru's father would look at the leaves, and we barely talked, but I found an unexpected soothing in the *woosh* of the chair's tires and Otōsan's quiet breathing, his face turned to the sun. When we went to do errands or were on the way to the park, people would stare at us, and sometimes Otōsan and I would laugh about it: the wide-eyed curiosity over the light-haired woman in yoga pants and sneakers pushing a wool-vested, blanket-covered, graying Japanese man.

On the phone, my family asked when I'd be coming home. My hope had been to go back for an extended stay once my forty-fifth birthday passed in October. But by autumn, Otōsan was so sick and in need of such constant care that we couldn't find a way for me to leave. Neither Toru nor Kei could take enough time off work to allow me to go home even for two weeks.

In between our daily regimens of work plus housework plus visiting Otōsan plus trying to snatch a few moments to ourselves, Toru and I were trying to gauge my body's cycles without the clinic's help. Toru thought we still had a chance (though remote, he conceded) of conceiving a child without all the shots and doctors and medical interventions. But I'd read the studies and statistics, recalled all my dismal test results, and I knew he was wrong.

Once again, though, I'd come up with a plan, all neatly mapped. I'd give myself nine months to move on, claiming a kind of gestation period for my mourning. Speed-walking around Osaka Castle Park with my American friend Lisa (childless, single, safe), I detailed the perfect blueprint for my grief: a trimester of being a mess (Just like three months of morning sickness! Although now I can just be hungover!), a trimester of emerging from the thick swamp of sadness, and a trimester of preparing in earnest for a childless marriage, after which could bloom the resumption of a normal existence with new goals and hopes and a renewal of my part-time life in Boston. "And then we can start traveling together, too!" Lisa said, and, arms swinging under the shadow of the ginkgo trees, we guessed at new itineraries.

As I was talking from my living room one late-fall morning to my shrink in Cambridge with whom I had Skype sessions periodically, she asked in her even, therapeutic tone what would happen if I didn't insist on a strict plan, a black-and-white organization of my life. I could hear the ambulance sirens of a Central Square evening coming to me from the headset of my computer as I stared through the Osaka light, and I thought about her question.

I liked my crystal-edged intentions, so clean, so organized. My forty-fifth birthday had provided us a neat threshold from where I could begin to move on, and nine months later (What unexpected symmetry! What a clear path!) I'd stop my mourning and start the hard work of rebuilding all I'd relinquished when I narrowed my entire life down to medically enhanced baby-making in Japan.

But, of course, Toru and I hadn't stopped having sex now that I'd stopped all treatments. We still had an intense tenderness and bond, more so now because of what together we'd hoped for and lost. Combining that with an agreement to have sex as much as possible in the middle of every month covered all our bases. I even found an unexpected comfort, a surprising familiarity in the loose schedule of our intimacy. After more than four years of having our couplings monitored, mandated, or limited by fertility clinics, we didn't have to question how to restoke any original, more primal urge to be together.

This all felt too much to explain in therapy, though. I never liked talking about sex with someone I had to pay to listen. "Yeah," I said into the tail end of a long silence, "I guess we could still keep 'trying.' I mean, just by having sex and stuff." This could be a way to ease into the postbaby quest. Toru got to hold on to his optimism, while I could still feel close to him without holding on to any false hope, without pretending I didn't know my fertility was now statistically considered gone.

When I switched topics to Toru's father, my shrink didn't press the issue. In the same therapeutic tone, she asked a question I could have anticipated even in a coma from any twenty-first-century therapy session between a Northeast female doctor and an overeducated female patient: What was I doing to take care of *myself*, to prioritize *my* needs, while I tried simultaneously to care for my father-in-law?

A few nights later, on Skype with my stepmother, I said Toru and I were beginning to look for nursing homes, called "care houses" in Japan, although we knew Otōsan didn't want to move to one. "I just never thought," I told my stepmother, "that I'd be changing diapers now, only to have them be my father-in-law's." She told me again how sorry she was that we hadn't been able to have a baby. "But you know, honey," she said, the Skype connection crackling beneath her Texas twang, "in life, things just have a way of happening for a reason."

My eyes narrowed to slits. I stared venom into the pixels of my computer screen. My stepmother was trying to be helpful. But I didn't care. I ended the conversation quickly.

I knew there was no reason, no redemptive message, in our not being able to have a child. I had no patience for anyone's well-intentioned efforts to push a silver lining my way. Yes, I believed Toru and I could make a good life without having made a baby. I knew eventually I'd write about what we'd done and felt and learned about finding joy in a barren marriage. And, of course, that was all a gift. But one gift didn't exist to justify the losses that had preceded it. Why, I wondered, must we rush to make it seem so? What we'd gone through had been a testament of our love for our baby-who-never-was, but that didn't mean it was the right outcome.

Instead of redemption or meaning, what you have to find in the trail of years of failures, I was coming to believe, is the determination to go beyond those failures. To build a full and meaningful life not because of but in spite of them. When friends or family talked about "gestating" a book or any other opportunity instead of a baby, I gritted my teeth. I counted their children in my bitter brain. Cast aspersions on their flimsy need to make a neat narrative out of grief. (Ignored, at least at first, the way their neat narratives mirrored my own determination to meticulously map each step of my own mourning.)

Our grief was small compared to many people's. We'd lost embryos, not children; chances, not lives. But it did teach me one modest lesson about loss: usually, it leaves no meaning in its wake. Just the responsibility to build beyond it.

EVERY WEEKNIGHT that fall, after I fixed Otōsan's dinner, Toru and I would eat at a restaurant, and then either he or I would give his father a shower and put him to bed. I learned to kneel on the bathroom floor and keep my eyes lowered while I wrapped a towel around Otōsan's waist and slid the diaper pad up or down, or hold him under his arms and stare at the wall over his bony shoulder while together we crab-walked into his shower room, then lowered him onto a plastic stool. My eyes would turn to examine the shower knob as if it were a device of endless fascination, and then I'd turn it on and angle the spray toward Otōsan's stool, staring at the plastic seat legs hovering near the drain. After his shower, I knelt again on the hard floor of the changing room, raised a towel to his waist, and lowered my head, saying repeatedly *"Sumimasen!"* ("Please excuse me!"). For the first time, I felt grateful for Japanese protocol, which now gave me postures and polite apologies in deference to Otōsan's immutable dignity as the elder and my eternal humility as daughter-in-law, traditions helping to soften the brittle truths in the bathroom alongside us.

Afternoons when I came over, Otōsan would spend long minutes straining to lift himself from his wheelchair or put on his own pair of socks. Then he'd fail and try again. I'd wait until he lifted his head and nodded at me, and then I'd intervene. Afterward, he always said, *"Domo arigato gozaimasu,* To-ray-shee," thanking me as formally as possible. I longed to tell him how his quiet persistence in the glare of time's iron destruction gave me strength and inspiration. That he was teaching me the rarest of life's lessons: how to face the inevitable declines of age, how to lose our bodies without ever giving up the fight to remain in dignity. But I never did.

I thought about his huge loss happening just after my and Toru's smaller one. How my body had revealed its first signs of irreversible aging as his began to swoon under its final wane. How his face never cracked with strain or anger as his body remained an elusive stranger to his mind, his foot like a foreign country to the sock clutched in his fist. He'd just try again, completely absorbed in the challenge.

I also never told Otōsan how I began to find the strangest source of solace in his body, in the chance to comfort him even though he never wanted that. How after his shower I'd pat down his spindly torso and his legs that were like winter trees, and some small measure of my grief would soften over the loss of another body, a baby's body, to fuss over. Then I'd feel guilty—a terrible, dark, dirty guilt—that I could conjure any kind of consolation from his suffering.

Some nights, the phone would ring at three or four in the morning, and Otōsan would tell Toru that he had fallen, he wasn't sure where—maybe he was outside now, at their friends' summer cottage where they went when Toru was a child? Or at home but he'd need to leave soon for the office? He would guess at possibilities, slumped in the dark against his hospital bed, and Toru and I would drag ourselves onto our bicycles and pedal through the empty city streets. When we got to the apartment, Toru would distract his father with a change of pajamas or another shower while I scrubbed the rug, praying Otōsan wouldn't notice. On these nights, I didn't feel consoled at all; I felt as overwhelmed and sad and guilty as I knew Toru felt all the time.

One morning, just after Toru left for work, the phone rang at seven-thirty. "To-ray-shee," I heard Otōsan say, "SOS!" Then the helper-*san* took the phone. She spoke fast in Japanese, and I had no idea what she was saying. I hung up and called Toru, who was on the train. He got off at the next stop to call his father, then called me back. The helper had found him on the floor and couldn't lift him.

Soon after I got there, another helper-*san* arrived, along with Otōsan's care manager. Together, they bathed and dressed him while I wiped the kitchen floor where Otōsan had fallen in the middle of the night after, I imagined, tumbling into his wheelchair and pushing himself painstakingly forward, eager for an early breakfast, or just unsure where he was.

I called Toru again. "How am I supposed to behave with the helper-*sans*!" I asked, panicky. "I know it's rude for me to do their jobs, because I'm not supposed to suggest that they aren't doing them properly. But I can't help feeling like it's totally rude of me to just stand here and let them clean up! And I don't want them to think I'm not willing to clean or help Otōsan!" I couldn't believe I was fretting about etiquette at a time like this, one half of my brain trying to gauge the cultural expectations, the other half stunned with worry about Toru's father.

"Maybe just heat his breakfast?" Toru suggested. "But no need to help them wash him." I flew around the kitchen, my face hot, my nerves buzzing, turning on the coffeepot, heating Otōsan's toast, arranging the butter this way and that on the table, as if angling the dish called for consummate precision.

A few days later, when I came to take Otōsan for a walk, he was sitting in his wheelchair in the kitchen. "To-ray-shee," he said, and he tapped his forehead. Then in English, "I think, maybe, something's wrong with my head."

By late fall, Toru had finally convinced his father to go to a nursing home, and after New Year's, we moved him into a private one nearby, partly subsidized by Japan's nationalized health system, partly by Otōsan's life savings. "How long can he, and then we, afford that?" I asked Toru, who calculated ten years. I felt thankful that Otōsan would have a private room—not available at any public care house near us—and grateful that together we had enough savings for longer than he'd probably live. Then I felt guilt and sadness again to think we were budgeting a man of seventy-three to die by his early eighties.

The morning before Otōsan's move, I covered the walls of his tiny sterile-clean new room with a dozen old family photos, as if they could distract him from his loss of home. Toru felt relief and also a deeper kind of guilt, but for me, the daily visits had become much simpler. No cleaning, no struggling with the wheelchair ramp up the steps to Otōsan's apartment. Now, I'd push the chair through the spare, gleaming care house lobby and bow my head to the row of receptionists behind the desk, and they'd flip some switch behind their counter that opened the glass doors to outside. Then we'd walk along the streets of Shinsaibashi and watch the people watching us, or we'd stare into shop windows or restaurant displays, their plastic models of faux udon or curry angled toward the sidewalk, all glossy with shellac.

Sometimes at night, I'd sit with Toru's father in the care house dining room while he had dinner. The facility was still new, Otōsan's floor not yet filled, and around us, four or five other men would sit alone at tidy tables, bowing their heads slightly when the white- or pink-clad helper-*sans* brought fish and rice and vegetables. They'd stare at the wide-screen TV while they ate, and I'd sit nervously next to Otōsan, wondering whether or how often to help him lift the spoon to his mouth, not wanting to embarrass him, not wanting the staff to think me cold, then praying they wouldn't try to talk to me in Japanese. After he finished eating, a helper-*san* brought Otōsan his medicine, a little clear packet with his name printed in black, and below that, a pink Hello Kitty figure winking out at us with her huge eyes and absent mouth.

One cold afternoon, I tried to turn on the heating unit in Otōsan's room, which was tucked between a wall and the ceiling. "Why is this closed?" I asked in Japanese, forgetting the word for "turned off." Otōsan just shook his head. I grabbed the remote and stared at its buttons, each one labeled in *kanji*. The unit had options for cooling, heating, fan, timer, and the like, but I couldn't tell which was which, so I pushed various buttons, and Otōsan and I lifted our heads to watch, hearing beeps that told us nothing, seeing lights change in indication of who knew what. "*Gomen,* Otōsan," I said, "Sorry," and then I lapsed into English. "Sorry, but I'm confused!"

"Me, too, To-ray-shee," he replied.

IN FEBRUARY, four months past my forty-fifth birthday and with Otōsan settled in the care house, I finally took a three-week trip home to Boston. Originally I'd planned to go for longer, but we still didn't want to leave Toru's father without a daily family visit, and it was hard for Toru to get off work by the time visiting hours ended at eight p.m. Kei was trying to plan time off from her job in Tokyo that summer, so I intended to go home again in July and August for at least six weeks.

At home, I began to think again about how we could afford to buy a small studio apartment somewhere in the Boston area now that we weren't going to have a child. I drank coffee every morning and wine each night, went to a hot yoga class and heard my heart beat too fast in my ears, and felt a delicious release at not caring about any of it. When I went running around the reservoir across from my mother's apartment, my muscles felt weaker than they had years earlier when I jogged three times a week, but my body felt both looser and sharper, as if without the constant hormone treatments a thick haze had begun to burn off.

I even resumed Four Stories, holding an inaugural return event. For opening night, I bought new grayish-blue suede boots and got my hair cut, highlighted, and blown out, and I drank cocktails and laughed and blabbed at the microphone and felt grateful when a crowd once again showed up. Somewhere deep inside I still felt the hollow space of sadness and disbelief that Toru and I wouldn't have a child. But I also felt my old self coming back.

In Boston, now meeting face-to-face, my shrink wanted to discuss my feelings about the baby-not-to-be. I had nothing specific to say. She raised her eyebrow. I didn't feel like I was avoiding the topic; I was in a place where conversation didn't necessarily serve.

Silently, I recognized that my perfect plan hadn't rolled out exactly as expected, that instead of tumbling into my scheduled first trimester of gut-deep grief, I felt more numbness than anything, despite the melancholy that lingered at its edges. On one hand, I tried to explain, my life was no different than it had ever been: I'd never had a child and didn't have one now. On the other, I still felt sad and shocked, like I'd lost something, but what? It was all just one more emotional push-pull. Before, the contradiction was between terror that I'd be a bad mother and terror that I'd never get to meet our baby. Before that, it was between wanting to be with Toru and not knowing if I could survive Japan, or even marriage. Now, the friction was between everything being the same and different at the same time. But wasn't that life? To hold two contradicting truths at one time and to keep on holding them?

OTŌSAN ONLY MADE IT a few months in the care house. One early morning soon after I got back to Osaka, a nurse called. Toru was on a business trip in Hong Kong, and I grabbed the phone from the bedside table, staring through slit eyes at the clock. Just past six-thirty. I knew something must have happened even before I heard the nurse's rush of Japanese. Within her explanation, I could only understand a few random words. *Byoin,* "hospital," and *netsu,* "fever" (or was she saying *natsu,* "summer"? But, no, that wouldn't make any sense, would it?), and then a string of sharp syllables that remained opaque to me beyond the urgency in her voice.

By the time I had called Toru in Hong Kong and he had phoned the care house and then his sister in Tokyo and then called me back, Otōsan was in an ambulance. I sped to the hospital on my bike, the March air damp and cool on my skin. I waited almost an hour on the orange vinyl seat of the hospital's lobby couch, Toru calling back and forth between me and the care house, me trying to explain to the man behind the square information window that I was looking for my father-in-law, then urging my cell phone toward him and pleading with him to talk to Toru as he reared back from the handset thrust in his face by the frantic foreigner. Finally, we realized Otōsan had been brought to a different hospital. The one where I waited, where Otōsan's regular doctor worked, apparently did not accept emergency admissions between the hours of eight p.m. and eight a.m. The ambulance had searched for a hospital that both had a bed and took critical patients anytime. Later, as Toru explained all this to me, I couldn't stop shaking my head into the phone. *What, they only take emergencies on a strict schedule in this country?* I couldn't tell if I was misunderstanding the culture or Toru's explanation. It turned out, not unusually, to be the former.

The bed they found Otōsan was in a ward for ten men, their various illnesses rising in a swamp of smells from their parchment skin. The doctors lowered Otōsan's fever from more than 103 degrees Fahrenheit with an IV drip, then diagnosed acute pneumonia. When he opened his eyes, he looked around as if he had landed in another country. He was too weak to speak. Over the next month, we'd explain that he'd gotten very sick, and now he was in the hospital about a mile from the care house, still close to his own apartment. But he'd forget again and again where he was.

A few of the men around Otōsan moaned, others swatted at the bars along their beds with mitten-covered hands while scaly or weeping splotches bloomed on their ankles, legs, or forearms. A couple were unconscious, hooked up to beeping monitors. Many had pee bags attached with catheters, the yellow liquid sloshing in clear plastic until someone came around with a bucket to empty them. The other men wore diapers, and twice a day the nurses would shoo me and any other visitors out of the room and close the heavy iron door to change their patients in semiprivacy. Windows along the wall were shrouded with thin, papery-looking shades emitting weak streams of light, which loitered on the ceiling, blotched, like the men's limbs, with cracks and stains.

"Did they put him in a public hospital?" I asked Toru, when he got home the next day from Hong Kong, joining both me and Kei at Otōsan's bedside. "Not public, just old," Toru said, his eyes bleak. No wonder there had been an empty bed for his father, for who would choose a ward like that? But the doctors were reluctant to move him now.

I spent the next month steeling myself for the ward's smells and sounds each weekday when visiting hours started. Toru assured me I didn't need to stay long each afternoon, but Otōsan was so confused about where he was, and I got a feeling in my chest like paper being crushed into a tiny crinkled ball when I imagined him alone and bewildered as he woke each day, staring up at a dirty prewar ceiling. The nurses wouldn't let me use my computer or even my e-reader in the ward because of the patients on heart monitors, even though I explained I'd turned off the Web connection. Mostly, though, they were kind, and I didn't want to inhibit their desire to care for Otōsan by angering them, so I obeyed, bringing books and sitting by his bedside, breaking up the six hours of visiting time with trips to get tea or a late lunch until Toru could rush in from work for the last hour or so. Outside, I'd gulp at the fresh air.

In the hospital, sometimes I'd hold or stroke Otōsan's hand, and when he got a little stronger, I'd help him stretch his bone-thin legs in a vain attempt to prevent a loss of muscle mass. I held his foot in my hand and said, "Push!" and he'd push his toes against my palm with light, tentative pressure, and then I'd push back and try to move his whole leg back and forth, like a make-shift recumbent bike on a speed barely above "off."

"Thank you, To-ray-shee," he'd whisper, when we were done.

Toru and I were both so tired every night when we left the hospital, its smells and shadows clinging to our clothes, that we'd have dinner, go home and shower, and then tumble into bed. As we had over the previous half year or so, we tried to figure out when and if my body would release an egg that cycle, but when we only managed to have sex twice that month, we barely noticed.

WHEN THE HOSPITAL finally released Otōsan, on a cloudy Sunday five weeks after he had been admitted, I felt a surge of optimism as we drove back to the care house. Toru's father was in his own wheelchair on a ramp in the back of the first car Toru and I had ever owned: a tiny van, equipped with a handicapped ramp in place of a backseat. We'd bought the vehicle a few months earlier to bring Otōsan over for dinner on the weekends when it was too cold for him outside, but we'd barely used it before he'd been hospitalized.

Back at the care house, the staff lined up and bowed as we brought in Otōsan, and then they all called out, *"Okaeri,"* "Welcome home!" Toru's father nodded slightly, looking tired and a little confused.

In his room, the care house nurses examined him and found a raw, gaping bedsore spreading from the bony notch above his backside. They shook their heads and clucked their tongues at the hospital's negligence, then laid him on his side and tried to clean the wound and dress it while Otōsan trembled a little, his face to the wall. I turned my back to the bed and stared at the door, and when they had covered Otōsan's midriff again, I turned back around and saw that Toru had turned pale.

After the care house doctor arrived and put Otōsan back on antibiotics, the staff encouraged us to go home so Toru's father could rest. I promised Toru I would come back the following morning, bring my laptop, and sit with Otōsan most of the day to help him with the transition back. Then we went home, exhausted again, my earlier optimism turning gray but still not gone completely.

The next morning, the phone rang again at just past eight. It was Toru, calling from his way to work. "My father's fever is bad again," he told me. Otōsan needed to return to the hospital. This time, Toru insisted the care house bring him themselves and go directly to the correct hospital, where Otōsan's doctor worked and where we knew the care was good—and Otōsan could get a single room.

I was waiting in the lobby when the care house nurse and helper pulled up in a taxi with Toru's father. I rushed outside, but Otōsan didn't seem to recognize me, and he had white foam pooling from his mouth. I tried to wipe his chin as gently as possible while we waited for the nurse to fill out his admissions papers, and I listened to the wheeze of his labored breath. By the time Toru arrived a few hours later, the emergency room doctors had diagnosed acute pneumonia again and a fever of more than a hundred and four.

A few days later, the hospital added an additional diagnosis. One early evening, they called us into the nurses' station on Otōsan's floor and pulled up some pictures on a screen. By that time, the nurses all knew me by sight, because once again I tried to come every weekday for the full stretch of visiting hours (Toru and Kei took all the weekend shifts), although now I could bring my laptop and work while Otōsan slept, and the new hospital was so clean, so modern, compared to the old one that the visits felt like barely a hardship.

At first, each new nurse would come into Otōsan's room to check his IV or vital signs, and almost uniformly, they'd give a little start seeing a foreign woman sitting on the tiny vinyl couch, computer open on her lap. But each time I'd explain I was the *yome*, "daughter-in-law," and they'd nod or say, *"So, desuka?"* "Is that so?" and smile kindly at me. One was delighted by the foreigner on the ward. "I. Love. English talking!" she told me happily when she came to Toru's father's bedside, pointing to her own nose, then gently rearranging Otōsan's sheets around his legs.

Now, as I sat with Toru in the nurse's station, the white-skirted women all averted their eyes while the doctor—also a woman, but in a hospital coat and pants—pointed toward monochrome images on a screen. She spoke in low, gentle Japanese to Toru. I could barely follow any of her words, but I knew a few days earlier they had found a mass during a CT scan of Otōsan's torso, and I could tell the news wasn't good by her tone and by the white haze on the monitor inside what I guessed were grayer-shaped organs. And by the way Toru swallowed and tried to keep his voice low to match the doctor's.

Afterward, Toru and I went into the hall and whispered by the door to Otōsan's room. Cancer, Toru explained to me, pointing to his abdomen but shaking his head when I first guessed "stomach." After I supplied my next conjecture, he nodded, slowly at first and then more rapidly as he searched through his brain to confirm the English word for "pancreas." It was advanced. Too advanced to treat. "Normal person, they might live three to six months," Toru said, repeating the doctor's diagnosis. But with Otōsan's Parkinson's, dementia, and recurrent pneumonia, his prognosis was much worse.

SEVENTEEN

IN THE MIDDLE OF OTŌSAN'S first month in the new hospital, I had some mild spotting—"another early, ridiculously light period"—I reported to Toru. Neither one of us dwelled for long on the topic. Most of our mental space was taken up with Otōsan. Though I felt disappointed, I was also relieved that I could get my period without feeling like my chest was being crushed. When my stomach started to feel upset a week or so later, I tried to push away the thought that I might be approaching early menopause. I'd heard the hormone shifts of that milestone could cause queasiness. "Maybe I picked something up in the hospital," I said to Toru. For a brief flash, I wondered if it could be something worse, but then I pushed that thought aside, too.

I wasn't sick enough to stop visiting Otōsan, who actually seemed to be getting a little better despite the doctor's dire warnings. He was awake most of the day now, and often the nurses would put him in a wheelchair and I'd push him to the hospital's roof garden, where we could see Osaka Castle in the distance, and I'd ask Otōsan about various buildings, and sometimes he'd remember what they were. It was early June, and the air was warm but not too humid, a brief stretch of gentle summer before the rainy season set in, followed by the killing heat and humidity of an Osaka August. I'd wheel Otōsan to the corner of the roof deck that had a slice of sun, and he'd sit in the light and the breeze until he got tired and nodded when I suggested going back to his room. Despite his cancer and the welts that rose like bruised pillows on his arms and ankles from his months on an IV, the doctors thought he might even be able to go back to the care house soon.

One afternoon, when my stomach bug still hadn't gone away, I called Lisa and told her I was feeling too sick for our power walk. Lately, she'd been meeting me a few times a week near the hospital so we could loop around Osaka Castle Park. "I can meet you for dinner, though," I said. "I've been at the hospital all afternoon and really need to eat. Maybe just soup?"

Lisa felt like one of my few remaining lifelines in Osaka, someone I could commiserate and even laugh with over my failure to get pregnant while she complained about her latest boyfriend, a British pilot who came to Japan only a few times a year. Since she had never wanted children, I never had to worry about her prattling happily about kids or inviting me to spend time with a new baby.

When we met that evening at an udon soup place, she asked how Toru's father was. Then, peering into my face, "And how are you?"

"We're hoping he can go back to the care house soon. And I'm okay. A little sick. But maybe it's just stress."

I ordered a plain bowl of noodles, easy on the stomach, and she ordered soup with tempura. "Can you believe I haven't even been drinking lately?" I joked. "I'm really shirking on my commitment to nine months of boozing, now the treatments are over." Lisa raised her beer to me.

"I'm sure I'll be better by the weekend," I said, envisioning us in another restaurant, a bottle of red wine between us.

"Poor littlest," Lisa said, using the nickname she'd given me as the smallest among our circle of expat friends.

When our soup came, I eyed Lisa's tempura. Her beer held no appeal, but suddenly the batter-covered shrimp sent a bolt of hunger through me. "Oh, my God, gimme one of those, please? Think I'm getting better already."

After I ate the shrimp and finished my bowl of soup, my belly felt a little better.

"Leave it to me to crave tempura even when I have a stomach bug."

"Maybe you're pregnant!"

"Ha!" Then I added, "That would be like a granny getting knocked up. No way. I'm halfway to my forty-sixth birthday already. Think I'm just an oinker. Anyway, I just got my period, like, ten days ago."

"Poor littlest!" Lisa said again, downing the rest of her beer.

If someone who had kids had made a joke about my suddenly becoming pregnant, I would have been annoyed. But now we just laughed.

A FEW MORNINGS LATER, I finished an hour of slow yoga in our tatami room before heading to the hospital for visiting hours. I still felt a little sick, but I had no fever. As I finished my last yoga stretch, I lay on the soft tatami mats and felt my limbs, watery and loose. Breathing easily, I rested a minute longer, and Lisa's voice popped into my head. "Maybe you're pregnant!" Then, "poor littlest!" and our laughter.

After a few minutes, I went into the bathroom, peeling off my Lycra top and turning on the hot water. I opened the closet door to grab a towel. Reaching in, I saw an old pregnancy test. I hadn't used one in months. I turned it over, looked at the date stamped on the back of its shiny packaging. *Not yet expired. But almost.*

I let the shower run, waiting for it to steam, and felt the familiar tightening in my bladder from hearing water through a faucet. I stared at the package in my fist, then kept my palm curled around it while I streaked to our tiny toilet room next to the shower. *Might as well use it, just because,* I thought, looking again at the impending expiration date. I'd heard women approaching menopause sometimes got very faint false positives on early pregnancy tests from their hormones being so out of whack. *Maybe I'll get my first confirmation of perimenopause.*

A few minutes later, the shower still running but now way past steaming, my entire body naked and shaking, my arms feeling like they might abandon their sockets, I grabbed my cell phone and texted Toru at work. The pregnancy test was positive. Not a faint positive, but the darkest one I'd ever seen. "What should I do?" I typed madly into the phone.

Trembling, I waited for Toru's response. "Stay calm" came the first text. Then, "Keep warm your belly."

I went back to the clinic where I'd gone before I'd ever started IVF. After I passed a urine sample through a tiny white window in the bathroom wall, a nurse called me into a closet-sized room. She spoke no English, so I tried to explain that I'd taken a pregnancy test that morning and seen a strong positive, but I'd just had my period ten days ago, so how could that be? Was it early menopause? The nurse motioned me into a larger room next door, where I repeated my confused tale for a doctor I'd never met. She tipped a stick in front of her toward me. On their test, too, the second line was as dark as ink.

She asked me when my period before the last one had started, and I puzzled over dates in my head. About six weeks ago? I guessed. I expected her to suggest a blood test, but she motioned me into the examining room a few doors down. Minutes later, she shifted the ultrasound screen toward me. Then she pointed to what she explained was my uterus, circling her finger around a dark mass inside it. Together, we watched as a little white light beat rapidly at its center.

The doctor measured the blinking blob and estimated I was almost seven weeks along. My spotting three weeks earlier had been early pregnancy bleeding, and now the embryo inside me was already throbbing out a strong, steady heartbeat.

Standing outside the clinic, shaking once more, I called Toru, and we repeated over and over to each other how incredible it all was, how stunning the news. "I guess, there goes the theory that if you just relax or stop trying you'll get pregnant," I said, since technically we'd still been trying, although without medical intervention, and we both felt racked with stress from his father's illness.

Then we discussed telling Otōsan, even though with my history of miscarriage and my age, we knew the situation was precarious. "But maybe it might give him some happiness, some hope," I urged, and Toru agreed. His father might not even remember the pregnancy in a few days, so if I miscarried, we wouldn't have to tell him that. Yet the echo of hearing happy news now might linger somewhere in his mind, might fortify him somehow to think of a lasting legacy growing with the potential of a first grandchild.

"Otōsan," I said that afternoon at his bedside, trying to swallow down a pale wave of nausea, "I have a secret." He looked up at me and blinked, his body swathed in sheets and blankets, an IV line snaking from beneath. He was too weak to raise his head.

"Ninshin desu! Akachan-wa naka-ni!" "I'm pregnant! A baby is inside!" I patted my stomach to supplement my broken Japanese, then raised a finger to my lips. Otōsan's eyes went wider. He tried to clear his throat, considered the news for a moment, then whispered in English, "Does Toru know?"

I laughed. "Of course!" Switching back to Japanese, I attempted to explain the series of events: stomach felt sick, went to doctor, doctor gave me tests and looked and saw the baby inside, and Toru and I were so surprised. Otōsan mulled the details for another moment longer. *"Itsu?"* he asked. "When will the baby come?"

January, I told him, and then he grabbed my hand and kissed it, and then he burst into tears.

BY THE TENTH week of my pregnancy, the clinic urged me to find a maternity hospital where I would be assigned an OB and, we hoped, give birth. They recommended screenings, too, because of my age and the increased incidence of genetic abnormalities for babies born to mothers past thirty-five. We had my first screening in my thirteenth week, a high resolution "nuchal" scan that tracks fetal measurements coinciding with Down's syndrome as well as spinal and heart defects. The baby's heart and spine looked fine, the doctor told us. But the fluid around its neck was just slightly more abundant than usual. Combining this measurement with my age, we were looking at a one-in-five chance of Down's.

Driving to see his father that day after the scan, Toru remained upbeat, even though by now Otōsan was hardly able to whisper. His veins were sometimes too weak for the IV, his wrists, arms, and ankles covered with bruises from where the nurses tried, and failed, to jam the line into a viable spot, and the hospital had encouraged Toru to begin looking for hospices. About the baby, though, he remained confident. "I really think baby is fine," Toru told me, his hands clasped lightly on the wheel as he turned through traffic. "But I worry you," he said, after I had burst into tears in the doctor's office, the scan results pinned to the wall in front of us while a nurse reviewed them in Japanese and Toru translated. As usual, he was more optimistic than I. But now I wasn't only scared, I was also torn.

When we had started trying to have a baby, five years earlier, Toru and I had agreed that if we learned the child would have a serious genetic abnormality we would terminate the pregnancy. Because of our age, Toru had said, we probably wouldn't survive long enough to care for an adult child who couldn't live alone. I'd agreed, not knowing in my heart whether I could even care for a baby who was healthy, let alone one with special needs.

Now, though, I sat in the car and stared dumbly at the dashboard, and the maze outside the windshield barely registered. I knew this was not the time to talk about terminating a pregnancy, or not terminating one and signing up for a lifetime of caretaking—exhausted and headed as we were to ache over the bedside of Otōsan as his body faded further. But I also knew I wasn't sure anymore I could stick to our original agreement. I didn't know how Toru felt, but it seemed inconceivable to me that we would not do everything we could to finally hold this baby, in whatever form it came to us. Especially when Otōsan was slipping away from us at the same time.

At the hospital, Toru asked his father to name the baby, although by now we all knew he'd never get to meet it. Then, within a few days, Otōsan stopped being able to whisper, and he went silent, whatever names he'd chosen buried in a morphine haze. As I passed into my second trimester, the threshold beyond which the baby would most likely survive until birth, Otōsan died. It was a Saturday afternoon in late July, and Toru and Kei dressed their father, now gone but still in his hospital bed, two nurses by their side who helped remove his gown and cover him in the pants and button-down shirt in which he would be cremated.

A few days later, we gathered at the crematorium to bid Otōsan's body a final good-bye. I felt my hand go instinctively to my stomach as a uniformed man pulled a metal tray out of the elevator leading to the furnace, and Otōsan's bones emerged, pieces of his skeleton shockingly intact amidst layers of white ash. Then Toru and I, Kei and her husband, Michiko-*san* and Hamatani-*san*, and Otōsan's only surviving brother and his wife each took turns picking up pieces of the bones with chopsticks, while another attendant wrapped them in a white box and cloth, which we would eventually bury next to Toru's mother.

We had the baby's final screening soon after, derived from a sample of my own blood containing both my and the fetus's

DNA. Then we waited three weeks for the results, the air around me feeling lighter, grayer, as if an uncomfortable weightlessness had materialized, a vacuum in the sudden absence of Toru's father. I didn't bring up whether we would terminate the pregnancy depending on the screening's outcome, even though I knew I should discuss it with Toru. But how to broach that subject in the airless swamp of his mourning? *Besides,* I thought, *by the time we get the results, it will be almost twenty weeks. Almost too late to terminate.* I didn't have Toru's firm optimism about the baby being fine, but I was hoping time might make some decisions for us.

ONE MORNING IN mid-August, on another Skype call with my Cambridge therapist, she broached the topic of what we would do if the baby's results showed evidence of either Down's syndrome or a more serious chromosomal abnormality. She understood my reluctance to bring up the topic with Toru, given his recent loss, but she urged me to consider the repercussions of *not* discussing it: that when the test results finally came back, if the baby wasn't healthy, we wouldn't have a lot of time to make a joint decision, especially since we had spent years assuming we were on the same page about raising a child with a genetic disease.

I recalled the day we'd had the final screening. Before they drew my blood, the hospital had required us to meet with a genetic counselor who showed us a chart of statistics about chromosomal abnormalities and maternal age. The chart stopped at forty-four. "You'll be forty-five when you deliver?" she asked in

Japanese. "Forty-six. And a half," I said, peering at the paper. "But you look so young!" she assured me, and then she laughed and waved her hand over the list, as if to convince me not to worry that I was two years past its most dire statistic.

I knew my therapist was right. If the test came back negative, it would provide a 99 percent guarantee the baby did not have Down's, as well as significant assurance about two more serious conditions, putting our minds at ease. But positive results were more precarious to read and required follow-up testing, and then we'd have to wait for an amniocentesis, a more invasive procedure with a chance of causing miscarriage. Which would put us right near the twenty-four-week threshold, when abortion in Japan became illegal.

"It's not that I'm *sure* I wouldn't terminate the pregnancy," I tried to explain. "Although I really think I couldn't," I added quickly, my hand once more traveling to my stomach. I thought back to my earlier realization of what I'd learned from all my years of fertility treatments: that you never know what you'll choose when faced with difficult options, when reality is pushed up against your nose, despite what you always felt sure you'd do in the abstract. So I knew that, even though now I didn't think I could terminate this pregnancy, who could say how I'd actually feel if we learned our baby was nothing like we'd always pictured? If we were suddenly asked to devote the rest of our lives to caring for a child who might never grow to independence? Or, with one of the conditions more serious than Down's, an infant incapable of living past the first few days of life?

"If the baby has some kind of genetic disorder that would cause great suffering, would create great pain and an inability to survive much past birth, then, yes, probably I would need to face, to choose termination," I told my shrink. "Although I think that's unlikely, given that some physical evidence of this would have probably been visible on the nuchal scan.

"But Down's?" I said, after another moment. "Down's seems really different to me all of a sudden. Although who knows what I would think or choose if push comes to shove," I added, trying my hardest to be accurate. Then I thought about Toru's father, about losing him so close to when we might have to make a decision about losing the baby, and I felt my voice catch.

"Go on," she said, after a brief silence.

I stared around the living room, wrapped the headset cord around my index finger, then tried to steady my voice.

"It's just that . . . I think maybe a baby with Down's could have a good life, a fulfilling life, despite the chromosomal abnormality." I fell silent again for another minute, lifting my eyes to the ceiling while I tried to imagine a baby with half-Japanese, half-Western features and eyes slightly wider than average. I pictured walking down the sidewalk in our Osaka neighborhood with a little child toddling left and right, dark-haired and gentle. What would the neighbors notice first? Its Western traits or its slightly skewed expression?

Then I imagined reading everything I could about Down's syndrome, learning about all its different variations, throwing myself into theories about guiding a child with this genetic trait through a life as full and joyful as possible. I wondered about which hidden joys I myself might find therein, how the experience would shape me, might both limit and grow me, how I would draw a community of similarly configured families around me. It was something I could start to picture.

I began speaking again. "And I think, maybe, that I could be a good mother to a child with Down's syndrome." My shrink was silent.

After a beat, she let out a soft "Wow."

"What?"

"Wow," she said again. "It's just that I've never heard you say that. In all these years, Tracy, in all these years of trying, I've never heard you say that you thought you could be a good mother. To any kind of child. And now I hear that. I hear you, clear and sure." She stopped speaking for a moment, then added, "And that's huge."

"Huh," I said. I hadn't thought about it before, but now I realized she was right. Something in me *had* changed, something about my faith in my ability not just to survive but to prize the all-consuming demands of love. Then I knew: this is what Otōsan had given me.

After we hung up, I thought about all the challenges, the drudgery, really, of taking care of Otōsan as he declined and trying to be there for Toru while it happened. The diaper changes. The late-night showers, the furtive carpet scrubbings, the anxious hours in the hospital (surrounded once again by people who didn't speak my language). All of it made not just manageable but somehow, alongside the stress and the smells and the exhaustion, something precious, because it was a part of my bond with both of them.

It was only a year or so, I knew, of being bound to an illness bigger than us all. It was surely less demanding than the 24/7 commitment of motherhood. It had been thoroughly overwhelming. But when it ended, I'd wished we'd had more time. And in a flash, I'd choose to do it all again. *Maybe that's what makes love bearable,* I thought. The bond, the closeness, the interdependence, the white-hot desire to soothe, to care for, to be together for as long as possible. It wouldn't make the outsized stress of caretaking, or of parenthood—with any child, I assumed—go away. It just made it worth it. Gave us a shot at being bigger than all the ways love could take us away from ourselves and then eventually deliver us back.

EPILOGUE: LANDING

Toru and I are lying in bed, almost twenty-four weeks into my pregnancy. Less than a month earlier, we'd gotten the baby's test results, and I was bowled over that all were negative. As far as the doctors could tell, I would give birth to a healthy girl at the end of January. Toru nodded his head when we heard the news, my husband lightly confirming that, yes, once again, his immutable optimism had been proven correct.

I'm heading back to Boston in a few days to spend three weeks at home before I get too big to travel. I'm excited about being back in the U.S., about seeing my family and friends, eating all the American food I've been craving. I don't know how much longer my own parents will remain healthy, and now I have some small sense of what it might mean to lose them.

But I'm nervous, too. I never guessed when I left Boston last time that I'd be coming back again in less than a year, likely for the last time ever without a child—or at least the last time in eighteen years. How will I sustain my connection to Boston now that our baby is on the way? Could Toru and I move to the U.S. more easily now, or at least eventually, without his father to take care of? Could we even afford to have a baby and a vital connection to two countries at once? Although I realize Japan will never exactly feel like *home*, I can't deny it has become an eternal part of me: where my husband will always feel most grounded, where Otōsan's remains will rest forever, where my baby will be both born and from. In a sense, the country and culture have now become an irrevocable part of my body, the flesh of my flesh, deriving from a foreign world. How does one reconcile such paradoxes?

And how will a baby change my relationship with Toru? I don't know anyone with an infant who doesn't at one point or another hate her husband or partner. The stress of a newborn presents one of modern marriage's greatest challenges. Toru and I may have been blessed up to this point with a dynamic of uncommon ease, but the flip side of not being fighters is that you never really learn how to fight well. I'm nervous now about how we'll deal with this new trial. Have we developed the tools we need to manage a new gulf if one opens between us? (When I bring up this fear to Toru, he says with utter certainty, "It will be okay! Of course I can deal with your bad moods," which makes me think perhaps he's missed the point.)

I have no fixed answers, nor any firm plot beyond hopefully getting through my pregnancy, meeting our baby, and surviving childbirth without the epidural the Japanese prenatal nurse assures me they don't use. *"Ja, ganbatte, ne!"* "So, just buck up, okay!" she tells me with a cheerful smile before she settles down to chastise me for all the weight I've gained. I don't tell her that, according to my American pregnancy books, my size is right on track. Since my first appointment over the summer at the hospital where I'm to give birth, she has been fretting about my "fat."

"Americans, you like juice! But you must stop drinking

juice!" she'd commanded, even though Toru assured her that despite my nationality I wasn't partial to the beverage. I was frequently too nauseated for anything but ice cubes. By August, the nurse had started reminding me of December's culinary dangers. She looked at me with a mix of sternness and pleasure on her face when she enthused, "The holidays are coming up. So please don't enjoy!" Although she speaks some English, Toru had to translate my explanation that I'm Jewish, so I don't celebrate Christmas, nor do I tend to eat more in December. She'd stopped a moment when Toru tried to clarify this, asked some questions in Japanese about what Jewish meant and what our winter holiday was called. Toru attempted to explain Chanukah, though I added that, really, Chanukah was a holiday for children, and as an adult, I didn't celebrate it anyway. Taking in this strange new information, the prenatal nurse paused a moment longer, tipping her round face in contemplation. Finally, she straightened and smiled brightly, eyeing me directly once more. "Well," she said, "you'll still probably be too fat in December!" Then she turned back to Toru with more admonishments for him to translate. He told me she suggested I weigh myself "one time every morning and one time every night," so I don't forget how fat I'm getting, and then, despite ourselves, he and I both burst into laughter.

Soon, although I'm at the doorstep of my sixth month, my neighbors begin to ask excitedly if it's twins. One points to my belly, holding up two fingers, and I laugh and say no, lifting up just one. When the same neighbor, a mother with three children of her own, repeats this same question every time she sees me, I smile a little tighter. *Does she think they're going to suddenly discover a second fetus growing at twenty-four weeks into my pregnancy?*

Another neighbor stops me at a little place around the corner from our apartment where I buy smoothies. She has an answer for my conundrum about my baby being simultaneously like I am—American—and from a foreign country. Instead of both, the child is apparently *"hafu,"* meaning "half." Not both anything, not double, not even a whole, apparently, but half Japanese, as if no other half exists or needs be named. She points excitedly to my belly and tells the two cashiers that she is my neighbor, that my husband is Nihonjin, Japanese, and that the baby inside is *hafu*. The three of them coo and smile and chatter about how cute *hafu*s are, reminding me I must bring the baby in after she's born so they can see her. Meanwhile, at another café down the street, the cashier looks happily at my stomach and asks *"Sugu?"* "Isn't the baby coming soon?"

But as long as the little one and I are healthy, I remain unconcerned about my weight gain. Beyond the birth itself, I'm still terrified of motherhood, even while I feel something miraculous is happening to me. It's uncomfortable, scary sometimes—a lot of times—but I know now that this discomfort, this disorientation, this is life. Not a failure to plan. Not a mistake in decisions made or destinations chosen. Just the inevitable arrival hall where reality continually delivers us, again and again. If we're lucky.

I spent so much of my early adulthood terrified of losing myself, grasping on to some illusion of having firm control over life, an unshakable plot. But I'm starting to realize—after having immersed myself so deeply in the quagmire of Japan, of Otōsan's illness and death, and of modern marriage—that you can't properly find yourself if you haven't let yourself get lost in the first place.

·   ·   ·

IN BED, I cup my bulging belly, shifting from my back, where I know I'm not supposed to rest for long (something about the fetus's growth and the blood supply to the placenta, I've read). I stretch out beside Toru. He leans over to talk to the baby, whispering as he does every night in Japanese, saying who knows what. (Probably "Don't listen to the foreigner," I joke to my friends.) He puts his lips to my belly button and converses, as if it were a phone line to my uterus, some intergenerational portal connecting past to present to future. Then he lays his face against my abdomen and I feel the scratchy stubble of his chin on the surface of my skin, and then the baby kicks from inside, and he lifts his head up and smiles.

"Is it lovely?" he asks me, and the word sounds a little like "rubbery" from his accent, and it takes me a moment to understand what he means. "To feel the baby inside?" he says.

"Well, it's actually a little odd," I say. "But, yes, it's very lovely."

I think back to a night years earlier, when we'd lain together in bed just after we'd been married, before either birth or death had become such loaded or real topics to us. That night, Toru had been tipsy, tossing about in an uncharacteristic attempt to get comfortable. He'd just come home from an afterwork *nomi-kai*, a drinking party, a ubiquitous part of Japanese corporate culture that neither wives nor partners are invited to join.

Suddenly, he paused his quest for sleep's perfect pose, raised his head to look at me, narrowed his eyes. Then he broached a grave issue: if I'd gargled that evening with antiseptic, another of

Japan's beloved health obsessions alongside keeping one's belly warm.

"You must keep safe," he told me, throwing his head back on the pillow when I'd admitted that, no, once again I hadn't been able to toss the Betadine-like substance down my throat. "Then you'll live to be a hundred and twenty," he said, "like really old people in Okinawa." He thought for a minute, started to hover toward sleep. "I'm younger than you," he eventually mumbled, "and I'm Japanese, so I'll live longer."

"But I'm a woman, and women live longer than men."

"But if we both live to be a hundred and twenty," he'd said, his voice fading, "then I'll still live longer than you, because you'll be reaching a hundred and twenty before me.

"But that's okay, that's good," he'd said, his voice a dream-filled mutter. "Because then, then I can send you," he'd murmured softly, and fell fully into sleep.

Now, in bed and forty-six and pregnant, I remember this night while I stare at him, resting heavily on my elbow. He turns to lie peacefully on his back, his hand lingering on my stomach before he pulls it away and allows sleep to pull him gently under. *This is a man who plans, without one doubt, to stay beside me always,* I think, *until he can help me through the hardest and most terrifying journey of all*—the last arc into death. Then I know I really am home, at least in one of life's most fundamental ways, even if I still don't know exactly where I am or how to guarantee a home's fixed location.

For just a second, I sense a faint, residual reluctance to admit I've proven both so dependent and such a cliché: a woman who has realized that "home" and "life" and "love" and "husband," and now maybe "child," too, all comprise each other; a woman who once gave up her own plans and world for a man. But in doing so, I grew a greater sense of rootedness, a new kind of faith in some fixed strength within my skin, an internal place of permanence even more personal, more *mine*, than any cartographic coordinate. Knowing this, a deeper truth dawns on me: of my incredible good fortune, despite all my foiled plans, to have spread my singular little arms across the globe, let go, and ended up holding such a cliché as my own.

ACKNOWLEDGMENTS

I am very grateful to my family: to my parents and eldest sister, who were reluctant to have private conversations and memories aired publicly but still supported, with immense generosity, my writing of this book; to my brother Scott, who gave me endless encouragement; and to my middle sister Lauren, who never failed to welcome my own efforts to write, and whose prose—in its sheer beauty—will always awe me and give me something to aim for. Deepest thanks as well to the entire Hoshino clan, who welcomed me in and taught me not just about Japan but about what it means to be family.

Without my editor, Sara Minnich Blackburn, this book would not exist. Her insight, wisdom, support, and encouragement got me through the writing of this memoir, but it also gave me something hopeful to work toward during dark times, so I am profoundly grateful to her both as a writer and a person. I still can't believe my luck that I got to work with her. Ditto for the entire Putnam team that helped create, design, and support this book, including especially Stephanie Hargadon for all her work and guidance on publicity. I also feel lucky to have had the chance to work with my agent, Rachel Sussman—my literary hockey mom!—not just for how she helped me as a new author navigate the world of publishing but for our fun conversations along the way. Without Eve Bridburg, I never would have found Rachel. I also want to recognize Dorian Karchmar: I so appreciate your kindness and your advice about agents when I was looking for representation. In addition, I'm grateful to KJ Dell'Antonia from the *New York Times* blog *Motherlode,* who was the first to invite me to tell parts of this story publicly.

So many friends helped me with the writing of this book. Jennifer Ivers, Mark Kaufman, and Sari Boren were incredible editors as well as unspeakably generous readers, as were Megan Sullivan, Jessica Goodfellow Ueno, Jodi Harmon, Peter Kreig, Lisa Theisen, Colleen Shiels, Susan Blumberg-Kason, Paul Morrison, Mary Hillis, Zoe Jenkins, Sasti Lavinia, Tracy Nishizaka, and Alexandria Marzano-Lesnevich from Grub Street Boston. Tim Huggins helped immeasurably not just as a friend but also with advice about publishing, publicity, and bookselling, as did Michael Lowenthal, Jennifer Haigh, Elyssa East, Kaitlin Solimine, Elizabeth Mckenzie, Elizabeth Searle, Don Lee, Bret Anthony Johnston, Ethan Gilsdorf, Leza Lowitz, Alison Lobron, Linda Schossberg, and Heidi Durrow.

I offer great thanks to the authors who have read over the years at Four Stories, not just for your generosity in sharing your work at the events but for all you've taught me about writing and reading narratives that transport. As a group, you've moved, inspired, and wowed me.

I'm also fortunate to have gotten great support from the instructors and students in my Mediabistro courses. Jill Rothenberg and Kelly McMasters, I don't believe I could have written a successful proposal without your guidance! Megan Parks, Scott

Rodbro, Robert Henderson, Karla Bruning, Marin Heinritz, John Dillon, Isabelle Marinov, Pete Evanow, and the rest of the Mediabistro crew, I'm so glad I got my start on this book with all of you.

Finally, I want to thank Toru, although in so many ways I don't properly have the words to do so, and Elli, who gave me a happier ending than I ever dared imagine.